Abby Merrill Adams

Sense in the Kitchen

A Guide to Economical Cooking

Abby Merrill Adams

Sense in the Kitchen
A Guide to Economical Cooking

ISBN/EAN: 9783744783576

Printed in Europe, USA, Canada, Australia, Japan

Cover: Foto ©Andreas Hilbeck / pixelio.de

More available books at **www.hansebooks.com**

SENSE IN THE KITCHEN.

A GUIDE TO

Economical Cooking.

BY

ABBY MERRILL ADAMS.

SYRACUSE, N. Y.:
A. S. HUNTER, PUBLISHER.
1881.

C. W. BARDEEN, Printer.   A. J. CROOK, Binder.

PREFACE.

The peculiar and distinctive features of SENSE IN THE KITCHEN to which we would call special attention, are:

1st. It is the result of experience, every recipe having been tested and known to be *the best*.

2nd. The recipes are simple and plain, the work being primarily designed for the home, rather than for the ho tel and restaurant.

3d. The full and explicit directions with each recipe cannot fail to please every young housekeeper.

4th. The chemistry of Food is fully and clearly treated so that one learns not only *how* any kind of food should be prepared but *why* it should be so prepared.

5th. Particular attention is paid to the hygienic effect of different kinds of food upon the different systems.

6th. In the part devoted to etiquette and ceremonious entertainments we try to meet the needs of those who wish such help and yet who do not wish to follow the extremes of social life.

In the preparation of this work the following well known authorities have been consulted: "Johnson's Agricultural Chemistry," "Youman's Chemistry and Household Science," Edwin Smith's valuable work on "Foods," George H. Lewes' "Physiology of Common Life," "Wells' Chemistry," W. B. Tegetmeier's "Handbook of Household Management and Cookery," Marion Harland's "Common Sense," and "Breakfast, Luncheon and Tea," Mrs. Cornelius' "Young Housekeeper," also "Chicago Home," and "Kansas Home."

We owe much to friends of the compiler who have kindly furnished many valuable recipes, and we are under special obligations to Mrs. Leonard, of La Crosse, Wis.

INDEX OF SUBJECTS.

	PAGE.		PAGE.
Arranging the Tables	311	Hygiene of Drinks	291
Bills of Fare	324	Ice Cream	246
Bread	130	Introductory	7
Cake	163	Meats	36
Canned Fruit	264	Meat Maxims	78
Catsups	115	Milk, Butter and Cheese	71
Confectionery	271	Miscellaneous	300
Drinks	278	Pies	196
Elements of Animal Food	9	Poultry	56
		Puddings	208
Elements of Vegetable Food	83	Pudding Sauces	227
		Pickles	105
Eggs	67	Salads	118
Etiquette	316	Sauces for Meat and Fish	64
Fancy Dishes for Dessert	235	Sugars	160
Fish	21	Sauces, Preserves and Fruit Jellies	251
Fritters	155		
Flavored Vinegars	104	Soup	11
Game	62	Sick Room	291
Gravies (*See Sauces for Meat and Fish.*)		Sweetmeat Maxims	188
		Vegetables	88
Griddle Cakes	151	Vegetable Maxims	157
Hygiene of Animal Food	80	Vegetable Acids	102
Hygiene of Vegetable Food	158	Waffles	151
		Yeast	125

We may live without poetry, music or art
We may live without conscience, and live without heart;
We may live without friends; we may live without books;
But civilized man cannot live without cooks.
He may live without books,—what is knowledge but grieving?
He may live without hope,—what is hope but deceiving?
He may live without love,—what is passion but pining?
But where is the man that can live without dining?
—Owen Meredith.

FOOD.

Food is required by the body for two chief purposes, viz: to generate heat and to produce and maintain the structure under the influence of life and exertion. The duty assigned to food is to supply the materials which are lost by the waste which is continually going on in the body; so that bone must be renewed by materials which compose bone; flesh by flesh.

Flesh in its fresh state contains water, fat, fibrine, albumen and gelatine, besides compounds of lime, phosphorus, soda, potash, magnesia, silica and iron, and certain extractives. Blood has a composition similar in elements to that of flesh. Bone is composed of cartilage, gelatine, fat and salts of lime, magnesia, soda and potash combined with phosphoric and other acids.

The brain is composed of water, albumen, fat, phosphoric acid, osmazome and salts.

Hence it is required that the body should be provided with salts of potash, soda, lime, magnesia, sulphur, iron, as well as sulphuric, phosphoric acids and water. Thus a knowledge of the composition and requirements of the physical system leads to a proper combination of food; and these combinations have been effected by investigation and experience which protect even the most ignorant from evil consequences.

All animal food is rich in the four most essential elements to man, viz: carbon, oxygen, hydrogen and nitrogen, as well as many other very important elements to our well being; such as phosphorus, sulphur, chlorine, potassium, lime, iron and water which is a compound. Phosphorus is found in all animals in the state of phosphoric acid. This united with lime forms the phosphorate of lime, never absent from bone.

Sulphur is found in all animal substances.

Chlorine is one of the parts of salt.

Potassium is formed in a very small degree in animals and is the base of potash.

Iron in the state of oxide is found in minute portions in all animals.

Water, composed of hydrogen and oxygen, is found ready formed. Blood contains 80 per cent. water, flesh 75 per cent.

It is calculated that the human body makes up three-fourths of its weight in water.

These are called the elements; the first four named are the principal or essential elements. The proximate principles of animals are fibrine, gelatine, albumen, oils and fats, osmazome and caseine. These elements will be found discussed under such heads of food as they form an essential part.

ELEMENTS OF ANIMAL FOOD.

It is well known that the flesh of nearly all grazing animals, either wild or domestic, is good for food. It contains the proximate principles of animals, viz., albumen, fibrine, fat, gelatine, water, salts and osmazome.

ALBUMEN is found the most pure in the egg, and will there be more fully discussed.

FIBRINE is found in the animal body in two distinct states, viz., in a solid condition in muscular flesh, and as a fluid in the blood. That which we will discuss is the solid fibrine, which is the fleshy part of meat when freed from fat, and forms the base of the meat; when boiled sufficiently long to become tender, unites with the gelatine and is nutritive and strengthening.

FAT in animal flesh is found in the form of suet, marrow and leaf, or what is known as lard when tried out. Fat or oily substances are furnished to the system, mingled by nature with nearly all the food we eat. Milk contains three or four per cent. of it, and ordinary meat, fourteen per cent; while in butter, gravies and fat we have it concentrated and almost pure. Fat in small quantities is found to be an essential agent in promoting digestion, while an excess of it exerts an injurious effect especially in persons of weak digestion.

Cooking generally renders fatty substances less agreeable to the stomach especially if the organ is weak. In frying, the temperature runs high, tending to decomposition and the production of various acrid and irritant fatty acids. Fatty matters thus changed are liable to become rancid by the fermenting action of the stomach producing heart-burn and nausea.

GELATINE.—Various parts of the animal body such as the skin, tendons, cartilage and soft portions of the bones dissolve completely by long boiling and form, when cold, a jelly, called gelatine, which is exclusively an animal product, and is never found in plants; that which forms a jelly in plants is pectine. Gelatine is rich in nitrogen and also contains some sulphur. Common glue is dried gelatine.

Ising-glass, which is the purest variety of gelatine, is mainly procured from the air bladders of several varieties of fish, especially of the sturgeon. As an article of food gelatine is used largely in soups, jellies, etc. Although it has been proved to have little nutritive value, but is regarded in the sick-room, in the form of jelly, as an agreeable accompaniment to more nutritious food.

OSMAZOME is a substance which has a reddish brown color and gives the smell and flavor to meats; it varies with various animals and increases with their age. It takes its name from two Greek words, meaning smell and soup.

FLESH OF FISH differs little in chemical composition from animal flesh except in phosphorus, but greatly from it in flavor and texture. In different varieties the proportion of fat and oil varies, being much greater in some than in others, it is also found in greater proportion in them, than in quadrupeds. The eel contains fifty per cent. of fat; herring, thirty per cent; salmon, in good condition, ten to twenty per cent. Fish is rich in phosphorus; but it will not sustain full health and strength like flesh, although it is very good food. In countries where fish forms the main diet, leprosy is found to be a more common disease than in countries where a mixed diet is used. Oysters are delicacies rather than necessary food.

Lobsters and other kinds of shell fish are very indigestible and persons of weak digestion cannot eat them with impunity.

SOUP.

The base of soup should always be lean, uncooked meat; to which may be added chicken, turkey, beef or mutton bones well broken up. Wash the meat and put it in cold water without salt; soft water is best; if hard water is used, a little soda improves the water; let it come slowly to a boil. Always skim often, do not add the salt and other seasoning until the scum has ceased to rise. Let it gently simmer for eight or ten hours until the meat is in rags; then strain the stock into an earthen jar; do not cool in metal as there may be poison in the soldering or other parts; let it cool and remove all the grease. The stock will keep in a cool place several days, and from it can be made all the various kinds of soup. Be very careful in using cold meats and bones that none are tainted, as the soup may be ruined by the use of a very little tainted bone or meat. If the meat is cut in small pieces and bones well broken, the juices can be extracted much quicker than if used in large pieces. The neck and knuckle pieces are good for soup-stock. Whatever may be added to this stock when used, as rice, tapioca, vegetables, etc., must be cooked before being added, as much boiling injures the flavor of the soup. Thin soups must be strained. If it is to be made very clear, stir in one or two well-beaten eggs, with the shells, and let it boil half an hour, and then strain.

Flavors for Soups.

The following are most of the flavors used by the best French cooks, also those of Professor Blot and Soyer. Combinations are recommended by those authors in the following proportions:

¼ ounce thyme.
¼ ounce bay-leaf.
⅛ ounce marjoram.
⅛ ounce rosemary.

Dry the above when fresh; mix in a mortar, and keep them corked tight in a glass bottle.

Also the following in these proportions:

½ ounce nutmeg.
½ ounce cloves.
¼ ounce black pepper.
⅛ ounce cayenne pepper.

Pound, mix and keep corked tight in glass. In using these with salt, put one ounce of the last recipe to four ounces of salt. In making dressing, or force meat, and hash, use at the rate of one ounce of this spiced salt to three pounds of meat.

Soup Powder.

2 ounces parsley.
2 ounces summer savory.
2 ounces sweet marjoram.
2 ounces thyme.
1 ounce lemon peel.
1 ounce sweet basil.

Dry, pound, sift and keep in a tight corked bottle. Let the housekeeper add these flavors so that they will not be strong, but quite delicate, and then *make a rule for the cook*. The excellence of French cooking is the combination of flavors, all so delicate in force and quality that no one is allowed to predominate.

MEAT AND VEGETABLE SOUPS.

VEAL SOUP WITH MACARONI.

3 pounds of veal knuckle, with the bones broken and meat cut up.
3 quarts water.
¼ pound Italian macaroni.

Boil the meat alone in the water for nearly three hours, until it is reduced to shreds; put the macaroni in enough water to cover it, in a vessel by itself and boil until tender. The pieces should be only an inch in length. Add a little butter to the macaroni when nearly done. Strain the meat out of the soup, season to your taste, put in the macaroni, and the water in which it was boiled; let it boil up, and serve.

TURKEY SOUP.

Put all the turkey bones, and little bits left of a dinner into about three quarts of water. If you have turkey gravy, or the remnants of chicken, add them also, and boil them two hours or more. Skim out the meat and bones, and set the water aside in a cool place until the next day. Then take all the fat from the top; take the bones and pieces of skin out from the meat and return it to the liquor. If some of the dressing has been left, put that in also, and boil all together a few minutes. Add more seasoning if necessary. An onion should be boiled in it.

RICH BEEF SOUP.

6 pounds of beef.
6 quarts of water.
2 turnips.

2 carrots.
1 head of celery.
1 quart of tomatoes.
½ head small white cabbage.
1 pint green corn, or Shaker corn, (soaked over night.)

Simmer the beef in the water for six hours, using the bones, broken in small pieces. Cool it and take off the fat. Next day, an hour before dinner, take out the meat to use for hash or mince-meat, heat the liquor, throw in some salt to raise the scum, and skim it well. Then slice the vegetables small, and boil in a very little water. Cook the cabbage in two waters, throwing away the first. Boil the soup half an hour after these are put in. Season with salt, pepper, mace and wine to suit the taste.

MUTTON SOUP.

4 pounds of mutton.
4 quarts of water.
4 heaping teaspoonfuls of salt.
1 even teaspoonful of pepper.
2 teaspoonfuls of sugar.
1 small onion.
2 carrots.
2 turnips.
1 teacup of rice, or broken macaroni.

Boil the meat in the water two hours. Then add the vegetables, all cut fine, and the seasoning, and boil one hour and a half longer.

FRENCH VEGETABLE SOUP.

1 leg of lamb, of moderate size.
4 quarts of water.
Potatoes, carrots, cabbage, tomatoes and turnips, take 1 teacupful of each, chopped fine.
4 teaspoonfuls of salt.
Pepper to taste.

Wash the lamb and put it into the four quarts of cold water. Skim carefully. Cook two hours, then add the vegetables. Carrots require the most boiling, and should be put in first. This soup requires about three hours to boil.

Plain Calf's Head Soup.

Boil the head and feet in just water enough to cover them; when tender, take out the bones, cut in small pieces, and season with marjoram, thyme, cloves, salt and pepper. Put all into the pot, with the liquor, and four spoonfuls of butter; stew gently an hour; then, just as you take it up, add two or three glasses of port-wine, and the yolks of three eggs boiled hard.

Ox-Tail Soup.

Take two tails, divide them at the joints. Soak them a little while in warm water, then put them into cold water in a gallon pot or stew-pan, with a little salt. Skim off the froth. When the meat is boiled to shreds, take out the bones, and add a chopped onion and carrot. Use spices and sweet herbs as you prefer. Sprinkle in a little farina before serving. The bones and meat should be boiled the day before being served, and the next day take the fat off from the top of the liquor, and then add the vegetables and spice, and boil an hour and a half more.

Mock Turtle Soup.

1 soup-bone.
1 quart of turtle beans.
1 large spoonful powdered cloves.
Salt and pepper.
6 quarts of water.

Soak the beans over night, put them on with the soup-bone in nearly six quarts of water and cook five or six hours. When half done add the seasoning; when done, strain through a colander, pressing the pulp of the beans through to make the soup the desired thickness. Serve with a few slices of hard-boiled egg and lemon sliced very thin.

The turtle beans are black and can only be obtained from large grocers.

Vegetable Soup.

3 carrots.
3 turnips.
1 small cabbage.
1 pint tomatoes.

Chop the vegetables, except the tomatoes, very fine; have ready in a porcelain kettle, three quarts of boiling water, and put in all except the cabbage and tomatoes, and simmer for a half hour, then the chopped cabbage and tomatoes, the latter having been stewed; also a bunch of sweet herbs. Let the soup boil for twenty minutes, then strain through a sieve, rubbing all the vegetable through. Take two tablespoonfuls of best butter and one of flour, and beat them to a cream. Now, pepper and salt your soup to taste; add a teaspoonful of white sugar, a half cup of cream, lastly stir in the butter and flour. Let it boil up, and it is ready for the table. Serve with fried bread chips.

Green Corn Soup.

1 large fowl, or 4 pounds of veal.
1 gallon of cold water.

Put the meat in the water without salt, cover tightly and simmer slowly till the meat slips from the bone; do not let it boil to rags, as it will make a nice dish for breakfast. Set aside with the meat a cup full of the liquor. Strain the soup to remove all bones and rags of meat, grate one dozen ears of green corn, scrape the cob to remove the heart of the kernel; add the corn to the soup, with salt, pepper, and a little parsley; simmer slowly a half hour; just before serving, add a tablespoonful of flour beaten very thoroughly with a tablespoonful of butter. Serve hot. To serve the chicken or veal, put the cup of broth in a clean saucepan; beat one egg, a tablespoonful of butter, a tablespoonful of flour, all together very thoroughly, add to the broth, with salt, pepper, and chopped parsley; boil all together for a minute; arrange the meat on a dish, pour over the dressing while boiling hot, and serve at once.

Pea Soup.

2 quarts of good stock.
1 quart of split peas, or green peas.
1 tablespoonful of white sugar.

Soak the peas, if split, over night, and then boil tender in just enough water to prevent them from scorching; when tender, pass through a sieve, and add them to the stock; add pepper and salt to taste; let all come slowly to a boil. Let the soup simmer slowly for thirty minutes, and just before serving, stir in a teaspoonful of butter in which has been stirred a teaspoonful of flour. Serve hot with chips of fried bread.

Dry Bean Soup.

To 1 quart of stock, use
1 pint of dry beans.

Soak the beans over night, in the morning boil until soft; pass through a colander or sieve, and add to the stock, as in pea soup. A sliced onion may be added if desired. Salt and pepper to taste.

Asparagus Soup.

3 or 4 pounds of veal cut fine.
A little salt pork.
2 or 3 bunches of asparagus.
3 quarts of water.
1 pint of milk.

Boil one-half of the asparagus with the meat, leaving the rest in water until about twenty minutes before serving; then add the rest of the asparagus and boil just before serving; add the milk; thicken with a little flour and season. The soup should boil about three hours before adding the last half of the asparagus.

Tomato Soup

1 quart of stock.
1 quart of tomatoes.

Cook the tomato twenty or thirty minutes, or until it becomes a pulp; then strain. Add the tomatoes to the stock, and stir in one tablespoonful of flour rubbed smooth in a tablespoonful of butter. Cook the tomatoes in the stock gently for a half hour. Flavor with pepper. Celery also adds to its flavor.

NOODLES FOR SOUP.

Rub into two eggs as much sifted flour as they will absorb; then roll out until thin as a wafer; dust over a little flour, and then roll over and over into a roll. Cut off thin slices from the edge of the roll and shake out into long strips; put them into the soup lightly and boil for ten minutes; about a salt-spoonful of salt should be added while mixing with the flour.

CROUTONS.

Cut wheat bread in squares of one-half inch, and fry in butter until a golden brown. Take them up in a dish to drain some time before ready for table. Serve with soup instead of crackers.

FISH SOUPS.

Oyster Soup. No. 1.

1½ quarts of milk.
1 quart of oysters.
⅔ cup of butter.
A little salt.

Have ready a bright stew-pan or kettle, into which put the oysters and liquor, with sufficient boiling water to cover the oysters. Stew gently, stirring occasionally for fifteen or twenty minutes. As the scum rises it must be taken off. When the oysters are nearly done, add the milk; and lastly, the butter and salt.

Oyster Soup. No. 2.

1 can oysters.
½ cup butter.
1 tablespoonful of flour.
A little salt.

Drain the liquor from the oysters, and put it in a porcelain kettle, to which add an equal quantity of water. Mix butter and flour and stir in when the liquor boils. Last of all, pour in the oysters and dish as soon as they reach the boiling point. Many persons prefer a cup of cream or milk in addition.

Cove oysters cooked in this way are a very good substitute for fresh ones.

Clam Soup

1 quart clams.
1 small piece of salt pork.
1 large, or two small onions.
2 quarts of water.

1 quart raw potatoes, sliced.
1 tablespoonful flour.
1 pint of milk.
Butter, pepper and salt to taste.

Cut the pork in small squares and fry a light brown. Add onions cut very fine, and cook about ten minutes. Then put in the water and potatoes and let it boil, then add the clams. Mix the flour with milk, pour into the soup, and let it boil about five minutes.

LOBSTER SOUP.

1 large, or 2 small lobsters.
1 quart of milk.
1 pint of water.
1 pound of butter.
1 tablespoonful flour.

Pick all the meat from the shell and chop fine; scald the milk and water, then add the lobster, butter, and flour. Season with salt and red pepper. Boil ten minutes and serve hot.

CAT-FISH SOUP.

6 cat-fish, in average weight ½ pound apiece.
½ pound salt pork.
1 pint milk.
2 eggs.
1 head of celery, or small bag of celery seed.

Skin and clean the fish and cut them up. Chop the pork into small pieces. Put these together into the pot, with two quarts of water, chopped sweet herbs, and the celery seasoning. Boil for an hour, or until fish and pork are in rags, and strain, if you desire a regular soup for first course. Return to the saucepan and add the milk, which should be already hot. Next the eggs, beaten to a froth, and a lump of butter the size of a walnut. Boil up once, and serve with croutons.

FISH.

Purchase fish which have just been caught; of this you can judge by their being hard under the pressure of the finger. Fish soon lose their best flavor, and a few hours make a wide difference in the taste of some sorts. Cod are best in cold weather; mackerel in August, September and October; halibut in May and June. Oysters are good from September to April; but are not healthy from the first of May to the last of August. Lobsters are best at the season when oysters are not good. Pond fish should be soaked in strong salt and water to take out the earthy taste. Fish may be kept good several days, if frozen. All large fish need to be soaked in tepid water before being cleaned; which should be done with great care, all scales and shiny substance being removed with a knife.

BOILED CODFISH. (*Fresh.*)

Lay the fish in cold water, slightly salted, for half an hour before it is time to cook it. Wipe it dry and put it into the fish-kettle with water enough to cover it, in which a little salt has been dissolved. Let it boil quite briskly. A piece of cod weighing three pounds will cook in a half hour from the time the water fairly boils, if put in without a cloth. A better plan is, after wiping the fish, to wrap it in a clean linen cloth, which should be dredged with flour to prevent sticking. Sew up the edges, so as to envelope the fish entirely, but have only one thickness over any part. Fish cooked this way will require twice as long to boil as when put into the water without any covering; but the flavor is better preserved, and when unwrapped, it will not present the crumbling grain, that disfigures most boiled fish.

Rock-Fish.

Rock-fish and river-bass can be nicely cooked in the same way as codfish. It is not necessary to boil them as long.

Boiled Codfish. (*Salt.*)

The fish should be put in lukewarm water and soaked over night. Change the water once during the evening. In the morning change again, and wash off all the salt. An hour or more before dinner time, take it out and put in ice-water, which will make it firm and hard. Set it over the fire in lukewarm water, sufficient to cover, and boil a half hour. Drain it well, lay in a hot dish and pour over drawn butter, in which hard-boiled eggs have been cut up.

Codfish Sounds and Tongues.

Soak them over night, wash, scrape, and boil them gently a short time, in milk and water. To be eaten with drawn butter. If fresh, wash and dry them with a cloth; dip them in corn meal, and fry with a little salt pork.

Salt Codfish and Eggs.

Prepare the fish as for balls.
1 pint rich sweet milk.
3 eggs, well beaten.
1 tablespoonful of butter.
A little chopped parsley.
Pepper.
Heat the milk to near boiling and gradually stir into it the eggs, butter, parsley and finally the fish. Boil up after the fish has been stirred in and then pour it over buttered toast in a deep dish.

Broiled Fish. (*Fresh or Salt.*)

Wash and drain the fish, sprinkle with pepper, and lay with the inside down upon the gridiron, and broil over bright coals. When a light brown, turn for a moment on the other side, then take up and spread with butter. Serve at once.

Codfish and Potato Stew.

Soak, boil and pick the fish, if salt, as for fish-balls. If fresh, boil, and pick into bits. Add an equal quantity of mashed potatoes, a large tablespoonful of butter, and milk enough to make it very soft. Put into a skillet, and add a very little boiling water to keep it from burning. Turn and toss constantly until it is smoking hot but not dry; add pepper and parsley, and dish.

Codfish Balls.

Chop the cold boiled fish very fine. Add one-half as much more mashed potatoes as fish. Mix the potatoes and fish together and work into a stiff batter, adding a lump of butter, and sweet milk, and if you want to have them very nice, a beaten egg. Flour your hands, and make them into balls or cakes. Drop them into hot butter or lard, and fry to a light brown; or melt enough lard or butter in a frying pan, and cook them until they are well browned, taking care to use enough lard or butter, to prevent their sticking to the pan.

Salt Mackerel.

Put to soak over night as many as needed, in plenty of water; in the morning drain them out, put into a skillet and partly cover with hot water; let them stand on top of the stove, cooking slowly (much boiling toughens), for about five minutes. Pour off the water, leaving it dry; melt cream and butter together and pour over. If the fish is No. 1, it will pay for the trouble.

BROILED FRESH MACKEREL.

Open it down the back; wash, and sprinkle salt over, and let it lie for an hour. Grease the gridiron. Lay the skin side down first. The fire should not be hot enough to scorch; turn once or twice, and allow fifteen minutes to broil; lay on a hot dish and put on shavings of butter. The wire gridirons are most convenient for broiling fish, as they are turned without using a knife and fork.

FISH CHOWDER. NO. 1.

Take a pound of salt pork, cut into strips, and soak in hot water five minutes. Cover the bottom of a pot with a layer of this. Cut four pounds of cod or sea-bass into pieces two inches square, and lay enough of these on the pork to cover it. Follow with a layer of chopped onions, a little parsley, summer savory and pepper. Then a layer of split Boston, or butter, or whole cream crackers, which have been soaked in warm water until moist through, but not ready to break. Above this put a layer of pork, and repeat the order given above, until your materials are exhausted. Let the topmost layer be buttered crackers, well soaked. Put in enough cold water to cover all barely. Cover the pot, stew gently for an hour, watching that the water does not sink too low. Should it leave the upper layer exposed, replenish carefully with boiling water. When the chowder is done thoroughly, take out with a perforated skimmer and put into a tureen. Thicken the gravy with a tablespoonful of flour and about the same quantity of butter. Boil up and pour over the chowder.

FISH CHOWDER. NO. 2.

Take thin slices of salt pork and fry brown; leave the fat in the bottom of the kettle. Put in a layer of fried pork, then a layer of potatoes, a layer of fish, layer of crackers; if Boston crackers split them. Season each round of layers with salt and pepper. Fill the kettle in this way; on the top place small pieces of butter, and water sufficient to keep from burning. Cook slowly for one hour and a half. A saucer put in the bottom of the kettle will prevent it sticking to the bottom. If onions are used for seasoning, two or three are sufficient, slice, and put in with the other seasoning.

BROILED SALMON, OR STEAK.

Cut it in slices an inch and a half thick, dry it in a clean cloth, salt it, and lay it upon a hot gridiron, the bars having been rubbed with lard or drippings. It cooks very well in a stove oven, laid in a dripping-pan.

BOILED SALMON.

Clean a salmon in salt and water. Allow twenty minutes for boiling every pound. Wrap it in a floured cloth, and lay it in the kettle while the water is cold. Make the water very salt; skim it well; in this respect it requires more care than any other fish. Serve it with drawn butter and parsley. If salmon is not thoroughly cooked it is unhealthy. When a piece of boiled fresh fish of any kind is left of dinner, it is a very good way to lay it in a deep dish, and pour over it a little vinegar, with catsup, and add pepper, or any other spice which is preferred.

BAKED SALMON.

Wash and wipe dry, and rub with pepper and salt. Lay the fish upon a grating set over your baking pan, and roast or bake, basting it freely with butter, and, toward the last, with its own drippings only. Should it brown too fast, cover the top with a sheet of white paper until the whole is cooked. When it is done, transfer to a hot dish and cover closely, and add to the gravy a little hot water thickened with arrow-root, rice, or wheat flour, wet first with cold water; a great spoonful of tomato sauce, and the juice of a lemon.

SALMON TROUT. (*Baked.*)

Clean, wash and wipe the fish; lay at full length in a baking pan, with water enough to keep from scorching, add a very little salt, if needed. If the fish is large, cut across the back with a sharp knife, a few times. Baste often with butter and water, and bake slowly. When the fish is done, have ready a cup of rich cream, diluted with a few spoonfuls of hot water, in which you have stirred two spoonfuls of melted butter, and a little chopped parsley. Heat this in a vessel set within another vessel of boiling water; add the gravy from the dripping-pan, and boil up to thicken. Pour the gravy over the trout when ready for the table.

BOILED SALMON TROUT.

Clean, wash and dry the trout; envelope in a thin cloth fitted neatly to the shape of the fish, lay within a fish-kettle, cover with cold, salted water, and boil gently a half hour, or longer, according to the size. When done, unwrap and lay in a hot dish. Pour around it a cream sauce and serve.

BROOK TROUT.

Clean, wash and wipe the fish; roll in flour or corn meal, and fry in hot butter or a mixture of lard and butter. Fry them quickly to a light brown. If lard is used to fry them in, they should be seasoned with a little salt when done. Perch, White Fish, Pickerel and other small fish are cooked as above, except that they should be salted when rolled in the flour or meal.

CAT-FISH. (*Fried.*)

Skin, clean and remove the heads. Sprinkle well with salt an hour or more before ready to cook. Have ready a quantity of powdered cracker, and two or three eggs beaten to a froth. First, dip the fish in the egg and then into the powdered cracker and fry in hot lard or drippings.

BOILED SHAD. (*Fresh.*)

A roe-shad is best for boiling. Clean, wash and wipe the fish. Cleanse the roes, and season both eggs and fish with salt; wrap in separate cloths, and put in the kettle. Cover with water, salted, and boil from half to three-quarters of an hour, according to size. Serve with a gravy of drawn butter mingled with chopped egg.

Boiled Shad. (*Salt.*)

Soak the fish several hours in warm water (seven is not too much), changing it several times. Wipe off all the salt, and put it in ice-water for an hour. Put it in the kettle, with fresh water enough to cover, and boil fifteen or twenty minutes, according to size. When done, place a large lump of butter on the fish, and serve in a hot dish.

Fried Shad.

Clean, wash and wipe the shad, remove the head, tail and fins; split it open, and cut each side into four pieces. Season with salt and pepper; dredge with flour or cornmeal. Have ready in the frying-pan hot lard, or drippings; put in the fish and fry until brown. If it is a roe shad, fry the roe in the same way as the fish.

Baked Shad.

Only a large shad should be baked. Clean, wash and wipe the fish, and make a stuffing of grated bread crumbs, softened in sweet milk; add a little butter, salt, pepper and sweet herbs, moistened with a beaten egg. Fill the shad with the stuffing and sew it up. Put a cupful of water in the baking-pan to prevent scorching, and bake one hour. Baste frequently with butter and water. When done, make a gravy with the drippings, adding more water; thicken and season to taste. Turn the gravy over the fish, or serve from sauce boat. Take out the thread with which the fish was sewed before sending to the table.

Broiled Shad. (*Fresh.*)

Wash, wipe and split the fish. Season with salt and pepper; lay upon a buttered gridiron inside downward. Turn the fish when the lower side is brown. A medium sized shad will be done in about twenty minutes. Lay in a hot dish and spread a good piece of butter on the fish.

BROILED SHAD. (*Salt.*)

Lay in lukewarm water and soak over night. In the morning lay it in ice cold water for a half hour.

Wipe and broil in the same manner as fresh shad.

BAKED HALIBUT.

A piece weighing five or six pounds is large enough for baking. Lay it in salt and water for two hours. Score the outer skin and put it in the baking-pan in quite a hot oven, basting it frequently with butter and water, and bake an hour or until a fork will penetrate it easily. Make a gravy from the drippings, using additional water, a little butter, and flour to thicken. Serve the gravy in a sauce boat.

BOILED HALIBUT.

Four or five pounds of halibut is sufficient to boil for an ordinary family. Lay in cold salt and water for a half hour. Wipe dry and cut the skin in squares. Put in the kettle with cold water (salted) enough to cover it, and boil from half to three-quarters of an hour, according to the size of the piece. Drain and serve with egg sauce, or drawn butter poured on the fish, or in a sauce boat.

The remnants of the fish left over, can with the sauce and mashed potato, be warmed up together for breakfast. Season with salt and pepper.

HALIBUT STEAK.

Wash and wipe the steak dry. Dip each steak, after salting, into beaten egg and then in fine pounded cracker; then fry in hot fat or lard. Or the steak can be broiled upon a buttered gridiron; season first with salt and pepper; when done butter well. Lay in a hot dish covered closely.

SMELTS.

Soak smelts a little while in warm water; scrape them, and cut the heads so far that you can gently pull them off, and thus draw out the dark vein that runs through the body; then rinse and lay them into a dry cloth while you fry two or three slices of salt pork crisp. Dip the smelts into a plate of fine Indian meal, and fry them brown. If you fry them in lard or drippings, sprinkle them with salt when nearly done, as they will not brown as well if the salt is put on at first.

STEWED EELS.

An eel weighing a pound is better than one that weighs three. Skin and clean, carefully extracting all the fat from the inside. Cut into lengths of an inch and a half; put into a sauce-pan, with enough cold water to cover them; throw in a little salt and chopped parsley, and stew slowly closely covered for at least one hour. Add, at the last, a great spoonful of butter, and a little flour wet with cold water, also pepper. Serve in a deep dish.

FRIED EELS.

Prepare as for stewing; roll in flour and fry, in hot lard or drippings, to a light brown.

SHELL-FISH.

To Open Clams.

After washing them carefully, pour boiling water over, and let them stand awhile. The shells will open easily.

Boiled Clams.

To boil clams, wash them from the loose sand, put but very little water in the pot; as soon as the shells open they are done; take them out, wash each one carefully in the liquor, cut off the black portions, lay them in a sauce-pan with some of the liquor, a piece of butter rolled in flour, with a little pepper and vinegar; heat scalding hot and serve.

Clam Chowder. (*Canned Clams.*) No. 1.

Take two or three slices of salt pork, cut into small pieces and fry to a crisp; slice six or eight good-sized potatoes, and as many onions; take a large iron pot and put into it a little of the pork and of the fat; then a layer of potatoes; then a layer of onions; then pepper, salt and flour; then a layer of pork again, and repeat layer upon layer until the whole is arranged, then add hot water sufficiently to cover the whole, and let it cook slowly. When nearly done, add a half pound of butter, one quart of milk, and the canned clams. Cook until done, and just before serving, add a few large, hard crackers.

Clam Chowder. No. 2.

Fry five or six slices of fat pork crisp, and chop to pieces. Sprinkle some of these in the bottom of a pot; lay upon them a stratum of clams; sprinkle with pepper and salt, and scatter bits of butter profusely over all; next have a layer of chopped onions, then one of small crackers, split and moistened with warm milk. On these pour a little of the fat left in the pan after the pork is fried, and then comes a new round of pork, clams, onions, etc. Proceed in this order until the pot is nearly full, when cover with water and stew slowly, the pot closely covered, for three-quarters of an hour. Drain off the liquor that will flow freely, and when you have turned the chowder into the tureen, return the gravy to the pot. Thicken with flour, or better still, pounded crackers; add a glass of wine, some catsup, and spiced sauce; boil up and pour over the contents of the tureen.

LOBSTERS. (*To select, and open.*)

Buy those that have been boiled but a few hours. The heaviest, whether large or small, are best. Lobsters are sweet and tender early in the spring, and are good until September. In opening them, care must be taken to remove the poisonous part; this lies in the head, all of which must be thrown away, as well as the vein which passes from it through the body; all the other parts are good. Break the shells with a hammer, and cut open the body on the under side with a sharp knife. Carefully examine the tomalley, or green fat, to see that there is none of the poison vein in it. If you are going to stew the lobster or make salad, save the liquor to mix with the meat.

LOBSTER. (*To Serve.*)

Prepare the lobster as above. Put it on a platter, the meat from the body in the center, and that of the large claws at each end of the dish. Arrange some of the small claws around the edge. Garnish with parsley and lettuce leaves, and serve with vinegar, mustard, and pepper.

OYSTER FRITTERS.

Drain the liquor from the oysters. Then take,
1 cup of the liquor.
1 cup of milk.

3 eggs.
A little salt.
Flour enough for a thin batter.
Mix all together, and stir the oysters in the batter. Have very hot in the frying-pan a few spoonfuls of lard, and drop the oyster batter in by the spoonful. When cooked to a light brown, they must be taken up and served hot.

OYSTER PATTIES.

Line small patty-pans with a nice crust. When cool, turn them out upon a dish. Stew a pint of large oysters one or two minutes in their own liquor, with a heaping teaspoonful of butter, two blades of mace, and a little lemon-juice. Sprinkle in a little flour; take them up, and when they are cool, put two or three oysters in each puff and serve. If the patties are to be eaten hot, stew as above, and bake covers of paste on tins; put the oysters hot, into the puffs, and place over them the covers, fresh from the oven, and serve.

FRIED OYSTERS.

Lay them in a cloth a few minutes to dry them; then dip each one in beaten egg, and then into sifted cracker crumbs, and fry in just enough fat to brown them. Put pepper and salt on them before you turn them over.

SCALLOPED OYSTERS.

Put a layer of crushed crackers in the bottom of a buttered pudding-dish, wetting the layer with slightly warmed oyster-liquor and milk. Next, place a layer of oysters, sprinkled with pepper and salt; lay pieces of butter upon them, then put another layer of crumbs, and so on until the dish is full. Have top layer of crumbs thicker than rest, and beat an egg into milk, poured over them. Stick pieces of butter thickly over it; cover the dish, and bake a half hour.

Oyster Pie.

Roll out a nice puff-paste, a little thicker than for a fruit pie, for the top crust, and about the usual thickness for the lower. Line a pudding dish with the crust, and fill it with crackers or bread crust, to keep the upper crust in place. Cover the dish (having the edges well buttered) with the upper crust pressed down hard to prevent it curling up, and bake. Cook the oysters as for a stew, five minutes, after which add two eggs and a spoonful of fine rolled cracker. Prepare the crust long enough beforehand that the oysters will be done when the crust is baked. Remove the crust, take out the bread crusts, turn in the hot oysters and replace the cover. Serve hot.

Or,

Some may prefer this method. Cover a deep plate with puff paste; put an extra layer round the edge of the plate, and bake nicely. When quite done, fill the pie with oysters; season with butter, salt and pepper; sprinkle a little flour over it, and cover with a thin crust of puff-paste. When the upper crust is done, the oysters should be. Serve immediately, as the crust soon absorbs the gravy.

Raw Oysters.

Wash the shells very thoroughly, and wipe them **dry**. Open them, and remove the upper shell, but leave the under shell with the oyster in it. Place the oysters thus prepared on a dish, with one or two lemons cut in **halves**, and serve. They should be eaten with salt, **pepper, and** lemon-juice, or vinegar.

Pickled Oysters.

100 large oysters.
1 pint white wine vinegar.
1 dozen blades of mace.
2 dozen whole cloves.

2 dozen whole black peppers.
1 large red pepper, broken in bits.

Put oysters, liquor and all, into a porcelain kettle. Salt to taste. Heat slowly until the oysters are very hot, but not to boiling. Take them out with a perforated skimmer and set aside to cool. Add the vinegar and spices to the liquor which remains in the kettle. Boil up fairly and when the oysters are almost cold, pour over them scalding hot. Cover the jar in which they are, and put away in a cool place. Next day put the pickled oysters into glass cans with tight tops. Keep in the dark and where they are not liable to become heated. If you open a can, use as soon as practicable.

Oyster Omelet.

1 dozen oysters, if large; 2 dozen if small.
1 cup of milk.
1½ tablespoonfuls butter.
6 eggs.
Salt and pepper.

Chop the oysters very fine. Beat the yolks and whites separately; the whites to a stiff froth. Melt three spoonfuls of butter in the frying-pan, while mixing the omelet. Stir the milk, yolks and seasoning well together in a dish, and then gradually stir the chopped oysters into the seasoned milk. After they are well mixed pour in one and a half spoonfuls of melted butter, and lastly whip in the whites with as few strokes as possible. Put the omelet into the frying-pan and as soon as it begins to stiffen, slip a broad-bladed knife around the edges, and lift it, that the butter may reach every part. The omelet should not be stirred. When it is stiff in the center, turn it into a hot dish, with the brown side uppermost.

ADDITIONAL RECIPES.

MEAT.

Ox beef is the best; the next best is the flesh of the heifer; and both are in perfection during the first three months of the year. The lean of good beef is red and of a fine grain, and the fat is white. The flesh of diseased animals is sometimes sold in city markets; therefore never buy beef, the fat of which is very yellow, nor mutton and lamb unless the fat is white. Yellow fat indicates that the meat is not healthy. The best roasting pieces of beef are the sirloin; the second cut in the fore quarter; and the rump. If you buy a sirloin for a family of six or eight, get eight or ten pounds. Cut off the thin end in which there is no bone; it is very good corned, and not good roasted. The roasting-piece will still be large enough for the family dinner, and the corned piece will do for another day. The back part of the rump is a convenient and economical piece, especially for a small family. It is a long and narrow piece, weighing about ten pounds, and contains less bone and fat, than any other, equally good, in the ox. The thickest end affords nice steaks, and next to them is a good roasting piece, and the thinnest end, which contains the bone, is good corned or for a soup. The whole piece is excellent for roasting, in case so large a one is needed. The spring is the best season for mutton. Select that which is not very large; it should be of a good red and white color, and fine grained. Lamb is best in July and August; veal is best in the spring; it should look white and be fat; the breast is nice stuffed; the loin should be roasted. The leg is an economical piece, as you can take off cutlets from the large end, stuff and roast the center, and make broth of the shank. Roasting pieces of all kinds of ribbed meat, except beef should be jointed by the butcher, else the carving will be very difficult. Meat will keep in an ice-house, or a good refrigerator, several days in hot weather; if you have neither, take your meat the moment it is brought in, wipe it dry and hang it in the cellar; sprinkling first a little pepper and salt over it, especially the parts which flies are most apt to visit; in mutton and lamb, these are the tenderloin, and the large end of the leg. The pepper and salt will also tend to preserve the meat from taint. You can keep meat longer by wrapping it in a cloth, and laying it in a charcoal bin, with a shovel of coal thrown over it. A leg of mutton will keep several days wrapped in a cloth which has been dipped in vinegar, laid upon the ground of a dry cellar. Meat that is to be salted for immediate use, should, if the weather is cool, be hung up a day or two first. To thaw frozen meat, bring it over night into a warm room; or early in the morning lay it into cold water. If meat is cooked before being entirely thawed, it will be tough. It is best to preserve fowls without freezing; they will keep very well packed in snow; the liver, etc., being taken out and laid by themselves in the snow, and the body filled with it.

Directions for Boiling.

Fresh meat should be put to cook in boiling water, and the water kept boiling; when done, leave the meat in the pot, closely covered, until cool. Remove the scum at the first boil, from all meats. All salt meats should be put on in cold water. Ham should be skinned as soon as it is done. Corned beef will be more tender if allowed to cool in the water in which it is boiled. Allow twenty minutes to a pound of fresh meat; but a little more time is required to cook a hind than a fore quarter. Salt meat should boil longer than fresh; allow forty minutes for every pound. The two things most important in boiling meat, are, to boil it gently, and to skim it until no more froth rises. Have a spoon and dish handy, and the moment the froth begins to rise, skim it off. If the water boils fast before you begin to take off the froth, it will return to the water, adhere to the meat, and make it look badly. Some persons throw a handful of flour into the kettle to prevent scum from adhering to the meat. If the water boils away so that the meat is not covered, add more, as the part which lies above the water will have a dark appearance.

DIRECTIONS FOR ROASTING MEAT.

It is not well to salt meat at first, as salt extracts the juices. In roasting all meats, the art depends chiefly on flouring thoroughly, basting frequently, and turning so often as not to allow any part to burn. To roast in a cooking-stove, it is necessary to attend carefully to the fire, lest the meat should burn. Lay it into the pan with three or four gills of water in it. Turn the pan around often, that all the parts may roast equally. When it is about half done, flour it again, turn it over that the lower side may become brown. If the water in it dries away, add a little hot water. Allow about a quarter of an hour to a pound if you like the beef rare, more if you prefer it done. For gravy remove the beef to a dish, skim the drippings, add a cup of boiling water, a teaspoonful of flour stirred in cold water. Pepper and salt to taste.

BEEF STEAK. NO. 1.

The best slices are cut from the rump, or through the sirloin. The round is seldom tender enough, and is very good cooked in other ways. Do not cut your slices very thick. Have ready a good bed of live coals, and a heated gridiron. Turn the steaks in less than a minute; and turn them repeatedly. If the fat makes a blaze under the gridiron, put it out by sprinkling fine salt on it. Steaks will broil in about seven minutes. Have ready a hot dish, and sprinkle each piece with salt, and a little pepper; lay on small pieces of butter and cover close. This is a much better way than to melt the butter in the dish before taking up the meat. Some persons keep a small pair of tongs on purpose to turn beef steaks, as using a fork wastes the juice. Steaks should be served as hot as possible.

BEEF STEAK. NO. 2.

Have your frying-pan very hot, wipe the steak dry, place in it, and cover tightly. Turn frequently and keep covered. When done, add to the gravy a good sized lump of butter, salt and pepper to taste. Pour over the steak, and serve hot. If your meat is tough, pound *well* with a steak mallet on both sides.

TOUGH BEEF STEAK.

Set a large kettle on the stove until it is hot, but not so as to scorch. Put in the beef, turning frequently, until it is well browned. Then pour in water, about a pint to a pound of beef, and let it simmer slowly for about a half hour. Take out the beef, season the soup with salt and pepper, catsup, onions and tomato, if liked, and thicken with a little browned flour. Chop the meat fine, season with butter, salt and pepper, and lay on slices of toast.

CORNED BEEF. (*Boiled.*)

Wash the meat carefully. Corned beef should be put in cold water and boiled until tender; skim often. It is not too much to allow forty minutes for every pound, after it has begun to boil. If it is to be eaten cold, it should be put away in some flat-bottomed dish, with a weight over it. Let it stand until perfectly cold, and slice thin.

BEEF TONGUE.

A corned tongue may be put to boil as soon as washed; but one that has been long salted should be soaked over night. A smoked tongue should be well washed, then soaked in a plenty of water over night. All tongues should be boiled until so tender that a fork will go in very easily. This will require from three to five hours, according to the size. When they begin to boil, the water should be carefully skimmed. When you take up the tongue, while it is yet hot, remove the skin, which will easily pull off with the aid of a sharp knife. When it is cold, before sending to the table, trim off the roots. The fat on the water in which a corned tongue is boiled is nice for shortening; that from a smoked tongue must be put in the soap-grease.

DRIED BEEF.

Dried beef is commonly served by shaving off thin shavings or chips to be eaten uncooked. A savory dish may be made by putting chips of the beef into a frying-pan with enough boiling water to cover them. Let this set over the fire for a few minutes, to soften the meat, then drain off the water, and put into the pan with the bits of meat, a tablespoonful of butter and a little pepper. Beat an egg, or more, according to the quantity of meat, and pour into the pan with the chipped meat. Stir together for a minute or two, until the egg is cooked. Serve in a covered dish.

FRENCH METHOD FOR COOKING BEEF.

For a family dinner buy several pounds of solid lean beef, having it cut, if possible, from that side of the round where the flesh is thickest. Do not have it in steaks, but thick and square. Lard it very fully with strips of fat salt pork, tie it with a small cord to keep it in shape, and put it in a perfectly tight, covered tin pail. Put it in without water, and add one carrot chopped, one half slice of onion chopped, a little celery seed, a half teaspoonful of sage and the same of sweet marjoram and thyme, cover the pail in such a way as to entirely exclude the air, and put it in an iron pot of water and let it boil steadily. If the water in the outside vessel boils away replenish it with hot water from the teakettle, which can be kept at hand for the purpose. After three hours open the pail and turn the beef the other side up. Add salt and pepper and fill the pail nearly to the top with raw potatoes cut in thick slices; cover again and boil three hours longer.

Then take the cord off the meat and put it in the center of a large flat dish and surround it with boiled rice; put the potatoes upon the rice and pour over all the seasoned extract or gravy which will be found in the pail. If it is inconvenient to have the range occupied so long by the the kettle, set the pail in the oven and the result will be almost equal. In that case it will only require five hours cooking instead of six. It seems like a long process, but it requires very little care or watching, and if once successfully tried it is sure to become an oft repeated family institution. If it is properly prepared no one flavor predominates.

BEEF LIVER.

Cut in slices half an inch thick, and pour over them boiling water until the outside turns white; remove this white outer skin, salt, pepper, and flour each slice, and fry in hot lard or butter, turning often. When done, take from the frying-pan, and pour into it a cup of sweet cream, add a little pepper and salt, a teaspoonful of flour made smooth with water; boil up once, pour over the liver and serve.

BEEF HASH.

Corned beef is best for a hash, but any kind can be used. Take about equal quantities of meat and potato. Chop the meat very fine and add the mashed potato; season with salt and pepper. Melt a good sized piece of butter in the frying-pan, and put in the meat and potato with a cupful of milk. Set it over the fire for a few minutes, stirring often to prevent burning.

If you prefer you can mould the mixture into flat cakes, dip them in beaten egg, and fry in hot drippings.

MEAT PIE.

Take pieces of meat, either steak or roast, and put them into water and cook until very tender. Line a pudding-dish with paste, put in a layer of the meat, and season as for chicken pie; fill the dish. A chopped onion and sliced parboiled potatoes can be added if desired. Pour over this the gravy in which the meat was cooked, thicken with a little flour and cover with a crust. Bake until the crusts are well cooked. Make a slit in the upper crust, before baking, for the steam to escape.

Crust for Meat Pie.

1 quart of flour.
3 tablespoonfuls of lard.
2½ cups of milk.
1 teaspoonful of soda, dissolved in hot water, and stirred into the milk.
2 teaspoonfuls cream tartar sifted in the dry flour.
1 teaspoonful of salt.
Work up quickly and lightly, and do not get too stiff.

Beef Omelet.

4 pounds of round beef, uncooked, chopped fine.
6 eggs beaten together.
5 or 6 soda crackers rolled fine.
A little butter and suet.
Pepper and salt.
Sage if you choose; make two loaves, roll in cracker; bake about an hour, and slice when cold.

Beef Croquettes.

Chop fine some cold beef; beat two eggs and mix with the meat and add a little milk, melted butter, and salt and pepper. Make into rolls and fry.

Pickle for Beef, Pork and Tongues.

4 gallons water.
1½ pounds of sugar, or molasses.
2 ounces saltpeter.
6 pounds salt.
If to last a month or two, this quantity of salt is sufficient, if over summer, nine pounds of salt. Boil all together gently; skim and let cool. Put the meat in the

vessel in which it is to stand. Pour the pickle on the meat until it is covered. Keep the meat under the pickle with a stone. Use the above proportions for a larger quantity if required. This is sufficient for one hundred pounds of beef.

BEEF. (*To corn.*)

To each gallon of cold water, put one quart of rock salt, one ounce of saltpeter and four ounces of brown sugar (it need not be boiled), as long as any salt remains undissolved, the meat will be sweet. If any scum should rise, scald and skim well; add more salt, saltpeter and sugar; as you put each piece of meat into the brine, rub over with salt. If the weather is hot, gash the meat to the bone, and put it in salt. Put a flat stone or some weight on the meat to keep it under the brine.

VEAL STEAK.

This should be thinner than beef-steak and should be thoroughly cooked. Broil upon a well-greased gridiron, over a clear fire; turn frequently while the steaks are cooking.

VEAL CUTLETS.

Sprinkle the cutlets with pepper and salt. Dip them in beaten egg, roll in fine cracker crumbs, and fry in hot drippings or lard. For gravy, add a little water, thicken with flour and cook for a few minutes. Serve in a sauce-boat. Another way is, to rub the cutlets in melted butter and broil on a gridiron as beef-steak, and butter well before sending to the table.

VEAL CHOPS.

Veal chops are more juicy and less apt to be tough than cutlets. Trim as in mutton chops, and fry in butter or lard. Dip the chops in beaten egg and fine cracker crumbs. The gravy is made in the same way as for cutlets and can be seasoned with parsley or any other seasoning desired.

MEATS.

BROILED VEAL.

It must not be done too fast, and will take longer than beef. It is a great improvement to broil pork and lay between the slices of veal. Lay them upon the meat while it is broiling, and if they are not brown when the veal is done, put them a few minutes longer on the gridiron. If pork is not used, season with butter. Add pepper and salt.

VEAL PIE.

Take about two pounds of veal from the loin, fillet, or any odd pieces you may have. Parboil long enough to clear of the bone, cut in thin even slices. Line a pudding-dish with a good paste. Put a layer of veal in the bottom, seasoned with salt and pepper. Enrich with butter or slices of salt pork, and dredge in a little flour. So proceed until all is in. Pour in a portion of the water in which the meat was boiled. Cover with a crust and cut a little hole in the top for the escape of steam. Bake one hour and a half.

ROAST FILLET OF VEAL.

Veal requires more time for roasting than any other meat except pork. It is scarcely ever done too much. A leg weighing eight or nine pounds should roast three hours. Prepare a stuffing of bread, pepper, salt pork, and sweet marjoram; make deep incisions in the meat and fill them with it. Fasten the fold of fat which is usually upon the fillet over the stuffed incisions with a skewer. Roast it slowly at first. Put into the dripping-pan some hot water with a little salt in it or some of the stock. When the meat has roasted about an hour, flour it thickly, and skewer upon it four or five slices of salt pork; after the flour becomes brown, baste the veal every fifteen minutes. In cutting the incisions, endeavor to make them wider inside than at the surface, so that the stuffing may not fall out.

Veal Pot Pie.

Take the neck, the shank, and almost any pieces you may have. Boil them long enough to skim off all the froth. Have ready a kettle; put in a layer of meat, then flour, salt and pepper, and add a little butter or a slice or two of salt pork, as your choose. Do this until you have laid in all your meat; pour in enough of the water in which the veal was boiled to half fill the kettle, then lay on a top crust which has been rolled about half an inch thick, and make an incision in it to allow the escape of the steam. Watch that it does not burn, and pour in more of the water through the hole in the crust if necessary. Boil an hour and a half. The objection to this dish is, that boiled crust is apt to be heavy, and therefore unhealthy; but if it is made after the recipe for cream tartar biscuit, it will be light.

A Loin of Veal.

A breast or a loin of veal should be basted a great many times and roasted thoroughly. It is an improvement to put on slices of pork as in cooking the leg. Allow two hours for roasting; more, if it is large. Flour it well.

Veal Loaf.

3½ pounds raw veal (lean and fat).
1 slice salt pork.
6 small crackers rolled fine.
Piece of butter, size of an egg.
2 eggs.
1 tablespoonful salt.
1 tablespoonful pepper.
1 tablespoonful sage.
3 tablespoonfuls extract celery.

Chop the veal fine, and mix the ingredients thoroughly. Pack tightly in a deep square tin; cover with bits of butter, and sprinkle fine cracker-crumbs over the top. Cover with another tin. Bake two hours, uncover, and brown the top. A nice relish for tea, and should be sliced thin when cold.

VEAL OMELET.

4 pounds lean veal.
1 pound salt pork, chopped fine.
1 tablespoonful salt.
1 tablespoonful pepper.
2 tablespoonfuls sage or thyme.
4 tablespoonfuls bread crumbs.
4 eggs (beaten).
½ pint sweet cream.

Mix the eggs, cream, and bread crumbs together, then add the other ingredients. Bake in a deep dish three hours and a half; put small pieces of butter on the top before baking. When done turn out on a platter.

SWEETBREAD. (*Fried.*)

Scald in salt and water, take out the stringy parts; then put in cold water a few minutes; dry in a towel; dip in egg and bread crumbs, and fry brown in butter; when done place in a hot dish. Pour into the pan a cup of sweet cream, a little pepper and salt, and a little parsley chopped fine; add flour, and when boiling pour over the sweetbreads.

SWEETBREAD. (*Broiled.*)

Parboil, rub them well with butter, and broil on a clean gridiron; turn them often and now and then roll them over in a plate containing hot melted butter, to prevent them from getting hard and dry.

MUTTON STEW.

Take three or four pounds of meat; cut it in small squares, crack the bones and remove all the fat. Put meat and bones in enough cold water to cover well, and set it where it will gradually heat. Cover closely. When it has stewed an hour, put in half a pound of salt pork cut in strips, a chopped onion, and some pepper. Cover and stew until the meat is tender. Make a paste like meat pie crust, roll and cut in squares, and drop in the stew, and cook ten minutes. Keep closely covered after the dumplings are put in or they will be heavy. More seasoning, such as parsley and thyme can be added when the dumplings are added. Finally thicken with two spoonfuls of flour broken up in cold milk, and boil up once more. The stew is greatly improved by the addition of green corn, if in season, which should be added an hour before it is taken from the fire. The grains from six or seven ears, cut from the cob, are sufficient. A stew made in this way from lamb, is even better than mutton.

Roast Mutton.

The parts roasted are the shoulder, saddle, loin and chine. Wash the meat well, and dry it with a cloth. Put the meat on with a little water (which should always be done for roast meats). If your fire is hot, allow for roasting twelve minutes to each pound of meat; baste with salt and water, then with the drippings; thicken the gravy with browned flour.

Broiled Mutton, or Lamb Chops.

Have the leg cut into steaks at the market, or by the butcher. Have the slices about the thickness of your finger; separate them from the bone neatly. Dip each in beaten egg, roll in pounded cracker, and fry in hot lard or drippings. If the fat is not salt, sprinkle the chops with salt, before rolling in the egg. Serve up dry and hot.

Or,

The egg and cracker may be omitted, then broil on a gridiron over a brisk fire. Salt, pepper and butter each chop before they are sent to the table. Lamb chops may be cooked in the same way.

BONED LEG OF MUTTON.

Have the bone taken out of a nice, fat leg of mutton. Make a rich stuffing of bread crumbs, hard boiled eggs chopped fine, butter, onions chopped fine, a little sage, a small quantity of black pepper, some pickled pork, cut up. Fill the leg with this forcemeat, and bake, basting often.

BOILED MUTTON.

Wash a leg of mutton clean and wipe dry. Do not leave the knuckle and shank so long as to be unshapely. Put into a pot with hot water (salted) enough to cover it, and boil until you ascertain, by probing with a fork, that it is tender in the thickest part. Skim off all the scum as it rises. Allow *about* twelve minutes to each pound. Take from the fire, drain perfectly dry, and serve with melted butter. If you wish to use the broth for soup, put in very little salt while boiling; if not, salt it well, and boil the meat in a cloth.

MUTTON CUTLETS.

Cut the cutlets from the neck and trim neatly. The trimmings and bits of bone may be used for gravy. Lay them in melted butter for fifteen or twenty minutes, taking care that the butter does not harden. Then dip each cutlet in beaten egg and fine cracker crumbs, and put in the dripping-pan with just water enough to prevent them from scorching. Baste often with butter and water, and bake quickly. Put the bones and bits of meat in just enough cold water to cover them, and stew sufficiently long to extract all the substance from them. Strain, season, and thicken with a little flour; then pour it over the cutlets when ready for the table.

PORK.

Lard.

Leaf lard is the nicest for all cooking purposes. Skin all the fat that is to be tried into lard; if the fat is not skinned before trying, the gluten in the skin will make the lard impure and frothy. Cut the leaves into small pieces, put them in a clean kettle over a slow fire, or in a larger vessel of water; throw in a little salt to make the sediment settle. Great care must be taken that it does not burn, for that will spoil the whole. A teacupful of water added before it becomes hot will prevent burning. Dip off the fat as fast as it liquefies and strain it through a cloth; when all is strained that can be dipped off, squeeze the remainder by itself through the cloth. If the cloth becomes clogged with the cold fat, dip it in hot water. Lard keeps much longer in small vessels than in large. Bladders tied over the jars are the best protection; next to these, paper, and outside of this, cloths dipped in the melted lard. To use up the refuse pieces of fat, take the fat to which the small intestines are attached (not the large ones), and flabby pieces of pork not good for salting; try these in the same way as the leaf lard, and set the fat thus obtained where it will freeze, and by spring the strong taste will be gone, and it can be used for frying.

Roast Pig.

It should not be more than a month old, and should be killed on the morning of the day it is to be cooked. Sprinkle fine salt over it an hour before it is put to the fire. Cut off the feet at the first joint. Make stuffing enough to fill it very full. When placed in the roaster, confine the legs in such a manner as to give it good shape. Rub it all over with butter or sweet oil, to keep it from blistering. Flour it at first a little; as soon as it begins to brown, dredge on a *very* thick covering of flour. If the flour falls off, instantly renew it. When it has all become of a dark brown color, scrape it off into a plate and set it aside. Put a piece of butter into the gravy in the roaster, and baste the pig very often, until it is done. The feet and liver should be boiled an hour or two, and the gravy from the roaster be poured into the water in which they were boiled. The gravy should be thickened with the browned flour reserved in the plate. A pig a month old will roast in two hours and a half.

SHOULDER OF PORK.

One weighing ten pounds will require full three hours and a half to roast it. For a small family divide it, and roast one half and corn the other. With a sharp knife score the skin in strips about an inch wide. Make a dressing, and put this into deep incisions made in the thick part of the meat. Rub a little fine powdered sage into the skin where it is scored; and then rub the whole surface with sweet oil, or drippings, to prevent its blistering. Baste often and frequently turn the meat. Pork burns very easily, and both the taste and appearance are much injured by its being burnt. While cooking, flour it often.

SPARE-RIB, OR CHINE.

A spare-rib requires an hour and a half or two hours, according to the thickness. A very thin one will roast in an hour and a half. Flour it well, and take care it does not burn. Baste it often. The chine requires a longer time being a thicker piece. It is more healthy, because less fat than the spare-rib, and having more meat in proportion to the bone, is a more economical piece. Before roasting either, trim off neatly all the fat which can be removed without disfiguring the piece, and set it aside to be tried and used as lard.

Pork Steaks.

Cut slices from the loin and neck. To fry pork steaks requires twenty-five or thirty minutes. Turn them often. If they are quite fat, pour off all that fries out when they are half done and reserve it for some other use. Then dip the steaks in crumbs of bread with a little powdered sage, and lay them back into the frying-pan. When done through take them up, dredge a little browned flour into the gravy, put in salt, pour in a gill of boiling water, and turn it instantly, as it boils up, upon the dish of steaks.

To Make Sausages.

6 lbs. lean fresh pork.
3 lbs. fat fresh pork.
12 teaspoonfuls powdered sage.
6 teaspoonfuls black pepper.
6 teaspoonfuls salt.

Grind the meat, fat and lean, in a sausage-mill, or chop it very fine, and the latter can be done much easier when the meat is frozen. Mix the seasoning in with your hands, taste, to be sure all is right, and pack in stone jars, pouring melted lard on top. Another good way of preserving them is, to make long, narrow bags of stout muslin, large enough to contain, each, enough sausage for a family dish. Fill these with the meat, dip in melted lard, and hang from the beams of the cellar. If you wish to pack in the intestines of the hog, they should be carefully prepared, as follows: Empty them, cut them in lengths, and lay for two days in salt and water. Turn them inside out, and lay in soak one day longer. Scrape them, rinse in soda and water, wipe and blow into one end, having tied up the other with a bit of twine. If they are whole and clear, stuff with the meat; tie up and hang in the store-room or cellar.

To Fry Sausages.

These are fried in the cases, in a clean, dry frying-pan until brown. If you have the sausage meat in bulk, make in small, round flat cakes, and fry in the same manner. Some dip in egg and pounded cracker, others roll in flour before cooking. Their own fat will cook them. Send to table dry and hot, but do not let them fry hard. When one side is done turn the other. The fire should be very brisk. Fifteen or twenty minutes is long enough to cook them.

BOLOGNA SAUSAGE.

Take equal parts of veal, pork, and ham. Chop them fine and season with sweet herbs, salt, pepper (cayenne and black), and spices if desired. Stuff into beef skins; tie them up, prick the skins in several places to allow the steam to escape, and put them into hot water and gradually heat to the boiling point. Cook slowly for an hour, then take out the skins and let them dry in the sun. Rub the outside of the skins when dry, with oil, or melted butter, and hang in a dry, cool cellar. If they are to be kept some time, rub pepper over the outside of the skins. These can be eaten without more cooking, although some persons prefer to boil them in a little water before eating. Cut in round slices when sent to the table.

MOLASSES CURED HAMS.

Moisten every part of the ham with molasses, and then for every one hundred pounds, use one quart of fine salt, and four ounces of salt petre; rubbing them in thoroughly at every point. Put the hams thus prepared, in a tight cask for four days. Then rub again with molasses and one quart salt, and return to the cask for four days. Repeat this the third and fourth time, and then smoke the hams. This process takes only sixteen days, while other methods require five or six weeks.

BOILED HAM OR SHOULDER.

A ham, weighing twelve pounds, should be cooked four or five hours. Boil it slowly in a plenty of water half the time it should be cooked; then take off the skin and any excrescences that were not removed by washing. Cover the fat side with pounded cracker, and lay it in a dripping-pan, or iron basin, and put it into the stove. Let it remain the other half of the time. The baking roasts out a great quantity of fat, and leaves the meat much more delicate. In warm weather it will keep in a dry, cool place, a long time. If a ham is very salt, it should lie in water over night. In baking it, care should be taken that it is not done too much, and thus made dry. The fat which bakes out is good to fry eggs, or potatoes, and if not strong will do to use on the griddle.

HAM AND EGGS.

Cut thin slices and take off the rind; if very salt, pour hot water upon them, but do not suffer them to lie long in it, as the juices of the meat will be lost. Wipe them in a cloth; have the spider ready hot, lay in the pieces and turn them in a minute or two. They will cook in a very short time. The secret of having good fried ham is in cooking it quickly and not too much. The practice of cutting thick slices, laying them into a cold spider and frying a long time, makes ham black and hard. Have the eggs ready, and drop them, one at a time, in the hissing fat. Have a large pan for this purpose, that they may not touch and run together; in three minutes they will be done. The meat should be kept hot, and when the eggs are ready, lay one upon each slice of ham.

BROILED HAM.

Cut the slices very thin; pare off the rind, and lay them on the gridiron over hot coals. Do not leave them a moment, as they must be almost immediately turned, and will need attention to keep the edges from burning.

SALT PORK. (*Fried.*)

Cut into slices, and lay them in cold water in the spider; boil them up two or three minutes, then pour off the water and set the spider again on the coals and brown the slices on each side. Fried pork with baked potatoes, and fried sour apples makes a very good dinner. It is an improvement to dip the pork, after being parboiled, into Indian meal, before frying it.

PIGS FEET.

They should be thoroughly cleaned and thrown into salt water over night, then boiled until almost in pieces. While cooking drop in the water a small red pepper pod, a few whole cloves and allspice. When done and well drained, put the feet one by one into a jar and cover with good clear vinegar, and in two days they will be ready for the table. A nice breakfast dish is made by cutting the feet into halves, dipping them in a batter, and frying in hot lard till they are of a light brown.

HEAD CHEESE OR SOUSE.

This is made of the head, ears, and tongue. Boil them in salted water until very tender. Strip the meat from the bones and chop fine. Season with salt, pepper, sage, sweet marjoram, and half a cup of strong vinegar. Mix all together thoroughly, taste to see that it is flavored sufficiently, remembering that the spice tends to keep it; pack hard in moulds or bowls. Press down and keep the meat in shape by putting a plate on the top of each mould (first wetting the plate), and a weight upon this. In two days the cheese will be ready for use. This is generally eaten cold for tea, with vinegar and mustard; but it is very nice cut in slices, seasoned slightly with mustard, and warmed in a frying-pan with enough butter to prevent burning.

TRIPE.

Boil it until tender. When cold, cut it in pieces four or five inches square; flour it a little, grease the gridiron and broil over a clear fire; lay it in a hot dish, add pepper and salt and butter and serve. To fry it; lay two or three slices of fat pork into a spider, and when these are crisp, dip the pieces of tripe in a beaten egg, and sprinkle them with fine crumbs of bread or cracker and fry brown. They are sometimes dipped in batter.

Baked Pork and Beans.

For a family of six or seven, take a quart of white beans, wash them in several waters, and put them into two or three quarts over night. In the morning boil them until they begin to crack open; then put them in a brown pan, such as are made for the purpose; pour upon them enough hot water to cover them. Take a pound of salt pork and cut the rind into narrow strips; lay it on top of the beans, and press it down so that it will lie more than half its thickness in the water. Bake several hours, four or five is not too much. Where a brick oven is used, it is well to let beans remain in it over night. If they are baked in a stove, or range, more water may be necessary, before they are done. Many persons think it an improvement to put in a large spoonful or two of molasses. Those who object to the use of pork, can have a very good dish of beans by substituting fat beef, and adding two teaspoonfuls of salt. To heat over baked beans, put them in a spider with a little water; heat them slowly at first, and cover closely. If they are too moist, remove the cover and stir often.

POULTRY.

A young turkey has a smooth leg, and a soft bill, and if fresh the eyes will be bright, and the feet moist. Old turkeys have scaly, stiff feet.

Young fowls have a tender skin, smooth legs, and the breast bone readily yields to the pressure of the finger. The best are those that have yellow legs. The feet and legs of old fowls look as if they had seen hard service in the world. Young ducks feel tender under the wing, and the web of the foot is transparent; the best are thick and hard on the breast. Young geese have yellow bills, and the feet are yellow and supple; the skin may be easily broken by the head of a pin; the breast is plump, and the fat white. An old goose is unfit for the human stomach.

ROAST TURKEY OR CHICKEN.

Dress and wash the fowl inside and out in two or three waters; in next to the last, mix a teaspoonful of soda, the soda is very cleansing. Fill the body with the soda water, shake well, empty it out and rinse thoroughly with clear water. Salt and pepper the inside, and fill the body and breast with the dressing given below. Sew it up with a needle and coarse thread; tie the skin over the neck with a thread or piece of twine. Sprinkle pepper and salt on the outside, and dredge thickly with flour. Put in a slow oven allowing fifteen minutes to the pound; as a general rule that is sufficient, but of course one must be guided by the age of the fowl. Baste frequently; stew the giblets in a sauce-pan, when cooked chop fine, add the water in which they were boiled, to the gravy of the roast fowl, also the chopped giblets; thicken with a little flour previously wet in water. Boil up once and pour in a gravy boat. If the fowl is very fat, skim the drippings well before putting in the giblets.

Dressing for Turkey or Chicken.

Grate bread crumbs fine, and mix with them butter, pepper, salt, thyme, marjoram or sage; wet with hot water or milk. You may, if you like, add the beaten yolks of two eggs, or mince a dozen oysters and stir into the dressing, and if partial to the taste wet the bread crumbs with the oyster liquor. Stuff the craw with this and tie a string tightly about the neck to prevent the escape of the stuffing; then fill the body of the fowl and sew up with a strong thread. This and the neck string must be removed when the fowl is dished.

Boiled Turkey or Chicken.

Take a young fowl, fill the inside with oysters and dressing, and baste about it a thin cloth fitted closely to every part; the inside of the cloth should be dredged with flour to prevent the cloth sticking to it. Place in a kettle of boiling water, enough to cover it well. Boil until tender. There will be a gravy in the kettle from the juice of the fowl. Make this into a white sauce with the addition of a little butter or cream. Add oysters, or serve up plain; the addition of a little parsley is an improvement.

Pressed Turkey or Chicken.

Boil one or two chickens in enough water to cook very tender. Take them out when done, remove all the bones, mincing the meat very fine; season with salt, pepper and butter, and return them to the water in which they were boiled. Cook them until the liquor is nearly gone; then pour the contents into a deep dish, lay a plate over it, put on a weight and set away in a cool place. When eaten, cut in slices. It will be as firm as cheese, and is very nice for tea.

POULTRY.

FRICASSEED CHICKEN.

Boil them until tender in water enough barely to cover them. Take off the scum as fast as it rises. Take them up and carve in the usual way. Put part of the water in which they were boiled into a spider or stew-pan. For two chickens rub a piece of butter as large as an egg, and a spoonful of flour together, and stir into the water as it boils up. Add some salt, and a gill of cream or milk. Lay in the pieces of chicken, cover the pan close, and stew them gently twenty minutes. Parsley cut fine is a decided improvement.

FRIED CHICKEN.

Cut the chicken in pieces, lay it in salt and water, which should be changed several times. Roll each piece in flour, beat two eggs, dip each piece in this and fry in hot lard. Season with salt and pepper. For gravy use cream or rich milk, seasoned with salt and pepper, and butter rubbed into flour. Stir constantly until it boils again.

BROILED CHICKEN.

If you are not sure your chicken is tender, it can be prepared in the following way: Lay some sticks across a dripping-pan filled with boiling water, and place the fowl on the sticks, after splitting it open through the back. Cover with a pan and steam for half an hour in the oven, and then transfer to a buttered gridiron, inside downward; broil slowly and let care be taken that they do not burn; turn in ten minutes. To keep them flat lay a tin sheet upon them with a weight. Turn several times; broil half or three-quarters of an hour. They can be broiled best in charcoal.

PICKLED CHICKEN.

Take in the fall, large, fat chickens, dress and boil whole until the meat will slip easily from the bone; place them in earthen jars, and pour over hot vinegar. When cold, they are ready for use. A nice relish for the tea-table, and much more wholesome, and quite as palatable, as pickled pigs feet.

Chicken Pie.

Boil chickens in water barely to cover them, until tender. Skim the water carefully. Take them out in a dish, cut them up, and remove the larger bones. If the skin is very thick, remove it. Have ready, lined with a thick paste, a deep dish, of a size proportioned to the number of chickens you wish to use; put in the pieces, with the hearts and livers, in layers; sprinkle each layer with flour, salt, and pepper, and put on each piece of chicken a thin shaving of butter; do this until you have laid in all the pieces; put rather more flour and butter over the top layer than on the previous ones, and pour in as much of the liquor in which the chickens were boiled as you can without danger of its boiling over. Lay on the upper crust, and close the edges very carefully with flour and water; prick the top with a knife. Cut leaves of crust and ornament it. Bake two hours. The crust for chicken pie should be twice as thick as for fruit pies.

Prairie Chickens, Quails and other Small Birds.

Dress with care, using a little soda in the water in which they are washed, then rinse and wipe them dry, and fill with dressing; sew them up neatly, and bind down the legs and wings with cords. Put them in a steamer and let them cook until just done. Then set them in the oven, in a pan, with salt and a small piece of butter, and baste often until they are of a nice brown, which ought not to take more than fifteen minutes.

Broiled Prairie Chicken.

Broil like other chickens, but longer, because they are larger, and the meat is thick. The fire should not be very hot, as they should broil gradually. Lay upon a hot platter, sprinkle with salt and pepper and put on a plenty of butter. The meat is very dry, therefore considerable butter is necessary.

Fricasseed Prairie Chicken.

Remove the inwards, wash the chickens, and boil an hour, or a little more. Skim carefully. Strain the liquor into a stew-pan. When it boils up, add, for one chicken, a spoonful of butter, two or three teaspoonfuls of browned flour, salt, and a little pepper, and stew ten minutes.

Roast Duck.

Clean, wash and wipe the ducks very carefully. To the usual dressing add a little sage, and a minced shallot. Stuff and sew up as usual, reserving the giblets for the gravy. If they are tender, they will not require more than an hour to roast. Baste well. Skim the gravy before putting in the giblets and thickening. The giblets should be stewed in a very little water, then chopped fine, and added to the gravy in the dripping-pan, with a chopped shallot and a spoonful of browned flour.

Roast Goose.

Wash thoroughly, using a little soda, rinse and then boil half an hour to take out the strong, oily taste; stuff and roast it exactly like a turkey. If it is a young one, an hour's roasting will be sufficient.

Roast Pigeons.

Pick out the pin feathers, or if there are a great many, pull off the skin. Examine the inside very carefully. Soak them half an hour in a good deal of water, to take out the blood. Then boil them with a little salt in the water, half an hour, and take off the scum as fast as it rises. Take them out, flour them well, and lay them in a dripping-pan; strain the water in which they were boiled, and put a part of it into the pan; stir in it a little piece of butter, and baste the pigeons often. Add pepper and sweet marjoram if you prefer. Roast them nearly two hours. Pigeons need to be cooked a long time.

Pigeon Pie.

Pick, soak and boil pigeons with the same care as directed in the recipe for roasting them. Make a crust as for chicken or veal pie. Lay in the pigeons whole, and season with pepper, salt, shavings of butter, and sweet marjoram; flour them thickly, then strain the water in which they were boiled, and fill the dish two-thirds full with it. Lay the top crust over and close the edges well. Make many incisions with the point of a knife, or a large fork, and bake an hour and a half.

GAME.

TO KEEP GAME FROM TAINTING.

Draw as soon as they come into your possession; rinse with soda and water, then with pure cold water; wipe dry, and rub them lightly with a mixture of fine salt and black pepper. If you must keep them some time, put in the cavity of each fowl a piece of charcoal; hang them in a cool, dark place, with a cloth thrown over them. Small birds, unless there are too many of them, may be kept in a refrigerator after you have drawn, washed and wiped them. The charcoal is an admirable preventive of decomposition.

VENISON.

Roast a haunch like a loin or leg of veal, and about as long. Flour it thickly. Put some of the stock for gravies, or water in which beef has been boiled, into a pan, and baste it often. Half an hour before serving it, add a tablespoonful of butter to the gravy, and baste it again and again. Most persons like venison cooked simply without spices. But if you prefer a dressing, make it as for veal, with the addition of powdered clove.

Venison steaks are cooked like beef steaks.

RABBITS AND SQUIRRELS.

Clean and wash them well; scald them fifteen or twenty minutes in just water enough to cover them. Skim the water, cut them up, and dip the pieces in beaten egg, and roll in bread crumbs or pounded crackers, with salt and a little pepper. Fry them brown in butter; lay them in a fricassee dish. Put a little of the water in which they were boiled into the spider; rub two spoonfuls of browned flour smooth in some of the water, and stir into the spider, and pour over the pieces. If the gravy does not seem rich enough, stir into it a small spoonful of butter. Rabbits are also stuffed and roasted.

Roast Fawn.

Clean and wash thoroughly; stuff with a dressing made of bread crumbs, chopped pork, pepper and salt. Moisten with water and cream, bind with beaten egg and melted butter. Sew up the fawn, turning the legs under, and binding close to the body. Cover with thin slices of fat pork, bound on with pack thread, crossing in every direction, and roast at a quick fire. Allow twenty-two minutes to a pound. Twenty minutes before it is dished, remove the pork and set down the fawn to brown, basting with melted butter. At last, dredge with flour, let this brown, froth with butter and serve. A kid can be roasted the same way, also hares and rabbits.

Boiled Partridges.

Put them in a floured cloth into boiling water, and boil them fast fifteen minutes. For sauce, rub a very small piece of butter into some flour, and boil in a teacupful of cream. Add cut parsley if preferred.

Roast Partridges.

Prepare them like chickens, and roast three-quarters of an hour.

SAUCES FOR MEAT AND FISH.

Gravy.

When ready to make the gravy, remove the roast from the dripping-pan and stir into the stock which is in the pan, flour sufficient to thicken the gravy, be careful to break the flour thoroughly in a little water, then pour over the thickened stock, boiling water and place over the fire, about five minutes, stirring constantly. If there is but little fat in the stock, as will be the case in veal or venison, add some butter when ready to stir in the flour. Strain when done.

Gravy for *Poultry* is made by boiling the giblets (necks, gizzards, hearts and livers,) by themselves in five or six gills of water. Skim carefully as a great deal of scum will rise. After an hour or more, take them out, and pour the water into the dripping-pan. Chop the liver fine, and add this to the gravy, and a bit of butter, some wet flour, and if you choose, a little sweet marjoram. In making gravy for a goose, pour off all the drippings, and put in some of the stock or meat liquor.

Melted or Drawn Butter.

3 tablespoonfuls of flour.
½ cup of butter.
1 pint of water or milk.
A little salt.

Break up, and beat well, the flour in milk or water. Cut the butter in small bits and put it in the water, in a vessel on the stove and when hot stir in gradually the thickening; taking care that it does not form lumps. If milk is used, the vessel should be placed within another containing water. Mix with milk for puddings, with water for fish and meat.

Egg Sauce.

Make a sauce of drawn butter as in directions above. Chop fine three hard boiled eggs, and stir into the drawn butter. This is used for fish and some kinds of vegetables. For fish, add capers or nasturtium seeds. The hard boiled eggs can be omitted, and two raw eggs well beaten, stirred into the drawn butter.

Oyster Sauce.

1 pint of oysters.
2 tablespoonfuls of butter.
½ lemon.
1 teacupful milk or cream.
1 teaspoonful of flour.
Cayenne and nutmeg to taste.

Stew the oysters in their own liquor five minutes, and then add the milk in which the flour has been broken up. Put in the butter and pepper, boil for one minute and remove the sauce-pan from the fire. Squeeze in lemon-juice when ready to serve.

This sauce is used for boiled halibut, cod and other fish; also for boiled turkey, chickens, and any other kind of white meat.

Celery Sauce.

Put a pint of milk to boil in a tin pail set in a kettle of boiling water. Cut fine six stalks of celery, and add to the milk, with a little salt. When the celery is soft, which will be in about an hour, stir in a spoonful of butter rubbed into half a spoonful of flour. If the sauce seems too thick, add enough milk to make it of the consistency of good cream. Let it remain a few moments, stirring constantly, and then serve.

SAUCES FOR MEAT AND FISH.

Caper Sauce. (*For Boiled Mutton or Lamb.*)

½ pint milk.
1 teaspoonful cornstarch or flour.
1 teaspoonful butter.
2 tablespoonfuls capers.

Boil the milk, then stir in the cornstarch or flour rubbed smooth in cold milk, and then the butter. Last of all, add the capers, and let it boil up.

Anchovy Sauce.

Pound three anchovies, and rub through a sieve. Stir them into half a pint of drawn butter. Add, also, lemon-juice, and a pinch of cayenne pepper.

Mayonaise Sauce.

Yolks of 2 raw eggs (not a particle of the white or your sauce will curdle).
1½ mustard spoonfuls of mixed mustard.

Beat the yolks of the eggs and mustard together; add very slowly the best salad oil, stirring constantly until you can reverse the dish without spilling; then add one tablespoonful of vinegar, and cayenne and black pepper to taste; half a teaspoonful of salt. Stir briskly until quite light colored, and serve on lobster, lettuce or fish.

Mint Sauce for Roast Lamb.

2 tablespoonfuls of green mint chopped fine.
1 tablespoonful powdered sugar.
½ teacupful of vinegar.

Soak the mint to remove all the gravel and chop very fine. Mix the sugar and vinegar (taking care that the sugar is all dissolved before sending to the table) in a sauce-boat, and stir in the mint. This gives a very fine flavor to lamb.

EGGS.

ELEMENTS OF EGGS.

Eggs contain two distinct substances, the yolk and the white, and in the latter is found a greater proportion of albumen than in the yolk. The white contains fifteen parts albumen out of every one hundred parts, the remainder being water. After the white has been heated it changes its transparent color, hardens, and becomes an opaque white, from which it derives its Latin name albas, white. The yolk also contains a considerable quantity of albumen, also drops of yellow oil. This oil forms about two-thirds of the weight of the yolk. Sulphur is also found in large proportion in the yolk, which causes silver to tarnish, when used in eggs which have been cooked; this also produces the offensive smell when the eggs are rotten. Vegetable albumen differs in no respect from that contained in eggs which is composed of carbon, oxygen, hydrogen, a large proportion of nitrogen and sulphur, except that albumen of eggs contains a slightly larger proportion of sulphur. Eggs form a very valuable food, for like milk they contain all the material required for the growth of the body, as is demonstrated in the chicken, which is formed from the materials within the shell. The digestibility of eggs greatly depend on the manner of cooking. When raw or lightly cooked, they are more readily digested than when hard boiled or fried.

SCRAMBLED EGGS.

6 eggs.
1 teaspoonful salt.
1 tablespoonful butter.
Put the butter in the frying pan, and when hot drop in

the eggs (unbeaten) which should be broken into a bowl. Stir in the pepper and salt, and keep stirring without cessation for three minutes. Serve in a hot dish, or upon toast. Do not let them remain in the pan until stiff.

PLAIN OMELET.

6 eggs.
1 cup milk.
Butter, salt and pepper.

Beat the whites to a stiff froth that will stand alone, the yolks to a smooth, thick batter. Add to the yolks, the milk, pepper and salt, lastly stir in the whites lightly. Have ready in the frying-pan a good lump of butter. When it hisses pour in the mixture and set over a clear fire. It must not cook longer than ten minutes. Do not stir, but as the eggs "set" slip a knife under the omelet to guard against burning at the bottom. When done, lay a hot dish bottom up on the pan, and upset the latter to bring the brown side of the omelet uppermost. Eat soon, or it will fall.

OMELET. (*Fried.*)

6 eggs.
6 tablespoonfuls milk.
½ cup butter (melted).
A little salt.

Beat the eggs well, and add the milk, butter and salt. Fry on a griddle hot enough for cakes; buttered to prevent sticking. Drop them on the griddle like large cakes. When they begin to set, turn up the edge, and as they brown fold them over and over. Then let them lie a moment more. Serve as hot as possible.

POACHED EGGS.

6 eggs.
1 pint milk.
1 teaspoonful salt.
1 tablespoonful butter.

Set a tin pan or pail on the stove containing the milk. Beat the eggs well. When the milk is nearly boiling put in salt and butter; then add the eggs, and stir steadily until it thickens, which will be in a minute or two. Set it off before it becomes very thick, and continue to stir it a minute more. Have ready in a warm dish, a few slices of toasted bread spread with butter, and pour the egg over it. It should be a little thicker than boiled custard.

POACHED EGGS. (*à la Crème.*)

Nearly fill a clean frying-pan with strained water boiling hot; strain a tablespoonful of vinegar through double muslin, and add to the water with a little salt. Slip your egg from the saucer upon the top of the water (first taking the pan from the fire). Boil three minutes and a half, drain, and lay on buttered toast in a warm dish. Turn the water from the pan and pour in half a cupful of cream or milk. If you use the latter, thicken with a very little cornstarch. Let it heat to a boil, stirring to prevent burning, and add a great spoonful of butter, some pepper and salt. Boil up once and pour over the eggs. A better way still is to heat the milk in a separate saucepan, that the eggs may not have to stand. A little broth improves the sauce.

BOILED EGGS.

New laid eggs require half a minute longer to cook than others. The fresher they are the better, and the more healthful. Eggs over a week old should never be boiled; they will do to fry. Put them into water that boils, but not furiously, as it will crack them. If you like them very soft, boil them three minutes. If you wish the yolk hard, boil them five minutes. To be served with salad, they should be boiled twelve minutes.

FRIED EGGS.

After you have fried ham, drop in the eggs one at a time. In about a minute dip the boiling fat with a spoon over them again and again. This will prevent the necessity of turning them which is difficult to do without breaking the yolks. Take them up in about two minutes and a half, with a skimmer. The fat that roasts out of a ham that is browned in an oven, is good for frying eggs.

Dropped Eggs.

Drop fresh eggs into a sauce-pan of boiling water with salt in it. Put them in gently, so as not to break the yolks. Have ready slices of buttered toast, and either take up the eggs with a skimmer, or pour off the water, and then turn them out upon the toast. Add more salt if they are not seasoned enough by that which is in the water.

Packing Eggs.

Pack in bran or salt, with the small end downward if you wish to use within a few weeks. If to be kept for a longer time, a surer method is to smear them well with linseed oil, or a weak solution of gum tragacanth, or varnish, this excludes the air. Another method is to make a pretty strong lime water; allowing a pound of lime to a gallon of boiling water; when perfectly cold, fill a large jar with it, in which you have packed the eggs, small end downward. Lay a saucer, or light weight on the top to keep them under water, and keep in a cool place. Renew the lime water every three weeks. You may add an ounce of saltpeter to it.

MILK, BUTTER AND CHEESE.

Milk.

Milk consists of water in large proportion, caseine, or curd, butter, sugar of milk, and saline matter, in small proportions. Caseine in many of its properties closely resembles albumen. If a little sulphuric acid be stirred in some skimmed milk, it will coagulate in a short time, and form a curd, from which can be obtained pure caseine, which forms one of the chief ingredients of cheese.

Caseine is found also in beans, peas, and perhaps in all vegetable juices. So large a proportion of caseine is found in peas that the Chinese make a cheese from them, which in time acquires the smell and taste of milk cheese, and is a favorite article of food when fresh. The caseine found in vegetables is called legumine, to distinguish it from that of milk. When milk has been exposed to the air for a length of time, it acquires a sour taste which gradually increases in intensity till at length the whole begins to ferment. This sour taste is owing to the production of a peculiar acid, which is called acid of milk, or lactic acid. The same acid is formed during the fermentation of the juice of beets, in sour cabbage (sauer kraut), and in many other kinds of vegetables which are allowed to ferment. The souring of milk arises from the action of caseine by converting the sugar in the milk into an acid. If milk be kept at low temperature it may be preserved sweet for several days. The quality of the milk depends largely upon the race and size of the cow. As a general rule small races, or small cows of a larger race, give the richest milk from the same kind of food. From extensive experiments made in England it was found that the Holderness breed gave the largest quantity of milk, and second the Alderney. Either of these varieties will be found well suited for family or town dairymen who wish to use the milk and cream for market. Mr. Youatt states that the "milch cow should have a long, thin head, with a brisk but placid eye; she should be thin and hollow in the neck, narrow in the breast and point of the shoulders, and altogether light in the fore quarters, but wide in the loins, with little dewlap. The udder should be especially large, round and full, with milk veins protruding, yet thin skinned, but not hanging loose or tending far behind. The teats should also stand squarely, all pointing out at equal distance and of the same size, and although neither very large nor thick toward the udder, yet long and tapering toward a point. Her feeding should be carefully attended to; great care should be taken not to give food which will injure the flavor of the milk. She should have a teacup of salt at least once a week. Be careful that she is not allowed to run from the pasture.

BUTTER.

Butter prepared in any of the usual ways contains more or less of all the ingredients contained in milk, but consists more essentially of the fat of milk intimately mixed with greater or less proportion of caseine, water, and a small quantity of sugar of milk. The nature of the food must in all cases affect the proportion of fatty and cheesy matter in our domestic butter. Besides the caseine and sugar, butter usually contains some coloring matter derived from the substance on which the cow has been feed. From experiments in England it has been proved that Ayrshire cows produced the largest amount of butter. The constitution of the animal will affect the quality of the butter, as there are some cows from which good butter can never be made, however well they may be fed. The chances of good butter at all seasons of the year are in favor of churning the whole milk, instead of the cream; but when the milk is churned, the temperature should be higher than for cream alone. This course is only practicable in large dairies. Cream should not be warmer when the churning begins than 55° F. Milk ought to be raised to 65° F. It is almost needless to allude to cleanliness, as being necessary for good butter, but we do wish to impress the fact upon the minds of those who may have had no experience in butter making. Cream is remarkable for the rapidity with which it absorbs, and becomes tainted by, unpleasant odors. It is very necessary that the air of the milk-room should be sweet and often renewed, and be careful to have it away from the direction whence bad odors come. Also strict cleanliness and care must be taken with all dishes used in the dairy. If butter is to be kept for a length of time, great care must be taken to exclude the air from every part. In butter to be salted the sooner it can be done and the butter packed close, the better and sweeter it will remain. The salt should be as pure as possible, free from lime and magnesia as it can be obtained, since these substances are apt to give it a bitter or other disagreeable taste. Common salt can be easily purified from these by pouring a couple quarts of water upon fifteen or twenty pounds of salt, stirring the whole occasionally for two hours and then straining it through a clean cloth. The water which runs through is a saturated solution of salt and contains all of the impurities, but may be used for common culinary purposes, or fed to the cattle. The salt which remains on the cloth is free from the soluble salts of lime and magnesia, and may be hung up in the cloth until it is dry enough to be used to mix with the butter and cheese. The point in salting butter is to take care that all the water which remains in the butter shall be fully saturated with salt, that is to say, shall have dissolved as much as it can possibly take up, and that in no part of the butter shall there be a particle of cheesy matter which is not also in contact with the salt. It is not uncommon to employ a mixture of salt, saltpeter, sulphur and sugar for the preservation of butter.

BUTTER MAKING.

As experienced butter makers have their own way of making butter, we do not presume to show a better way, but for the benefit of any who wish to make their own butter, or for market, and are inexperienced in the art, we have copied from the "New York Tribune" the directions given by John Stuart, Manchester, Iowa, who received a gold medal for best 50-pound package of butter at the Centennial display in June. These directions, although applying to a large dairy can be made useful for family butter making.

Mr. S. describes his mode of making as follows: His pans are 2 feet wide by 4 feet long and 14 inches deep. During warm weather they are set in vats of cold water, in a room of 62 to 65 degrees which raises the cream in 36 hours, when it is skimmed. In warm, muggy weather and thunder showers, it is skimmed sooner. He considers it important to skim at just the right time. His churning is done by horse power in a rotating, rectangular box churn, having neither floats nor dasher inside. The churning is done upon the first appearance of acidity, and is put into the churn at 58 to 65 degrees according to outside temperature. Time of churning, 30 to 45 minutes. Churning ceases as soon as butter comes, and before it is gathered into a mass. The butter-milk is then drawn off, and clear cold brine put in, and the churn gently agitated, till the brine, butter and butter-milk are well mixed, when it is drawn off and more cold brine is added, and the same process repeated till the butter-milk is all removed, as it will quickly be, without working the butter at all, and the butter left in fine hard granules or lumps, and in the best possible condition for receiving salt. The butter-milk being out, the butter is seasoned with three-quarters of an ounce of salt to the pound, and set away till the next day, when it is worked and packed in tubs prepared by soaking in strong brine.

Cheese.

When milk is left to itself for a certain length of time it becomes sour and curdles, but the curd and whey do not readily separate unless a gentle heat is applied, when the curd contracts in bulk and floats upon the whey, or is placed in a perforated cheese vat which allows the whey to flow from it. The natural curdling of the milk is produced by the lactic acid, but in the manufacture of cheese it is not usual to allow the milk to sour and curdle of its own accord. The process is hastened by the use of acids or of some substance such as rennet. A good way to prepare the rennet is to cut it in small pieces, put it in a jar with a handful or two of salt in one or two quarts of water and allow it to stand for two or three days, afterwards pour on it another pint and allow it to stand two days more, then strain and bottle the whole for future use. In this state it may keep for several months. The milk should be raised to a temperature of 90°, or 95° F., and the rennet mixed with it. The quantity used varies from a tablespoonful to half a pint for thirty or forty gallons of milk. The time for the complete fixing of the curd also varies from fifteen minutes to an hour or more. Great care should be taken in warming the milk, that it is not singed. In large dairies, a safe way is to have a pot with a double bottom after the manner of a glue pot, and have the space filled with water. In heating it is desirable not to raise the temperature too high, as great heat is apt to give an oiliness to the fatty matter of the milk. The curd should be broken up as soon as it coagulates, as the longer it stands after this the harder and tougher it becomes. The quantity of the rennet should be regulated carefully, as too much makes the curd tough, and too little causes loss of time, and will permit a large portion of the butter to separate from the curd. In salting cheese, as in butter, the salt should be pure, and can be obtained for that purpose in the same manner. Cheese, like butter, depends in a great degree for its richness on the richness of the milk, and is also susceptible to the various flavors which affect the milk. It may be improved in quality by the addition of cream or butter to the dried and crumbled curd but it must be thoroughly worked in. The Ræckem cheese of Belgium is made by adding half an ounce of butter and the yolk of an egg to every pound of pressed cheese. New varieties of cheese are formed by mixing vegetable substances with the curd. A green decoction of two parts sage leaves, one of marigold, and a little parsley, gives color and flavor to the green cheese.

The method of curing has a great effect upon the cheese; care in salting, warmth of the place where kept, temperature and closeness of cheese-room in which they are stored, often turning, and cleaning from mould, and rubbing with butter. All these have due influence upon the cheese. Time and care must be bestowed in cheese making in order to produce rich cheese, and by varying the mode of curing, and especially the temperature at which they are kept, an almost endless variety may be produced. In conclusion we will recommend to all who may be interested in cheese making, a thorough study of Johnson's Agricultural Chemistry, to which we are largely indebted for what we have written on milk, butter and cheese. The result will richly repay one for the study.

Cheese Making.

Strain the night's milk into the tub; in the morning take off the cream, put it over a clear fire, stirring constantly, when hot, add part of the milk; heat it enough to make the milk which is still in the tub quite warm, but not hot; pour it back into the tub, and strain in the morning's milk. Put in a spoonful or two of rennet, stir it well, and let it stand half an hour; if the curd does not form well by that time, add more rennet. When the curd is well formed, cut it in squares, making the knife go down to the bottom of the tub at every stroke; let it stand fifteen minutes for the whey to separate. Then break it up gently, putting the spoon down through all parts; it must be done gently, or some of the milk will be lost in the whey.

This causes white whey; the greener the whey, the richer the cheese. Lay the strainer on top of the curd, and dip off the whey that presses up through, until you have taken about a third of it; put this over the fire to heat. When hot, pour it back upon the curd, and break it up small and as quickly as possible; then lay the strainer into the cheese basket, and pour the curd in to drain. When this is done, return it to the tub, salt it, put it again into the strainer, and then into the cheese hoop. Lay the strainer over smooth; lay a follower upon it, put it into the press, and press it tight; let it stay two days, and increase the pressure four or five times, turning the cheese over each time. Then turn the cheese out upon a shelf, in a dark closet, or room, secure from flies. Every day rub the side that has lain upon the shelf, and turn it over; rub it *all over* with butter often; these things must be done for six months.

If cheese is rich, a strip of new cotton as wide as the thickness of the cheese, should be sewed tight around it, when first taken from the press, else it would soon melt out of shape. Cheese rubbed now and then with butter sprinkled with red pepper, will be a good plan when flies are about.

COTTAGE CHEESE.

Let the milk be turned by rennet, or by setting it in a warm place. It must not be *heated*, as the oily parts will then pass off, and the richness is lost. When fully turned, put in a coarse linen bag, and hang it to drain several hours, till all the whey is out. Then mash it fine, salt it to the taste, and thin it with good cream, or add but little cream, and roll it into balls. A little butter improves it.

MEAT MAXIMS.

Meats roast much better in a closely covered dish made for the purpose.

If fresh meats become soiled before cooking trim the soil off. Do not wash it.

If meat or fish *are* washed, they should be carefully dried with a napkin before cooking.

To boil or roast fresh meat it should, at the first instant, be plunged in boiling water.

Salt meats should be put to cook in cold water.

Meats should not boil furiously, but simmer.

Much good meat is spoiled by not being skimmed properly.

Corned beef should be allowed to cool in the liquor in which it is cooked.

Nothing improves a piece of meat so much as a sharp knife with which to cut it.

There is as much in cutting a roast as in cooking it.

Many people sharpen the table knives; it makes the meat seem tenderer.

Do not season food too highly; people differ in tastes.

Pork and fish should cook slowly.

If eggs are cooked too fast or too long, they become wheyey.

To make browned gravies, brown the flour as you brown coffee. You can keep a little stock of it in store.

If milk gravies are cooked too much or too fast they are apt to curdle.

To heat over oyster soup, skim out the oysters, heat the liquor and turn over them. They are as good as when fresh cooked.

MEAT MAXIMS.

If you cannot open clams, pour boiling water over them and they will open themselves.

Lard or grease may be cleansed by slicing raw potato into it, and boiling it. Fat in which fritters or cakes have been cooked, also sausage grease, may be cleansed in this way.

To cleanse rancid butter boil it with twice the amount of water and shake it well, and repeat till cleansed.

Custards put in the cups and steamed for ten minutes are fully as nice as when baked.

Tainted meat or fowl may be made sweet by boiling with a piece of charcoal.

Scrambled eggs overdone, are spoiled.

Meat hash on toast is nice for breakfast.

Dropped eggs on toast are nice for tea.

Never put butter or meat on to cold iron to cook.

Pork steak is nicer baked than fried.

Keep milk, butter and eggs at a good distance from anything having a rank odor, as onions, lobster, fish, etc.

Beef steak can be nicely broiled in a spider, by having the spider *hot*—not warm—when it is put in. Do not salt till it is done.

HYGIENIC EFFECT OF ANIMAL FOOD.

Soup

Soup has but little nutritious value compared with most kinds of food. The joints of meat, which are usually selected for soups contain a great amount of gelatine which has very little nutrition, and is principally useful as waste matter to keep the bowels in action. To a person of sedentary habits or who is costively inclined, they are excellent for this purpose, but they form but little blood, bone or muscle, and give but little heat to the body.

Lean Meats. (*Fresh.*)

Lean beef contains about twenty-five per cent. of material for muscle, but can never be eaten alone, not having the necessary carbon to produce heat. Either fat or starchy food is required to supply the lungs with fuel, fat being best in winter and starch in summer. The lean meat (muscle) of an animal which has led an active life is much harder and firmer and takes more time to digest than one that has only lived in a stall. Tender meats are more digestible than tough ones because they can be so separated by the teeth that gastric juice can act upon them better. Lean beef, veal, mutton and pork do not vary greatly in their elements nor hygienic effects. They all tend to produce muscle, and are best adapted to the laboring man. Veal is more difficult to digest because it is slippery and difficult to chew properly

Fat Meats

contain a great amount of carbon which goes to produce heat. Fats are much better food in cold climates and in cold weather than in those which are warmer. A due amount of fatty matter is most necessary to produce heat, but an excess is very hurtful, especially to persons of weak digestion; during the process of digestion it becomes rancid and partially decomposed and often produces heat-burn and nausea.

A surplus of carbonaceous food is apt to induce inflammatory troubles, as gout and inflammatory rheumatism. When such food is used, it should always be accompanied by acid fruits and foods. The use of too great an amount of carbon food is said to aggravate any scrofulous tendancy.

Salt Meats

do not digest so quickly nor so perfectly as fresh meats. For this reason they are preferred by laboring men, as they remain longer in the stomach, and are, as they say, "better to lean upon." Scrofulous diseases, as erysipelas and salt rheum, are often produced and always aggravated by the too liberal use of salt and fat food.

The five principal meats may be classed as follows, the first mentioned under each head standing first, and the last mentioned standing last:

For *heat* and *fat*—pork, mutton, lamb, beef, veal.
For *muscle*—beef, veal, mutton, lamb, pork,
For *brain* and *nerve*—beef, veal mutton, lamb, pork.

Fish.

The hygienic effect of fish depends much upon the kind of fish. The most active fish as trout, pickerel, shad, etc., contain more muscle and brain food than common fish, as white fish, cod and haddock. But all kinds of fish are alike in having a greater amount of brain material than almost any other kind of food. Prof. Agassiz thought so highly of fish for students and thinkers that for years he used hardly any other kind of animal food. But good medical authorities claim that this was really the cause of his death, as fish do not supply sufficient of many of the elements which the system requires. Except the fatty fishes most of them require to be cooked in lard, fat pork or butter, and to be eaten with potatoes or some farinaceous food to supply the requisite carbon.

Shell-Fish.

Lobsters, crabs, prawn, shrimp, etc., are hard to digest, and though good strong food, cannot be eaten with impunity by persons of weak digestion, and are most miserably misapplied to evening entertainments in form of salads.

Oysters are unsatisfactory food for laboring men, but will do for the sedentary and for a supper to sleep on.

Eggs

contain all of the elements necessary to preserve health, and are healthful when cooked in any of the numberless ways common.

Cheese

has more than twice the amount of nourishment of any other known substance. It must therefore be used in small quantities and with such articles of food as fine flour or fruit which contains little nitrogen. It is hard of digestion, but there is much in being accustomed to it.

ELEMENTS OF VEGETABLE FOOD.

When wheat flour is mixed up into a dough and washed on a linen cloth or sieve, under a stream of water, a milky substance passes through and gradually settles to the bottom of the vessel. This substance, when dried, will be found to be a fine, snow-white powder known as *starch*.

Starch is found in (nearly) all kinds of grains, seeds, roots, bark, stems, pith and fruit of many plants. The various kinds of vegetable food which contain more or less starch as well as other principles will be considered in the following:

The Potato.—Of all the vegetables which grow in the temperate climate, the potato is used the most generally by all classes of people. It appears daily on the table of the rich and poor. The chemical elements of the best varieties do not vary greatly; these *do* however, vary greatly with the season, ripeness and soil. The solid part of the potato consists *mainly* of starch. It contains about 75 per cent. water, and also fat, sugar and salts in smaller proportion than starch. There is in the potato a bitter principle which is poisonous, and causes it to turn green if exposed to the light while growing. Cooking changes this principle, therefore the water in which potatoes are boiled, should never be used in the preparation of other kinds of food.

Parsnips, *Carrots* and *Turnips* contain a greater proportion of water than potatoes, and are less valuable as articles of food. Parsnips and carrots contain more sugar than potatoes, and all of them less starch. Turnips are of these three, the least valuable as an article of food.

The Beet is especially valuable as an article of food on account of the sugar which it contains. The French prepare a large amount of sugar from it, and make it an article of export.

Cabbage, Parsley, Mustard and all similar kinds of vegetables are essentially alike in chemical composition, containing water in large proportion, woody fibre, gum and sugar. They should be well cooked, indeed can hardly be too much cooked, and even then are found to require a longer time for digestion than animal food.

Rhubarb contains an agreeable acid principle in so large proportion that it is used for a home-made wine. It also contains certain medicinal qualities which are found in the root.

The Onion contains a large amount of nitrogenous matter, and is for that reason very nutritive. It also contains a strong smelling, sulphurized oil, which gives it its strong odor; this is also found in garlic; sugar and vegetable albumen is found in it.

Indian Corn, or *Maize* contains more oil or fatty matter than any other vegetable, also albumen, starch and sugar, which adapts it for sustaining life, and furnishing all the materials required for life, and is, perhaps, used more universally for human and animal food than any other vegetable.

Oat Meal stands first in all grains in point of nutriment, being first in nitrogenous element. It ranks next to Indian corn in quantity of fat or oil which it contains. It is rich in starch, also contains sugar.

Rice is remarkable for its starchy property, possessing more of it, than any other grain or vegetable, but is most deficient in oil.

Buckwheat consists of starch in large proportion, and contains sugar and gluten.

Seeds.—Of the seeds, such as peas and beans, they vary but little in chemical composition. Peas contain more starch and vegetable caseine or legumine than beans. These take the first rank among nutritive foods, but being considered difficult of digestion are usually eaten with other kinds of food.

Sago Starch is procured from the pith of several varieties of the palm tree. It comes in various forms. Sago meal or flour is a whitish powder.

Pearl Sago, the kind in general use for domestic purposes, consists of pinkish or yellowish grains, about the the size of a pin's head. Common or brown sago consists of much larger grains, which are of a brownish white color, each grain being brownish on one side and whitish on the other.

As all kinds of sago contain coloring matters, they are considered inferior to those varieties of starch, as arrowroot and tapioca which are perfectly white.

Tapioca is a variety of starch which comes from South America, and is obtained from the root of a plant containing a poisonous milky juice. When it appears as a white powder, it is called *Brazilian arrow-root*.

The term tapioca is commonly applied to that form of it which appears in small irregular lumps, caused by its having been dried on hot plates, and then broken up into fragments.

Arrow-root.—A root growing in the West Indies containing a juice supposed to be capable of counteracting the effects of wounds inflicted by poisonous arrows. This root yielded a starch which took the name of Maranta arrow-root. But afterwards starches from other plants which had a resemblance to Maranta starch, took also the name of arrow-roots. Thus there is *Tahiti* arrow-root, Manihot arrow-root, from the plants which yield tapioca, and potato arrow-root, or British arrow-root, as it is sometimes called. Maranta arrow-root, which is a very pure, white, starchy powder, is the most prized of all varieties, but is often adulterated with other and cheaper kinds.

Corn Starch.—This is a preparation of the starch of

Indian corn which has been separated as perfectly as possible from the other constituents of the grain. Chemical means are used to effect the separation. The grain is reported to yield from 30 to 35 per cent. of pure starch which bears a general price about one-third greater than wheaten flour.

Starch does not dissolve in water. A starch grain is composed of coats or layers like an onion. By boiling, the layers exfoliate or unfold, and the grains swell to twenty or thirty times their original size and form a thick jelly.

A cold jelly of starch and water left to stand will gradually change, first into gum and then into sugar. This change will be slow and will take months before the whole is converted into sugar. If one or two per cent. of sulphuric acid is added to the water, and the starch is boiled for some time and then the acid by similar means is neutralized and removed, and the solution boiled down, it yields a rich syrup or a solid sugar.

Potatoes treated in this way, it is said, will produce ten per cent. of their weight in sugar. Any substance which contains starch, as paper, raw cotton, flax, linen, and cotton rags, and even sawdust, may be changed into sugar by the same means.

Starch has a constipating effect, because it is so completely absolved, and leaves no residue to excite the intestines to act. The gastric juice contains both acid and pepsin, or "ferment substance," these acting on starch tranform it into sugar, some of which enters into the blood, and it is burned away for the production of heat.

Starchy food, more especially than any other, should be thoroughly masticated before being swallowed, as its digestion depends almost entirely on its thorough intermixture with the saliva in the mouth. Those forms which are more solid, such as bread and potato, are better digested than when prepared in the form of slops, as sago, arrowroot, etc., because in the latter form it is swallowed without mixing with the saliva.

ELEMENTS OF VEGETABLE FOOD.

Flour is principally composed of starch, gluten, sugar and gum. Of these, the first two constitute about 70 per cent.

Gluten.—If dough is worked on a sieve under a stream of water we have seen that the deposit in the vessel below will, when dried, contain the starch, while that substance which remains on the cloth will be found to be a gray, elastic, tough substance, almost resembling a piece of animal skin in appearance, presenting when dried, a glue-like appearance; hence its name, *gluten.*

Good flour will absorb half its weight in water. The water combines with the gluten which becomes tough and elastic. The gluten acts upon the sugar, changing it into alcohol and carbonic acid gas. The tough nature of the gluten does not allow the gas to escape, and as it swells or expands, the dough will swell or "rise" to a much greater bulk.

The best flour is that in which there is the most gluten, and which is the toughest and most elastic when wet.

Whatever injury the flour may sustain is manifested in a change in the gluten, reducing the quantity and diminishing its tenacity.

Flour dealers and bakers determine the quality of flour by working a handful into paste with water, when its value is judged by the tenacity of the dough, the length to which it may be drawn into a thread, or the extent it may be spread out into a sheet.

Maccaroni and *Vermicelli* are pastes formed from wheat flour and made into various shapes by pressing the paste through holes in metallic plates. The flours, therefore, which are best for these preparations are those which make the toughest paste and are richest in gluten. The best maccaroni should retain its form, and only swell after long boiling, without running into a mass or falling to pieces.

VEGETABLES.

To Boil Potatoes.

The *best* potatoes are good boiled without paring, but even these are best pared; and poor potatoes are unfit to eat, boiled with the skins on. New potatoes are made watery by being laid in water, but late in the winter, and in the spring, they should be pared and laid in cold water an hour or two before they are cooked. Put them into boiling water, with salt in it, and allow thirty or forty minutes for boiling, according to the size. When they are done through, pour off the water, and take the kettle to the door, or window, and shake them. Doing this in the open air makes them mealy; return them to the fire a minute or two, and then serve. Potatoes require nearly an hour to bake in a cooking stove or range.

Potato Balls.

Mash boiled potatoes fine, stir into them the yolk of an egg, and make them into balls; then dip them into a beaten egg, roll them in cracker crumbs, and brown them in a quick oven; or fry them in a small quantity of nice drippings, and, in that case, flatten them so they can be easily turned, and browned on both sides.

Mashed Potatoes.

Boil them according to the directions in the preceding recipe, allowing twenty minutes more time before dinner, than if they were to be put on the table whole. When they are dried, set off the kettle and mash them in it with a wooden pestle. Have ready a gill or two of hot milk or cream; if you use milk, put a small piece of butter into it. Sprinkle salt into the potato and mash it until it is perfectly fine; then pour in the hot milk and mix it thoroughly. The more it is worked with the pestle, the whiter it becomes. Put it into the dish for the table, smooth the top into proper shape, and set it into the stove to brown. To prepare it in the nicest manner, beat the yolk of an egg and spread over the top, before putting it into the oven. If you do not care to take all this trouble, it is very good without being browned.

Fried Potatoes.

Pare, wash and slice the raw potatoes very thin; this can be done with a sharp knife, but an instrument for the purpose is much better. When they are sliced, lay them in ice cold water for half an hour, then dry them by spreading between two cloths. Have the lard boiling hot in the frying-pan, and fry the potatoes to a light brown. Take them from the frying-pan as soon as they are brown and drain in a colander for a moment. Sprinkle with salt, and lay on a napkin in a deep dish.

Old Potatoes.

When potatoes are poor, as they often are in the spring, pare, soak, and boil them as directed in the first recipe, then take two together in a coarse cloth, squeeze and wring them.

Potato Cakes.

Mould into flat cakes, cold mashed potatoes, salt them, and fry in hot lard or drippings until a light brown.

Potatoes Heated in Milk.

To make a very good dish for breakfast, cut cold potatoes quite small, and put them into a sauce-pan or spider, with milk enough to almost, but not entirely cover them. When the milk becomes hot, stir and mash the potatoes with a large spoon until there are no lumps. Add salt, and a small bit of butter, stir it often, until it is as dry as you wish to have it. It is a nicer dish, when prepared with so much milk that a good deal of stirring is necessary to make it dry, than if done in but a small quantity.

SWEET POTATOES.

They are best baked; are very nice boiled till tender, and then pared and laid into the oven to brown. They require a third longer time to cook than the common potato. Cold sweet potatoes are excellent sliced and browned on the griddle. When one side is done, sprinkle salt over before turning.

BOILED CABBAGE.

Pick off the outer green leaves, cut in quarters; examine carefully for the insects which may get between the leaves. Lay them for an hour in cold water; then put them in a pot of boiling water and cook twenty minutes, change the water, putting in more boiling water and cook until tender. It takes nearly an hour to cook a good sized cabbage, when young; and a longer time for an older one. When done, drain well, and serve.

LADIES CABBAGE.

Boil the cabbage, as directed in boiled cabbage. When tender, drain and set aside until cold. Chop fine, and then add and stir well together, two well-beaten eggs, one tablespoonful of butter, four tablespoonfuls of cream, a little salt and pepper. Put in the oven and bake until brown.

CABBAGE. (*Boiled in Milk.*)

Cut the cabbage as fine as it can be sliced, boil it in milk thirty minutes; then add butter, pepper and salt, and thicken with a little flour.

SAUER KRAUT.

Line a barrel, keg, or jar with cabbage leaves, on the bottom and sides. Chop the cabbage fine, and put in a layer three inches deep; press this down well, and sprinkle with four tablespoonfuls of salt. Pack in this manner four or five layers, press down hard with a board made to fit loosely the inside of the vessel used for the purpose. Place heavy weights on the board or pound it down with a wooden beetle, until it is a compact mass, then remove the board, and put in another layer, repeating the process of pressing until the vessel is full. Cover with leaves and replace the board and weights to keep it down. Let it stand to ferment; in three weeks remove the scum, and if necessary cover with water. This should be kept in a cool dry cellar. To be eaten raw or boiled.

BOILED CAULIFLOWER.

Pick the leaves and cut off the stalk close to the bottom of the bunches of flowers. It should be cut in quarters if very large. Tie it in a coarse lace or tarlatan bag to prevent it breaking, and put it into boiling water, salted, and cook until tender. When done, turn it in a hot dish and pour over it a large cupful of drawn butter. Do not let it stay in the water after it is done as it will darken. **Serve** hot.

BROCCOLI AND EGGS.

Boil two or three heads of broccoli until tender. Put buttered toast in the bottom of a deep dish and lay on the toast the heads of broccoli arranged with the stems downward, and pour over the whole two cupfuls of drawn butter, into which four eggs have been beaten while hot. Serve hot.

MASHED TURNIPS.

Peel the turnips and put them on to cook in cold water, slightly salted. Boil until tender; drain and mash with a wooden spoon or potato masher. Stir in a spoonful of butter, and season with salt and pepper.

SCALLOPED TOMATOES.

Peel and cut in quite thin slices; make a forcemeat of bread crumbs, butter, salt, pepper and a little sugar. Put in a pudding-dish the sliced tomatoes and forcemeat in alternate layers. Spread the forcemeat quite thick upon each layer; when the dish is nearly full put on a layer of tomatoes and a piece of butter on each slice. Sprinkle in a little sugar and pepper. Strew the whole with dry bread crumbs, cover and bake a half hour, then remove the cover and brown.

STEWED TOMATOES.

Loosen the skins by pouring scalding water upon them; peel and cut them up, extracting the hard part of the stem-end, and removing all unripe portions. Stew in a tin or porcelain sauce-pan, half an hour, when add salt and pepper to taste, a teaspoonful of white sugar, and a tablespoonful of butter. Stew gently fifteen minutes longer, and serve. Some cooks thicken the tomatoes with a little grated bread.

RAW TOMATOES.

Pare with a sharp knife, as it impairs the flavor to remove the skins with hot water. Slice and lay in a dish. Season with vinegar, pepper and salt. Pieces of ice laid on the slices improve them very much.

RAW CUCUMBERS.

Pare and lay in ice-water for a half hour or more, then wipe and slice thin. Season with salt, pepper and vinegar. They are improved by laying bits of ice in with the slices. Some people who cannot eat them in vinegar find them a very nice relish eaten with salt. Thin slices of onion laid in the dish with the cucumbers, are an improvement. Cucumbers should be kept in a cool place; they are better to be eaten the same day they are gathered.

FRIED CUCUMBERS.

Pare and lay in ice-water half an hour. Cut lengthwise into slices nearly half an inch thick, and lay in ice-water ten minutes longer. Wipe each piece dry with a soft cloth, sprinkle with pepper and salt, and dredge with flour. Fry to a delicate brown, in nice lard or butter.

Green Peas.

If peas are young and fresh (and none others are good) they will boil in half an hour or thirty-five minutes. They should be put into cold water, without salt. When tender, drain them through a colander, and dish, adding a little butter and salt. When the peas are old, put a little soda in the water in which they are boiled.

Asparagus. No. 1.

Wash it, trim off the white ends, and tie it up in bunches with a twine or a strip of old cotton. Throw them into boiling water with salt in it. Boil twenty-five minutes or half an hour. Have ready two or three slices of toasted bread, dip them in the water and lay them in the dish. Spread them with butter and lay the bunches of asparagus upon the toast. Cut the strings with scissors and draw them out without breaking the stalks; lay thin shavings of butter over the asparagus, and send it to the table.

Asparagus. No. 2.

Cut the asparagus in pieces a half-inch long, boil in water with a little salt, and add rich, sweet cream to thicken.

Asparagus. No. 3.

Take the green heads of young asparagus, and cut into pieces no larger than peas; put them in boiling water with a little salt, and boil ten or twelve minutes. Drain a minute or two on a napkin; then put into a stew-pan two tablespoonfuls of butter, a sprig of mint, a half cup of cream, a teaspoonful of salt, and as much sugar; stew for ten minutes; then stir in the beaten yolks of two eggs; and in three minutes more, turn the asparagus out on a dish, and serve in the sauce with sippets of fried bread.

VEGETABLES.

Boiled Onions.

Boil them one hour in salted water, or half an hour in clear water, then drain the water off, cover them with milk, and boil until tender. When dished, put a little butter and a very little pepper on them.

Fried Onions.

Cut the onions in thin slices; turn over them a quart of boiling water, let them stand half an hour; drain and wipe them dry with a cloth; dredge in a little flour, pepper and salt, and have ready some hot butter or nice drippings. Fry them a nice brown.

Stewed Green Corn.

Cut the corn from the cob, and stew fifteen minutes in boiling water; then turn off most of the water and cover with milk, and stew until tender. When nearly done, rub smooth a very little flour into butter and put in. Season with salt and pepper. Cold boiled corn can be used in the same way, using the milk only; stew for a few minutes.

Boiled Green Corn.

Throw the ears, when husked, into a kettle of boiling water, slightly salted, and boil thirty minutes. Serve in a napkin. Or, you can cut from the cob while hot, and season with butter, pepper and salt.

Hulled Corn.

The white, yellow, or sweet corn may be used. Soak the corn over night in warm water, and in the morning put it in an iron kettle with water enough to cover it. To each quart of corn, put in a rounding tablespoonful of soda or saleratus, and boil until the hulls come off readily; then wash in several clear waters, and after it is thoroughly washed, put it on to boil again in clear water. Boil until tender, and then salt it, and let it boil a little longer. Turn into a sieve and drain thoroughly.

SUCCOTASH.

Ten or twelve ears of sweet green corn, boiled on the ear, in a kettle containing a small piece of fresh beef; also one quart, or less, of Lima, or common garden beans. When done cut the corn from the ear, mix with the beans and a small quantity of the liquid from the kettle, one cup of cream or rich milk, with plenty of butter, salt and pepper. Place on the stove, allowing it to come to a boil; then serve.

CORN PATTIES.

Take a coarse grater, and grate green corn. To every quart add three eggs, and one pint of milk; thicken with flour to a stiff batter, and fry in lard mixed with butter and salt.

SPINAGE.

Put it into a net, or a bag of coarse muslin, kept for the purpose, and boil it in plenty of water salted, for half an hour. All kinds of greens should be boiled in plenty of water, else they will be bitter. Drain your spinage thoroughly, lay it in a dish, put upon the top hard boiled eggs, sliced, and pour melted butter over it. Another way, is to press it between two plates, then put it into a sauce-pan with a small bit of butter, salt, and a little cream, and boil it up.

BOILED CARROTS.

Wash and scrape well; if large, cut in a few pieces and lay in cold water. Put in boiling water, salted, and cook until tender. Large carrots will require an hour and a half to cook. Young carrots should not be scraped, only washed. Season with butter and serve hot.

SALSIFY, OR OYSTER PLANT. (*Stewed.*)

Scrape the roots and drop into cold water as soon as cleaned. Cut in pieces an inch long, and put into boiling water enough to cover them. Stew until tender; turn off nearly all the water and put in a cupful of cold milk; cook ten minutes after this begins to boil. Rub a little flour into considerable butter and put it in. Season with salt and pepper. Boil up once more and serve hot.

BEETS.

They must not be scraped or cut, as they would then lose their color and sweetness. Salt the water, and boil them for an hour in summer, and in the winter for three hours. Cold beets make a nice pickle, if cut in slices, and put into vinegar.

BOILED PARSNIPS.

Scrape if young, before cooking; if old, pare, and split if they are large. Put them into boiling water and cook from thirty to forty-five minutes. If they are full grown they will require an hour or more to cook tender. Drain them, slice lengthwise and butter when ready for the table.

FRIED PARSNIPS.

Boil until tender, scrape off the skin, and cut in thick lengthwise pieces. Dredge with flour, and fry in hot lard, turning when one side is browned. Drain off all the fat; pepper them and serve hot.

PARSNIP STEW.

Take as many slices of salt pork as you have people to dine. To six slices, put six good sized sliced parsnips, and eight or nine potatoes peeled and sliced. Let the pork boil fifteen or twenty minutes, then add parsnips and potatoes, and boil till tender. Add slices of bread, and salt if needed.

STRING OR "SNAP" BEANS.

Break off the tops and bottoms and "string" carefully. Then pare both edges with a sharp knife, to be certain that no remnant of the tough fibre remains. Cut the beans in pieces an inch long, and lay in cold water with a little salt for fifteen or twenty minutes. Drain them and put into a sauce-pan of boiling water. Boil quickly twenty minutes if well grown, less if small, or until tender. Drain in a colander until the water ceases to drip from them. Dish with a great spoonful of butter stirred in.

SHELLED BEANS, OR LIMA.

Shell, and let them lie awhile in cold water. Put them in boiling water, salted, and cook until tender. Large ones will require nearly an hour to cook; a half hour or forty minutes is long enough for small ones. Drain them and add butter and pepper.

BAKED SQUASH.

Cut in pieces, scrape well, and bake from one to one and a half hours, according to the thickness of the squash; to be eaten with salt and butter as sweet potatoes.

SUMMER SQUASH.

If the rind is tender, boil it whole, in a little bag kept for the purpose. Put it in boiling water, and cook three-quarters of an hour. Take the bag into a pan and press it with the edge of a plate or with a ladle, until the water is out; then turn the squash out into a dish, add salt and butter, and smooth over the top.

WINTER SQUASH.

Cut it up and take out the inside. Pare the pieces and stew in as little water as possible. If you have a tin with holes in it, which will fit the kettle and keep the squash from touching the water, it is the nicest way to steam it. Be careful it does not burn. It will cook in an hour. Mash it in a dish, or if watery, squeeze it in a coarse cloth like summer squash. Stir in butter and salt, and if you like add pepper.

Celery.

Cut off the roots, and take off the greenest, toughest stalks. Wash and scrape the blanched stalks which grow nearest the heart. Lay in cold water until it is sent to the table. Serve in a celery glass without seasoning. Each person will dip in salt for himself.

Radishes.

A little while before using, lay them upon ice, or put them in cold water. To prepare them for the table, cut off the leaves; then scrape them, and put them in a tumbler with ice-water. Serve with salt, or pepper and vinegar.

Fried Egg Plant.

Slice the egg plant half an inch thick; pare each piece carefully, and lay in salt and water, putting a plate upon the topmost to keep it under the brine, and let them lie for an hour or more. Wipe each slice; dip in beaten egg, then in cracker crumbs, and fry in hot lard until well done and nicely browned.

Mushrooms.

There is great difference of opinion in regard to the varieties of mushroom which can be safely eaten, and unless one has learned to distinguish between the edible kind and the poisonous, it is not safe to have any thing to do with them. If they have an offensive smell, a bitter astringent taste, or even an unpleasant flavor, they are unfit for food. Color and texture can not with absolute certainty be relied on. The pale or sulphur yellow, bright or blood red and greenish are generally poisonous. The safe kinds have mostly a compact brittle texture; the flesh is white; they grow more readily in open places, than in damp or shady spots. The edible kinds are most plenty in August and September. The heads of these are round when they spring up, and as they grow, the lower parts unfold, and show a lining fringed with salmon color, the stalks and top are a dirty white. The skin can be more easily peeled from the edges, than from the poisonous kinds. If an onion is boiled in the pot with the mushrooms and turns black, they are poisonous, or if in stirring them with a silver spoon, it blackens, they should not be eaten.

MUSHROOMS. (*Stewed.*)

Select button mushrooms. Cut off the stalks and wipe clean with a wet flannel cloth. Put them in a sauce-pan, cover with cold water and stew gently fifteen minutes. Rub a little flour smooth in a spoonful of butter and add it with a little salt. Whip up an egg in three or four tablespoonfuls of cream, and stir in without letting it boil, and serve.

MUSHROOMS. (*Broiled.*)

You must be careful to get a wholesome one; peel it carefully, grease the bars of a gridiron, lay your mushroom on with the stalk uppermost. Do not turn it; in seven minutes it will be full of delicious ketchup which you must be careful not to spill in taking off.

GREENS.

Cabbage plants, turnip or mustard tops, the roots and tops of young beets, cowslips, dandelions, and various other things, make a good dish in the spring. When boiled enough, they will sink to the bottom of the kettle. Some require an hour, and others less time. Turnip-tops will boil enough in twenty minutes. Put salt in the water, unless you boil pork with them.

BAKED MACCARONI.

Break half a pound of pipe maccaroni in pieces an inch long, and put into a sauce-pan of boiling water slightly salted. Stew gently twenty minutes. It should be soft but not broken or split. Drain well and put a layer in the bottom of a buttered pie or pudding-dish; upon this grate some mild, rich cheese, and scatter over it some bits of butter. Spread upon the cheese more maccaroni, and fill the dish in this order, having maccaroni at the top, buttered well, without the cheese. Add a few spoonfuls of cream or milk, and a very little salt. Bake covered, half an hour, then brown nicely, and serve in the bake-dish.

MACCARONI WITH CHEESE.

¼ pound of maccaroni.
2 ounces of cheese (near the rind.)
1 pint of milk.

Wash and break the pipe maccaroni in pieces an inch long, and let it boil gently in water slightly salted, half an hour. Strain it off and put in the milk, let it simmer one hour, and then spread in layers in a deep dish. Upon each layer spread the grated cheese and scatter in bits of butter, fill the dish in this manner. Brown it in the oven.

ADDITIONAL RECIPES.

VEGETABLE ACIDS.

The sourness of fruits and succulent vegetables is due to various acids produced in the plants, and which they contain usually in quite small quantities. They exist in two states: 1st, as pure acids, or free, when they are strongest, and 2d, combined with bases, as potash, lime, etc., by which they are partly neutralized, and thus rendered less pungent to the taste. Their nutritive value is very low.

Acid of Apples. *Malic Acid* was first obtained from the juice of the apple, but it is also found in numerous small fruits. It exists very abundantly in green apples, hence their acidity which diminishes as they ripen. No use is made of this acid in a separate state.

Acid of Lemons. *Citric Acid* is obtained chiefly from the lemon (citron). Citric acid is prepared by saturating the lemon juice with lime and then the citrate of lime, so formed, mixed with several times its weight of warm water is decomposed with sulphuric acid. The clear liquid is then drawn off and evaporated until the crystals of citric acid are deposited as the solution cools. Artificial lemon juice is produced by redissolving the crystals in water and flavoring with essence of lemon.

Acid of Grapes. *Tartaric Acid.* This acid in the free state exists in the grape and is found in some other fruits. When the expressed juice of the grape is fermented as in the manufacture of wine, the tartaric acid in combination with potash, separates from the liquor, and deposits itself as a crust upon the interior of the casks, and in this condition is known in commerce as *crude tartar*. The pure acid obtained from this source is a white crystallized solid, soluble in water and of an agreeable acid taste. Tartaric acid is chiefly employed in dyeing.

Oxalic Acid exists in sorrel and also in the garden rhubard or pie plant combined with and partially neutralized by potash or lime. It is a prompt and mortal poison when pure, and fatal results frequently occur from mistaking its crystals for those of Epsom salts, which they much resemble. It possesses an intensely sour taste which Epsom salts do not. The proper antidote for it is the adminstration of chalk or magnesia dissolved in water. This acid is extensively used in printing calico, and by straw workers to cleanse their wares.

Vegetable Jelly, or Pectic Acid is obtained from the juice of apples, pears, quinces, currants, raspberries and many other fruits; also from turnips, carrots, beets and other roots. It is commonly prepared by mixing sugar with the juice and allowing it to stand for some time in the sun, by which a portion of the water is evaporated; or it may be boiled for a short time. When long boiled it loses the property of gelatinizing by cooling, and becomes a mucilaginous or gummy nature. Isinglass is often used to promote the thickening of vegetable jellies. Sugar has a similar effect.

Acetic Acid, or Vinegar. This acid is in the most general use for culinary purposes and is obtained by fermentation. Good strong vinegar contains about 4 per cent. of the pure acid. Vinegar may easily be made at any time by adding yeast to water sweetened with sugar or molasses or any sweet vegetable juice and letting the mixture stand for a length of time to air in a warm place. Apple and grape juice allowed to stand will undergo a change which will convert them into vinegar, and are highly prized for all purposes of cookery.

FLAVORED VINEGARS.

Celery Vinegar.

Put into a muslin bag four ounces of celery seed, put the bag in a wide-mouthed bottle, holding three or four quarts, fill with the white wine vinegar, and cork tight; set the bottle in cold water, heat it to boiling heat, take it from the bath, cork tightly, and set it in a cool place; this will be found a good substitute for celery, in all salads where this flavor is required.

Peach Vinegar.

Blanch, by putting them in boiling water, one pint of peach pits; pour over them cold vinegar, as strong as can be obtained, and cork tightly.

Oyster Vinegar.

Boil oysters in strong vinegar, until the vinegar is highly flavored; add clove, mace, and pepper, to suit the taste, then strain and bottle.

Horse Radish Vinegar.

6 tablespoonfuls grated horse radish.
1 tablespoonful white sugar.
1 quart vinegar.
Scald the vinegar; pour boiling hot over the horse radish. Steep a week, strain and bottle.

PICKLES.

Use none but the best cider vinegar; especially avoid the sharp, colorless liquid sold under that name. If you boil pickles in bell metal, do not let them stand in it one moment when it is off the fire; and see that it is perfectly clean and newly scoured before the vinegar is put in. Keep pickles in glass or hard stoneware; they should never be kept in glazed ware; look them over every month; remove the soft ones, and if there are several of these, drain off and scald the vinegar, adding a cup of sugar for each gallon, and pour hot over the pickles. If they are keeping well throw in a liberal handful of sugar for every gallon, and tie them up again. This tends to preserve them, and mellows the sharpness of the vinegar. This does not apply to *sweet* pickle. Pickles, well made, are better when a year old than at the end of six months.

Keep your pickles well covered with vinegar. If you use ground spices, tie them up in thin muslin bags.

Cucumber or Gherkin Pickles.

Select the small, young and slender cucumbers, and leave about half an inch of the stem, as this makes them keep better. Put them in a strong brine as they are gathered; be sure to keep them under the brine by placing a plate or board on the top of the vessel. When you wish to green and prepare a portion of them, cover the bottom and sides of the kettle with vine or cabbage leaves, and lay in the pickles, cover with a layer of leaves and pour over cold water to cover. Set the kettle over a moderate fire and bring to a scalding heat; keep at that temperature until perfectly green, which they should be in the course of ten or twelve hours. If they do not become green in that time, repeat the process. When well greened, remove and drain; put them in a stone jar and pour over them enough best cider vinegar boiling hot, to cover them.

If you wish to make spiced cider pickles, allow to every gallon of vinegar,

1 cup of sugar.
3 dozen whole black peppers; same of cloves.
1½ dozen allspice.
1 dozen blades of mace.

Put these in the vinegar and heat boiling hot and pour over. Turn off the vinegar, scald and pour on again in two days. Repeat the process three or four times. Keep in a dry, cool place closely covered.

SALT CUCUMBER PICKLES.

Put them fresh, unwashed, into a vessel, and cover with boiling water; when cold, pour off and cover again with hot water. When cold, put them into a cask of brine sufficiently strong for salt to settle on the bottom. Stir thoroughly every time fresh ones are added, and see that salt remains on the bottom. When the cask is full, cover the pickles with a cloth and a slight weight. Remove the cloth occasionally, and rinse it. The pickles keep well, are easily soaked, plump and fresh.

PICKLED PEPPERS.

Cut the stems out in a circle with a sharp penknife, and preserve them; fill each pepper with a mixture of finely chopped cabbage, horse radish, mustard seed, and salt. Before filling, wash the peppers in cold water; then fill, replace the piece cut out, tie with coarse thread, pack in stone jars, and fill up with cold, sharp vinegar. They will be ready for use in two weeks.

CAULIFLOWER.

Cut a large cauliflower in several pieces; wash and examine carefully for any insects which may be in it. Put it into cold water with two spoonfuls of salt. Heat the water gradually, until it comes to a boil. Boil for ten minutes, then drain until perfectly dry and put them in a glass jar. Prepare a flavored vinegar by boiling in one quart of vinegar, one teaspoonful cloves, and two of mustard for a few minutes. Pour the vinegar over the cauliflower when cold, this should cover the cauliflower.

Red Cabbage.

In proportion to two heads red cabbage, put twelve peppers, each chopped fine. To a gallon of the mixture, add,

1 tablespoonful cloves.
1 tablespoonful ground cinnamon.
2 tablespoonfuls salt.
½ cup fine black mustard-seed.
A few pepper corns.

Mix well, lay it in a stone jar, and pour over enough boiling vinegar to cover. Keep in a cool place.

Pickled Butternuts, or Walnuts.

Gather them when they are soft enough to be pierced with a pin. Place them in a very strong brine of salt and water, and let them soak six days, changing this twice during the time. Drain them dry, and pierce each nut by running a large needle through it. Lay in cold water for six hours. Prepare the vinegar by allowing to each gallon,

1 cup of sugar.
4 dozen whole cloves.
3 dozen black pepper corns.
2 dozen whole allspice.
1 dozen blades of mace.

Boil together five minutes. Place the nuts in jars, and pour the flavored vinegar over scalding hot. Repeat the scalding of the vinegar twice during the week. Tie up closely and they will be ready to use in a month or six weeks.

BEAN PICKLES.

Procure young beans from the late crops; wash and boil in slightly salted water until tender; drain them through a sieve or colander, then dry with a cloth. Pour boiling vinegar, spiced to taste, over them, repeat this two or three days, or until they look green.

MANGOES.

Select small musk-melons (the common kind are much better for this purpose than cantelopes), cut an oval piece out of one side. You must have a sharp knife, and be careful to make a smooth incision. Take out the seeds with a teaspoon. Fill the melons with a stuffing made of cloves, mustard seed, pepper corns, scrapings of horse radish, and chopped onion if you like it. Sew on the piece with a needle and coarse thread, or bind a strip of old cotton around each one and sew it. Lay them in a jar, and pour boiling vinegar on them with a little salt in it. Do it two or three times, then lay them in fresh vinegar and cover close.

NASTURTIUMS.

Gather the seeds while green, let them lie a few days, then throw them into vinegar. They need no spice except a little salt, being themselves sufficiently spicy. Boil the vinegar and pour on them. They are considered by many persons better than capers, and are much like them. They should be kept six months, covered close, before they are used.

GREEN TOMATO PICKLES.

1 peck green tomatoes.
8 onions.
4 green peppers.
1 cup salt.
1 cup sugar.
1 tablespoonful of pepper.

1 tablespoonful whole cloves.
1 tablespoonful mustard.
1 tablespoonful cinnamon.
1 tablespoonful mace.

Slice the tomatoes, peppers and onions, put in layers, and sprinkle over them the salt, and let them remain over night. In the morning press dry through a sieve. Put in the spice (in a thin muslin bag) and cover with vinegar. Stew slowly about an hour, or until the tomatoes are as soft as you desire. The onions can be omitted if you wish.

Cucumber Chow-Chow.

To six large cucumbers, take six onions, peel and chop very fine, separately; add salt enough to season, and let them stand until the water rises on them; squeeze them dry, mix together; add a little pepper, and vinegar enough to cover. Bottle and seal up air tight.

Chow-Chow.

1 peck green tomatoes.
1 large cup salt.
6 green peppers.
6 onions.
6 or 8 large stalks of celery.
1 pound sugar.
2 tablespoonfuls ground mustard.
4 tablespoonfuls fine black mustard-seed.
1 tablespoonful pepper corns.
1 tablespoonful whole cloves.
1 tablespoonful ground cinnamon.
1 tablespoonful mace.
½ tablespoonful ground pepper.

Chop the tomatoes, and sprinkle over them the salt; let this stand twelve hours, then drain off the water, and mix with it the onions, pepper and celery, all chopped fine. Mix the spices with the sugar, Put a layer of the chopped mixture in a preserving kettle, and scatter over it some of the sugar and spice, and so on **alternately.** Then cover with vinegar and let it simmer two hours.

English Chow-Chow.

1 peck cucumbers.
1 peck onions.
½ peck string beans.
3 heads cauliflower.
3 bunches celery.
½ dozen sweet peppers.

Soak the whole in strong salt and water over night; in the morning drain off the brine and scald them all in weak salt and water, but before scalding cut them into shape so that they will go easily into glass jars. Add

¾ pound mustard.
2 packages curry-powder.
6 quarts good vinegar.

Put the mustard and curry-powder into the vinegar, and let it come to a boil; put the pickles into the cans, and pour the boiling liquid over them while hot. Do not cover while scalding.

SWEET PICKLES.

Sweet Tomato Pickle.

8 pounds ripe tomatoes, peeled and sliced.
4 pounds sugar.
1 ounce cinnamon and mace mixed.
1½ ounces cloves.
1½ quarts vinegar.
Mix all together and stew an hour.

Cucumber Sweet Pickle.

Take ripe cucumbers, pare and seed, cut in strips; soak them in vinegar twenty-four hours. Drain and boil until clear, in a syrup of equal parts vinegar and sugar, with spices to your taste.

Cantelope Pickle.

Take fine ripe cantelopes, wash, pare and cut into small pieces, taking out the seeds; cover them with vinegar for twenty-four hours; throw away one quart of the vinegar to each quart remaining. Allow three pounds sugar to a dozen cantelopes, three ounces stick cinnamon, two ounces cloves, two ounces allspice (spices whole), boil them with the vinegar, when well skimmed put in the fruit, boil fifteen minutes, then take out, boil and skim the syrup, and pour boiling hot over the fruit.

Damsons.

5 pounds sugar.
1 pint vinegar.
1 peck damsons.
2 tablespoonfuls ground cinnamon.

1 tablespoonful whole cloves.

Boil the sugar and vinegar for a few minutes. Skim; then add the damsons and spice. Boil gently three hours, stirring frequently.

SPICED PLUMS, OR ANY FRUIT.

7 pounds of plums.
4 pounds of sugar.
1 quart vinegar.
1 tablespoonful cinnamon.
1 tablespoonful cloves.

Put the plums into the kettle with alternate layers of sugar. Heat slowly to a boil; add the vinegar and spice; boil five minutes; take out the fruit with a perforated skimmer and spread upon dishes to cool. Boil the syrup thick; pack the fruit in glass jars, and pour the syrup on boiling hot. Examine every few days for the first month, and should it show signs of fermenting, set the jars (uncovered) in a kettle of water, and heat until the contents are scalding.

PICKLED PEACHES.

Do not peel the peaches, but wipe with a coarse cloth; stick three or four cloves in each peach. Heat the peaches in just water enough to cover them, until they nearly boil; take them out and add to the water sugar in the following proportions:

For every 8 pounds of fruit,
4 pounds of sugar.
Boil fifteen minutes, skim and add,
3½ pints vinegar.
1 tablespoonful (each) allspice, cinnamon and mace.

Put the spice in a thin muslin bag. Boil all together ten minutes then put in the fruit, and boil until they can be pierced with a straw. Take out the fruit with a skimmer; spread upon dishes to cool. Boil the syrup until it is thick; pack the peaches in glass jars, and pour this over them scalding hot. Pickle pears in the same way without peeling. Cinnamon in sticks is preferable to the ground.

Watermelon Rinds.

7 pounds of rinds.
3½ pounds sugar.
1 quart of vinegar.
½ ounce white ginger.
Cloves and cinnamon to taste.

Take the thickest rinds, and pare off the hard, green rind, and remove the seeds, slice and drain in a colander over night. In the morning put in a strong brine, changing every three days; in the last brine, put in a little alum to make the rinds hard. Make the syrup and when hot put the rinds in and cook ten minutes, then remove and cook the syrup fifteen minutes, and pour over the rinds. They will be fit for use in two weeks.

ADDITIONAL RECIPES.

CATSUPS.

Walnut Catsup.

The walnuts must be young, and tender enough to be pierced with a needle. Prick them in several places, and put them in a jar adding a handful of salt to every thirty, and sufficient water to cover them. Break them up and leave them in the pickle two weeks, stirring every day. Drain off the liquor and cover the shells with boiling vinegar to extract what remains in them. Mash and strain through a colander. Allow for every quart, an ounce each of pepper and ginger, half an ounce each of cloves and nutmeg, beaten fine. For every two quarts add a pinch of cayenne, and half a teaspoonful celery-seed tied in a bag. Boil all together for one hour, if there are four quarts of the mixture. When cold put in bottles, putting an equal quantity of the spice in each one. Butternuts make a very nice catsup, made in the same manner.

Currant Catsup.

5 pounds ripe currants.
4 pounds sugar.
2 teaspoonfuls cloves, pounded fine.
2 teaspoonful ground cinnamon.
1 pint vinegar.

Mix the currants, sugar and spice together, and boil two hours; then add the vinegar. Boil up once and remove from the fire.

Tomato Catsup.

1 peck ripe tomatoes.
1 ounce of salt.
1 teaspoonful cayenne pepper.

1 tablespoonful each of black pepper, powdered cloves and celery seed in a bag.
7 tablespoonfuls ground mustard.
½ ounce mace.

Cut the tomatoes in halves, and put in the preserving kettle. Boil until the pulp is dissolved. Press through a hair sieve. Return to the fire, add the seasoning and boil four hours, stirring frequently. When cold, add a pint of strong vinegar. Take out the celery seed, and bottle, sealing the corks. Keep in a cool, dark place.

Horse Radish.

Wash the roots, and scrape them free from the outside skin; grate the roots finely and mix with strong vinegar. Add to one pint of the grated roots a teaspoonful of loaf sugar.

Imitation Worcestershire Sauce.

3 tablespoonfuls cayenne pepper.
2 tablespoonfuls walnut or tomato catsup (strained through muslin).
3 shallots minced fine.
3 anchovies chopped into bits.
1 quart of vinegar.
½ teaspoonful powdered cloves.

Mix and rub through a sieve. Put in a stone jar, set in a pot of boiling water, and heat until the liquid is so hot you cannot bear your fingers in it. Strain, and let it stand in the jar, closely covered, two days then bottle for use.

Gooseberry Catsup.

2 quarts gooseberries.
1 pint water.
1 teaspoonful ground cinnamon.
1 teaspoonful mace.
½ teaspoonful pepper.
½ teaspoonful cloves.

Pick clean ripe gooseberries, and boil till the fruit is quite tender; then add the spice, stir them together, and let it simmer a few minutes; then press out all the juice; add to each quart, one pound of sugar; reduce until the syrup is nearly a jelly, then thin with the best vinegar until of the consistency of molasses. Bottle and cork tightly.

Ever Ready Catsup.

2 quarts of cider vinegar.
12 anchovies, soaked and pulled to pieces.
12 small onions, chopped.
1 tablespoonful, each, mace and cloves.
3 tablespoonfuls, each, salt, sugar and whole black pepper.
2 tablespoonfuls ground ginger.
½ tablespoonful cayenne.
1 quart sliced ripe tomatoes.

Put in the kettle and boil until the mixture is reduced to one-half its original quantity. Strain through a bag. Let it remain until the next day, then bottle, fill to the top and seal.

SALADS.

Sydney Smith's Recipe for Salad Dressing.

Two boiled potatoes, strained through a kitchen sieve,
Softness and smoothness to the salad give;
Of mordaunt mustard take a single spoon—
Distrust the condiment that bites too soon;
Yet deem it not, thou man of taste, a fault,
To add a double quantity of salt.
Four times the spoon with oil of Lucca crown,
And twice with vinegar procured from town;
True taste requires it, and your poet begs
The pounded yellow of two well-boiled eggs.
Let onions' atoms lurk within the bowl,
And, scarce suspected, animate the whole;
And lastly, in the flavored compound toss
A magic spoonful of anchovy sauce.
Oh, great and glorious! oh, herbaceous meat!
'Twould tempt the dying anchorite to eat;
Back to the world he'd turn his weary soul,
And plunge his fingers in the salad bowl.

Made Mustard.

Pour a very little boiling water over three tablespoonfuls of mustard; to this stir in slowly,
1 teaspoonful sugar.
1 tablespoonful olive oil.
1 saltspoonful salt.
Yolk of 1 egg, well beaten.
Add vinegar to suit your taste.

Cold Slaw.

1 cup vinegar.
A piece of butter size of a walnut.
1 egg.
1 teaspoonful mustard.
1 teaspoonful sugar.
1 teaspoonful salt.
1 teaspoonful flour.
½ teaspoonful pepper.

Boil the vinegar and melt the butter in it and pour over the above mixture; stir it well, then put it back on the stove to boil again about a minute; then pour the whole upon the chopped cabbage.

Horse Radish Sauce.

2 teaspoonfuls made mustard.
2 teaspoonfuls white sugar.
½ teaspoonful salt.
1 gill of vinegar.

Mix and pour over grated horse-radish.
Excellent with beef.

Lettuce.

Get that in which the head is hard and compact. Lay it in ice-water until nearly time to serve; then break off the imperfect leaves, and throw them aside. Cut off the remainder of the leaves from the root, and look them over carefully. Wash in two or three waters, and arrange the leaves in the bottom of a salad or other deep dish. Allow two hard-boiled eggs for each head of lettuce; have them ready, cold, to slice, and lay over the lettuce. Put bits of ice in here and there. Send at once to the table, and serve with sugar, vinegar, mustard and the best salad oil.

Celery Salad.

1 boiled egg.
2 raw egg.
1 tablespoonful salad oil.

2 teaspoonfuls white sugar.
1 saltspoonful salt.
1 saltspoonful pepper.
6 tablespoonfuls vinegar.
1 teaspoonful made mustard.

Prepare the dressing as for tomato salad; cut the celery into bits half an inch long, and season. Eat at once, before the vinegar injures the crispness of the vegetable.

TOMATO SALAD.

1 dozen medium sized tomatoes.
4 hard boiled eggs.
1 raw egg.
1 teaspoonful of salt.
1 teaspoonful cayenne pepper.
1 teaspoonful white sugar.
1 tablespoonful salad oil.
2 teaspoonfuls made mustard.
1 teacupful vinegar.

Rub the yolks to a smooth paste, and gradually add the seasoning, lastly the vinegar. Peel and slice the tomatoes a quarter of an inch thick, and put them on ice. Put a lump of ice in the dressing and let it remain until the dressing is cold, then remove and pour the dressing over the tomatoes and set it on the ice until ready to use.

LOBSTER SALAD. NO. 1.

Cut very small the meat of one good sized lobster. The hen lobsters are best for salad, because they contain the red meat called "coral," which is desirable for garnishing. Put it in a salad dish, reserving the coral for ornamenting the salad. Make a dressing as follows:

Yolks of 2 raw eggs.
Yolks of 2 eggs boiled hard.
1 tablespoonful made mustard.
3 of melted butter, or the best salad oil.
A little salt and pepper.
Vinegar to your taste.

Mash the yolks of the boiled eggs very fine, and mix with the beaten raw eggs. Add gradually the other ingredients. Beat the mixture a long time. Some persons like the addition of lemon-juice and a little brown sugar. Increase the quantity of dressing, as you may find necessary, according to the size of the lobster. Just before serving, take one or two good heads of lettuce which have been on the ice for several hours, and cut up very small the crisp inside leaves only. Put them over the lobster meat in the salad dish, first pouring over the lobster some of the dressing. Pour the remainder over the salad; garnish with the coral cut fine, the white of the two hard boiled eggs cut in rings, and two others boiled hard, and sliced. The salad is ready to serve.

LOBSTER SALAD. NO. 2.

Take one or two heads of white heart lettuce; they should be as fresh as possible; lay them in spring water for an hour or two; then carefully wash them, and trim off all the withered or cankered leaves; let them drain awhile, and dry them lightly in a clean napkin. Then take out the coral, or red meat, and mince the remaining parts very fine. Mash the coral fine, with the yolks of four hard boiled eggs, a little sweet oil, mustard, pepper and salt, all mixed well, and moistened with vinegar; incorporate this mixture thoroughly with the meat; put it on a dish; sprinkle the whole with lettuce minced very fine.

SALAD DRESSING.

2 raw eggs.
1 tablespoonful of butter.
8 tablespoonfuls of vinegar.
½ teaspoonful mustard.

Put it in a bowl over boiling water and stir until it becomes like cream; pepper and salt to your taste.

SALADS.

SUGGESTIONS.

Chicken for salad, should boil until it comes from the bone easily. It it better to shred it than cut or chop. Equal parts of butter and salad oil are preferred by many to the entire quantity of either. The addition of the liquor the fowl is boiled in, is an improvement to moisten the salad with. Put celery and cabbage in ice cold water for an hour or two before using for salads, to make it crisp.

CHICKEN SALAD.

The meat of a cold chicken or turkey (boiled or roasted).
¾ the same amount chopped celery.
2 eggs, boiled hard.
1 raw egg, beaten well.
1 teaspoonful of made mustard.
1 teaspoonful of salt.
1 teaspoonful pepper.
1 tablespoonful salad oil, or melted butter.
1 tablespoonful white sugar.
½ teacupful vinegar.

Shred the meat well, removing all gristle and skin; cut the celery into pieces half an inch long or less, mix them well, and then prepare the dressing. Rub the yolks to a powder, add the seasoning, and then the oil, beating hard and putting it in a few drops at a time. Then add the raw egg beaten to a froth, and pour in the vinegar slowly, beating the dressing well as you do it. Pour this over the meat and celery, tossing up lightly, so that all will become saturated. When ready for the table, turn into a salad dish and garnish with the whites of cold boiled eggs, cut into rings, and sprigs of bleached celery tops. If you cannot get celery, crisp white cabbage may be substituted for celery, and celery vinegar used in the dressing.

Turkey makes better salad than chicken. A fine salad may be made by using lean fresh roasted pork, instead of chicken.

Salad for Two Chickens.

Yolks of 8 eggs, well beaten.
¼ cup of sugar.
1 tablespoonful of salt.
3 tablespoonfuls prepared mustard.
Cayenne pepper to taste.
½ cup of cream.
1 pint of vinegar.
1 cup of butter.
Stir together until thoroughly mixed.

YEAST.

Good yeast is indispensable to good bread. Many of the compounds sold for yeast are unfit for use. Every housekeeper should make sure, by her own personal attention, that the yeast is properly made, and the jar well scalded. A jar having a close cover is best; bottles will burst, and you cannot be perfectly sure that a jug is cleansed from every particle of old yeast. To scald the jar, put it into a kettle of boiling water. This should be done every time you make yeast. Stoneware is liable to be cracked by the pouring of boiling water into it. Soft hop, or potato yeast, should be made once a week in the summer, and once in two weeks in the winter. No soft yeast can be fit for use if kept week after week; it may be rectified with saleratus, but the bread will not be very good.

POTATO YEAST. NO. 1.

4 large potatoes, or six small.
2 quarts cold water.
Double handful hops, tied in a coarse muslin bag.
4 tablespoonfuls flour.
2 tablespoonfuls white sugar.
1 tablespoonful salt.

Boil and mash the potatoes while hot, stir in the flour, sugar and salt. Boil the hops in water five minutes and pour the tea over the mixture. Strain through a colander and let cool. When still slightly warm add four tablespoonfuls of baker's yeast, or two yeast cakes. Set it in a warm place to rise until it ceases to bubble up, or until the next day. In summer it will work well in a few hours.

POTATO YEAST. No. 2.

4 good sized potatoes.
4 tablespoonfuls white sugar.
1 teaspoonful of ginger.
1 teaspoonful of salt.
2 cupfuls of flour.
1 pint of boiling water.

Boil and mash the potatoes, then add the other ingredients, and pour over this the boiling water, and beat until the lumps disappear. After it is cooled add to it one cup of baker's yeast, and set away to rise. After it is done rising, put it in a glass jar and close; set away in a cool place. Add six tablespoonfuls of this yeast to your sponge.

SALT RISING, OR MILK YEAST.

½ cup new milk.
1 cup of boiling water.
1 teaspoonful of salt.

Stir in flour enough to make a thick batter, and set it in a covered dish in warm water; keep it at an even heat until light.

To make the bread: Add a pint of warm water, or milk, and make a thick sponge, and let it rise. When light, knead well, and put into pans, and set to rise again, when it will be ready for the oven.

HOP YEAST. No. 1.

3 good sized potatoes.
A small handful hops.
1 teaspoonful sugar.
1 tablespoonful salt.

Peel and grate the potatoes, put in enough water to make two quarts of the mixture; then strain out the starch and let it settle, and return the water to the potatoes and boil them. Steep the hops and strain in when the potato is soft. Add the sugar and salt. Let the mixture boil up, then stir in the starch, that has settled. Have it about the right thickness without adding any flour. When cold, add two-thirds cup of lively yeast; set it in a warm place to rise. Keep in a cool place.

Hop Yeast. No. 2.

4 large potatoes.
1 handful hops.
4 quarts water.
3 large spoonfuls flour.
2 spoonfuls sugar.
1 spoonful salt.
1 spoonful ginger.
1 teacup yeast.

Put the hops in a coarse muslin bag. Boil in the water the hops and potatoes. When the potatoes are done, take out the hops, mash the potatoes and add the flour, sugar, salt and ginger. Scald the whole together; when cool add the yeast and set it to rise.

Yeast Cakes.

Handful hops in a bag.
3 large potatoes.
1 quart water (cold).
1 pint flour.
1 teacup sugar.
1 spoonful salt.

Peel and slice the potatoes and place with the hops in the water; boil until the potatoes are soft. Put into a pan the flour, sugar and salt; scald them with the hop-water and potatoes, mashing the whole until smooth. When cool add four yeast cakes which have been well soaked. When the yeast is light, stir in corn meal till stiff enough to cut into cakes for drying. If too stiff, the cakes will be too hard. Sprinkle the moulding board with meal and spread the cakes on it, turning them frequently until dry. In warm weather place them in the air, but not in the sun; in cold weather they will dry in a warm room near the stove. When dry, wrap in a paper and keep from the air.

Yeast without Hops.

1 quart boiling water.
4 ounces white sugar.
1 teaspoonful salt.
1 teacupful yeast.

Stir into the water enough wheat flour to make a smooth thick batter. While hot stir in the sugar and salt. When cold add the yeast, and when fermented place in a covered jar for use. One half teacupful is enough for two loaves of bread. This yeast is good for raising buckwheat cakes, and makes bread very light and white, when good flour is used.

ADDITIONAL RECIPES.

BREAD.

In the composition of good bread there are four important requirements; good flour, good yeast, thorough kneading, and proper baking. Flour should be white and and dry, crumbling easily again after being pressed hard in the hand. If in handling the flour you notice a heaviness like ground plaster; if in squeezing it tightly, it retains the prints of the palm and fingers, and lies in the tray like a compact roll, or ball; or if it is in the least musty, or sour, the chances are ten to one against your having good bread. Next to the flour in importance is the yeast. This should be light in color and lively, effervescing easily when shaken, and emitting an odor like ammonia. If dull or sour, it is bad. Knead your bread faithfully. Do not work the dough over without spending any strength. The hands should be shut closely, and the fists pressed hard and quickly on the dough (so as to separate the fibres). A half hour is the least time to be given to kneading a baking of bread, unless you prefer, after having kneaded it till you have worked in the proper amount of flour, to chop it with a chopping-knife, four or five hundred strokes. An hour's kneading is not too much. Young housekeepers, and often those who should have learned better, frequently fall into a mistake in the consistency of the dough. It should be mixed *as soft as it can be handled*. The dough should be set in a moderately warm place, and kept at an even temperature. If it is too cool, the fermentation is arrested, and the bread fails to rise; if it is too warm, the work goes forward too rapidly, and the bread is puffy and strong. The former difficulty may be remedied by more heat, and the latter by a little soda dissolved in water and worked thoroughly into the dough. While rising it is much better to cover closely with a tin dish, as this prevents the steam from escaping, or the forming of a crust before it is placed in the oven. The oven should not be too hot, as too much fire at first and then cooling it, forms a hard crust and leaves the middle undone, or what is termed "slack-baked." The heat should be uniform in all parts of the oven as this prevents the loaf from cracking open, or one side rising lighter than the other, and opening the oven door to turn the loaf injures the bread. When the loaves are baked do not lay them flat on the table, as it is apt to make them heavy. Set them on the edge and put a cloth closely over them. This keeps in the steam and makes the crust soft. Some of the best cooks think that covering a cloth over hot bread injures its flavor, and prefer to leave the crust hard to covering it.

BUTTERMILK BREAD.

1 quart of buttermilk, heated to scalding.
2 quarts of flour.
½ cup of yeast.

When the milk is slightly cool, pour over the flour the whey, and when cool enough, stir in the yeast. Beat well, and let it rise over night. Mix early in the morning adding as much tepid water as is needed for the required quantity of bread. Let the whole rise until quite light, then knead thoroughly and let it rise before baking.

HOP YEAST BREAD.

1 cup yeast.
1 quart new milk and water, or scalded milk and water.

Stir in flour enough to make a stiff sponge and let it rise over night. In the morning stir it down and let it rise again; then mould thoroughly and fill bread pans half full; let them stand until light and bake three-quarters of an hour.

BREAD FOR LARGE BAKING.

Take eight pounds of flour, sift into bread dish; rub well into the flour a tablespoonful lard or butter. Make a deep hole in the flour and having ready a quart of lukewarm water with a heaped tablespoonful of fine salt, mix with flour and yeast, and pour in the cavity. Take a large spoon and stir in flour for a thick batter, then scatter a handful of flour over the batter; cover up the bread dish, and keep in a warm place, if cold weather. If summer, any where will be warm enough. This is called setting the sponge. When the batter is fermented pour in as much warm water as will make it of proper consistency. Knead it well until firm and smooth. Put it in the bread pans which must be well greased. In about one-half hour it will be ready for the oven which must be properly heated beforehand.

MILK BREAD.

1 quart milk.
1 teacupful yeast.
¼ pound butter.
1 tablespoonful white sugar.

Stir in the milk, which should be made blood warm, a pint of flour and the sugar, lastly the yeast. Beat all together well and let them rise five or six hours. Then melt the butter and add with a little salt. Work in flour enough to make a stiff dough, let this rise four hours, and make into small loaves. Set near the fire for half an hour and bake. In warm weather, add a teaspoonful of soda, dissolved in warm water to the risen sponge as all bread mixed with milk is apt to sour.

PATTERSON BREAD.

1 quart flour.
1 teaspoonful soda.
2 teaspoonfuls cream tartar.
1 teaspoonful salt.
Piece of butter twice the size of an egg.

2 eggs well beaten.
2 teaspoonfuls sugar.
1 pint sweet milk.

Put into the flour the soda, cream tartar, salt and butter, before mixing with the milk; and bake in well greased gem pans, or little tins.

Milk Yeast Bread.

See direction for Milk Yeast or Salt Rising.

Bread Sponge.

6 potatoes.
2 tablespoonfuls white sugar.
2 tablespooofuls of butter.
1 quart of tepid water.
3 cups of flour.
6 tablespoonfuls of yeast.

Boil and mash the potatoes while hot; stir the ingredients to a smooth batter, then add the yeast. Set over night; in the morning knead in sufficient flour to make a stiff spongy dough; knead vigorously for fifteen minutes. Set away to rise, and when light knead for ten minutes, mould out into modern sized loaves. Let them rise until they are like delicate or light sponge cake.

Graham Bread. No. 1.

2 cups of sour milk or buttermilk.
½ cup of best sugar or syrup.
1 teaspoonful soda.
½ teaspoonful salt.

Stir with a spoon to a stiff mass (not too stiff, or the bread will be too hard). Put it in a three pint or two quart basin, well buttered, and place in the steamer over *cold* water, which gives the loaf more time to rise. Steam about two hours, then put in the oven just long enough to give a rich brown color.

GRAHAM BREAD. NO. 2.

2 cups Graham flour.
1 cup Indian meal.
2 tablespoonfuls molasses.
1 teaspoonful salt.
1 teaspoonful baking powder.
1 small teaspoonful soda.

Add enough milk (half sweet and half sour) to make it a little stiffer than pound cake, and bake in a quick oven.

CREAM BISCUIT.

These are made in the same manner as butter milk biscuit, except no butter is required. Cream will make them sufficiently short.

CREAM TARTAR BISCUIT.

1 quart flour.
2 teaspoonfuls cream tartar.
1 teaspoonful soda.
1 teaspoonful salt.
1 pint cold water.
Piece of butter size of an egg.

Rub the butter into the flour until there are no lumps, then add the salt, and scatter in the cream tartar. Have ready the water in which the soda has been dissolved, pour into the flour, stirring quickly with a knife. Do this until the ingredients are well mixed, then add flour enough to mould smooth. Bake in a quick oven. These can be made of unbolted flour if desired. Make one half the quantity for a small family.

STRAWBERRY SHORTCAKE.

Make cream of tartar biscuit dough, a little shorter than usual. Roll it quite thin, and lay in the pans in sheets. Bake quickly. Take fresh strawberries or raspberries, and stir sugar into them. Split the cake and butter both parts, and put on a layer of fruit and replace the upper half of the cake. To be set on the table uncut, and eaten hot. Use buttermilk, or rich sour milk for this cake if more convenient, but in that case omit the cream tartar.

Baking Powder Biscuit.

1 quart flour.
4 heaping teaspoonfuls baking powder.
A little salt.

Mix the powder and salt well in the flour. Wet up with sweet milk, stiff enough to roll, but do not knead. Cut with biscuit cutter and bake fifteen minutes. They are much nicer than with shortening. If desired one can use a piece of lard the size of an English walnut, well rubbed in the flour.

Raised Biscuit. No. 1.

1 pint of milk.
½ cup of yeast.
1 tablespoonful of sugar.
1 teaspoonful of salt.
A piece of butter the size of an egg.

Warm the milk and butter together. Set the sponge at night and mix hard in the morning.

Soda Biscuit.

To each quart of flour, add
1 tablespoonful of butter.
3½ teaspoonfuls baking powder.
½ teaspoon salt.
2 cups sweet milk.

If soda and cream tartar are used, use one teaspoon soda and two teaspoonfuls cream tartar. Mix the baking powder thoroughly in the flour, then wet with the milk; if water is used take double the quantity of butter. Knead but little and bake quickly.

Raised Biscuit. No. 2.

Cut off a portion of raised dough which has been made ready for bread. Roll it out, spread on a little shortening, and mould it in; cut the biscuit, and let them rise until light and then bake. These biscuit can be moulded in the morning when the bread is prepared, and placed in a cool place until tea, but must be raised before baking. Bake in a quick oven.

Buttermilk or Sour Milk Biscuit.

1 pint buttermilk or sour milk.
1 quart flour.
Piece of butter half the size of an egg rubbed into the flour.
1 teaspoonful soda, dissolved in hot water.
A little salt.

Rub the butter and salt into the flour and stir in the milk. Stir the soda in with a knife till well mixed. Add flour enough to mould it smooth. Roll and cut as tea biscuit. Bake in a quick oven.

Easter Buns.

3 cups sweet milk.
1 cup yeast.
Flour to make a thick batter.
Set this as a sponge over night. In the morning add
1 cup sugar.
½ cup butter, melted.
½ nutmeg.
1 saltspoonful salt.

Flour enough to roll out like biscuit. Knead well, and set to rise for five hours. Roll half an inch thick, cut into round cakes, and lay in rows in a buttered baking-pan. When they have stood a half hour, make a cross upon each with a knife, and put instantly into the oven. Bake to a light brown, and brush over with a feather or soft bit of rag, dipped in the white of an egg beaten up stiff with white sugar.

Buns.

1 pint warm milk.
½ cup white sugar.

½ cup yeast.
½ cup butter.
1 egg.

Beat up and sponge with flour, and rise over night; then knead and work up three times before baking.

Plain Buns.

These are made like the Easter buns, but not rolled into a sheet. Knead them like biscuit dough, taking care not to get it too stiff, and after the five-hour rising, work in two or three handfuls of currants which have been previously well washed and dredged with flour. Mould with your hands into round balls, set these closely together in a pan, that they may form a loaf, which can easily be broken apart when baked. Let them stand nearly an hour, or until very light; then bake from half to three-quarters of an hour until brown. Wash them over while hot with the beaten egg and sugar. These are generally eaten cold, or barely warm, and are best the day they are baked.

Butter Crackers.

1 quart of flour.
4 tablespoonfuls of butter.
½ teaspoonful soda dissolved in hot water.
½ teaspoonful salt.
2 cups of sweet milk.

Mix the butter in the flour as for pastry. Add the salt soda and milk, mixing well, mould it into a ball and beat with the rolling pin for a half hour, turning the mass often. Roll into a sheet one quarter of an inch thick; prick with a fork and bake hard in a moderate oven. Dry in a bag hung up in the kitchen.

Puffs.

6 heaping tablespoonfuls flour.
1 pint milk.
2 eggs.

A saltspoonful salt.

Bake in cups not quite half full. Put in the oven when you sit down to dinner, and they will be ready for desert. Serve with cream and sugar, or maple syrup.

CRUMPETS. (*Plain.*)

3 cups warm milk.
½ cup yeast.
2 tablespoonfuls melted butter.
1 saltspoonful salt.
1 saltspoonful soda, dissolved in hot water.
Flour to make a good batter.

Set these ingredients (leaving out the butter and soda) as a sponge. When very light, beat in the melted butter, with a very little flour, to prevent the butter from thinning the batter too much, stir in the soda hard, fill muffin-rings, or patty-pans with the mixture, and let them stand fifteen minutes before baking.

WAFERS.

1 pound flour.
2 tablespoonfuls butter.
A little salt.

Mix with sweet milk into a stiff dough, and roll very thin, cut into round cakes, and again roll these as thin as they can be handled. Lift them carefully and lay in a pan and bake quickly. They should be hardly thicker than writing paper. Flour the baking-pan instead of greasing. These are very nice, especially for invalids.

ROLLS. NO. 1.

½ pint milk.
½ cup shortening.
½ cup yeast.
6 cups flour.
2 spoonfuls sugar.

Mix early and set it to rise. Make out into rolls, let them rise half an hour in pans before baking.

ROLLS. No. 2.

2 quarts flour.
1 tablespoonful white sugar.
1 pint milk.
½ teacup yeast.
Butter the size of an egg.
A little salt.

Make a hole in center of the flour, put in the butter, salt and sugar; pour over this the milk previously boiled and cold, and also the yeast. When the sponge is light, mould for fifteen minutes. Let it rise again, and cut in long cakes. When light, flatten each cake with the rolling pin and put a small piece of butter on top and fold each over itself as a turnover. Put in pans to rise, and when light bake in a quick oven.

FRENCH ROLLS. No. 1.

Take out from the risen dough when ready to knead, enough for the tea rolls. Work into this dough a tablespoonful of lard or butter and let it stand in a cool place for four hours. Knead it and let it stand for three hours longer. Then make into rolls by rolling pieces of the dough into round cakes and fold these up like turnovers. Again let these rise for one hour. Bake half an hour or less if the oven is quick.

FRENCH ROLLS. No. 2.

1 quart of milk; new, warm milk is best.
1 teacupful of yeast.
1½ quarts of flour.
1 egg.
2 tablespoonfuls of butter.
1 teaspoonful of salt.
½ teaspoonful soda dissolved in hot water.
1 tablespoonful sugar.

When the sponge is light, work in the egg, well beaten, butter, soda, salt and sugar, and flour enough to make a soft dough. Let it stand five hours, then roll into round cakes and fold like turnovers. Set them closely together in the baking tin, let them rise one hour. Just before baking, draw a sharp knife across each roll to make them break in baking. Bake half an hour.

SWEET RUSK.

1 pint warm milk.
½ cup butter.
1 cup sugar.
2 eggs.
1 teaspoonful salt.
2 tablespoonfuls yeast.

Make a sponge with milk, yeast, and enough flour for a thin batter, and let it rise over night. In the morning add butter, eggs and sugar previously well beaten together, the salt, and flour enough to make soft dough. Mould with the hands into balls of uniform size. Set close together in a pan and let them rise until very light. After baking wash the tops with a cloth dipped in molasses and water.

RUSK.

When moulding bread into loaves, reserve sufficient for one loaf to make up into rusk. Add

1 large, heaping tablespoon of half butter and half lard (it should be fresh, sweet and cold).
Whites of two eggs, well beaten.
1 tablespoonful sugar.

Mix well, and set aside until very light; then mould into rather small rolls, let them stand half an hour, or until they look light and puffy. Wash over lightly with the beaten yolk of egg. Bake twenty to twenty-five minutes in a quick oven.

SALLY LUNN. NO. 1.

1 scant quart flour.
4 eggs.
1 teacupful milk.

1 teacupful lard and butter mixed.
1 teaspoonful cream tartar.
½ teaspoonful soda dissolved in hot water.
1 teaspoonful salt.

Beat the eggs very light, yolks and whites separately, melt the shortening, sift the cream tartar into the flour, add the whites the last thing.

MUFFINS. No. 1.

1 pint sweet milk.
1 quart flour.
1 egg.
3 large spoonfuls sugar.
2 teaspoonfuls cream tartar.
1 teaspoonful soda.
Piece of butter size of an egg.

MUFFINS. No. 2.

1 pint sour cream.
3 eggs.
1 teaspoonful soda.
1 teaspoonful salt.

Enough flour to make as stiff as you can stir with a spoon.

BUTTERMILK MUFFINS.

1 quart buttermilk.
2 eggs.
1 teaspoonful soda, dissolved in hot water.
1 teaspoonful salt.

Flour to make good batter. Beat the eggs well and stir into the milk, beating hard all the while. Add the flour and salt, and lastly the soda. Bake in a quick oven.

SOUR MILK MUFFINS.

1 pint sour milk.
1 egg.
1 teaspoonful saleratus.

1 teaspoonful butter.
1 teaspoonful salt.

Put the egg in the milk without beating. Melt the butter and saleratus in a spoonful of hot water. Make quite a thick batter and beat well. Have the griddle of moderate heat; grease it and also the rings, lay them on and fill only half full of the batter.

RICE MUFFINS.

1 cup cold boiled rice.
1 pint flour.
2 eggs.
1 quart milk, or enough to make thin batter.
1 tablespoonful lard or butter.
1 teaspoonful salt.

Beat hard, and bake quickly.

GRAHAM MUFFINS.

3 cups Graham flour.
1 cup wheat flour.
2 tablespoonfuls sugar.
2 eggs.
2 teaspoonfuls cream tartar.
1 teaspoonful soda.
A little salt.

Take piece of butter the size of an egg, put it into a pint of sweet milk, set it on the stove until melted, and mix together.

RAISED GRAHAM MUFFINS.

3 cups Graham flour.
1 cup wheat flour.
1 quart milk.
¾ cup yeast.
1 tablespoonful lard or butter.
1 teaspoonful salt.
2 tablespoonfuls sugar.

Set to rise over night; bake in muffin-rings twenty minutes in quick oven. Eat when hot.

Corn Meal Muffins.

1 cup corn meal.
1½ cups flour.
1⅓ cups sweet milk.
1 egg.
2 small tablespoonfuls shortening.
2 small teaspoonfuls baking powder.
1 teaspoonful salt.

The egg can be omitted. If baking powder is not used, take two teaspoonfuls cream tartar, and one teaspoonful soda.

Graham Rolls.

1 egg.
2 tablespoonfuls sugar.
½ cup molasses.
1 cup sour milk.
1 teaspoonful soda.
1 teaspoonful ginger.
½ teaspoonful salt.
2½ cups Graham flour.
Bake in gem pans.

Graham Gems.

1 pint of sour milk.
1 teaspoonful soda.
1 egg.
1 tablespoonful shortening.
Graham flour enough to make a stiff batter.
Bake in gem irons.

French Toast.

2 eggs.
1 pint cold milk.
1 teaspoonful salt.

Take thin slices of stale bread and dip into the eggs and milk after being beaten together. Drain off the milk from the bread, and brown both sides on buttered griddle; serve in hot covered dish. Eat with syrup or butter and sugar.

Milk Toast.

1 quart milk.
½ cup butter.
Thicken with flour broken up in cold milk or water, and scald for a few minutes. Brown the slices of bread, and dip into the thickened milk. It is well to soften the bread by dipping it in hot water, in which a little salt has been dissolved. This can be used for butter toast, by using water instead of milk, and using one cupful butter.

Johnny Cake. No. 1.

1 pint sour milk, or buttermilk.
1 egg.
2 tablespoonfuls flour.
1 teaspoonful salt.
1 teaspoonful soda dissolved in hot water.

Mix the egg, milk and flour, and add enough meal to make a thick batter; and finally add salt and soda after being dissolved in the hot water. Beat very rapidly, and bake quickly and steadily.

Johnny Cake. No. 2.

1 cup cream.
1 cup sweet milk.
2 tablespoonfuls sugar.
1 egg.
1 teaspoonful salt.
1 teaspoonful soda.
Meal to mix soft. The sugar can **be omitted.**

Johnny Cake. No. 3.

1 egg.
2 cups corn meal.
⅔ cup flour.
3 tablespoonfuls sugar.

2 teaspoonfuls baking powder.
Milk enough to make it soft.

Brown Bread.

1 quart sweet milk.
4 cups meal.
2 cups flour.
⅔ cup molasses.
1 teaspoonful salt.
1 tablespoonful soda.
Bake slowly for one hour.

Steamed Brown Bread.

2 cups sweet milk.
1 cup sour milk.
3 cups corn meal.
1 cup flour.
½ cup molasses.
1 egg.
1 teaspoonful soda.
1 teaspoonful salt.
Steam three hours.

Graham and Indian Bread.

3 cups Indian meal.
1 heaping cup Graham flour.
⅔ cup molasses.
1 teaspoonful salt.
1 teaspoonful soda.
1 cup sour milk.
Scald the meal over night; steam three hours, and bake to give a nice crust.

Boston Brown Bread.

2 pints Indian meal.
1 pint rye meal.
1 cup molasses.
1 tablespoonful soda.

Mix with sour or buttermilk quite soft, so it will pour. Put the soda into the molasses, and molasses into meal. Add a little salt. Steam five or six hours.

Raised Brown Bread.

1 pint warm water.
1 cup flour.
2 cups rye meal.
2 cups Indian meal.
1 cup molasses.
1 small cup good yeast
1 teaspoonful salt.
1 small teaspoonful soda.

Pour the mixture into a tin pudding pan or pail; let it rise three hours. Set it into a kettle of boiling water, and steam four hours.

ADDITIONAL RECIPES.

ADDITIONAL RECIPES.

ADDITIONAL RECIPES. 149

GRIDDLE CAKES AND WAFFLES.

GREEN CORN GRIDDLE CAKES.

Grate the corn from the cob, and allow one egg for every cupful, with one tablespoonful of milk or cream; beat eggs well, add the corn, salt to taste; add one tablespoonful melted butter to every pint of corn, stir in the milk, and thicken with just enough flour to hold them together, say one tablespoonful for every two eggs. Fry in hot lard; or better, cook on griddle.

BUCKWHEAT CAKES. NO. 1.

2 quarts buckwheat flour.
4 tablespoonfuls yeast.
1 teaspoonful salt.
1 handful Indian meal.
2 tablespoonfuls molasses, not syrup.
Warm water enough to make a thin batter.

Beat well, and set to rise in a warm place. If the batter is the least sour in the morning, stir in a little soda dissolved in hot water. Mix in an earthen crock, and leave a cupful or more in the bottom each morning to serve as sponge the next night, instead of getting fresh yeast. In cold weather, this plan can be pursued for a week or ten days without getting a fresh supply.

BUCKWHEAT CAKES. NO. 2.

1 quart warm water.
1 tablespoonful scalded Indian meal.
1 teaspoonful salt.
1 gill yeast.
Buckwheat flour enough to make a thin batter. Let it

rise over night, in the morning add a quarter of a teaspoonful of soda, do this whether the cakes are sour or not. Buckwheat cakes cannot be made in perfection without this addition; but it should never be put in until just before they are baked. They should be made as thin as they can be, and be turned on the griddle. All kinds of griddle cakes should be well beaten. Flour or Graham flour can be used with buckwheat; if used, omit the Indian meal, and take one-third as much wheat flour, or Graham as buckwheat.

Bread Griddle Cakes.

1 quart milk (boiling hot).
2 quarts fine bread crumbs.
3 eggs.
1 tablespoonful melted butter.
1 teaspoonful salt.
1 teaspoonful soda dissolved in hot water.

Soak the bread in the milk ten minutes in a covered bowl; beat it to a smooth paste, add the beaten yolks, the butter, salt, soda and finally the whites beaten stiff. Bake on griddle.

Rice Griddle Cakes.

Put a pint and a half of cold boiled rice, in warm water enough to cover it, and let it soak an hour. Mash the rice well, and make a batter with one quart of sour milk, one light quart of flour, salt to taste, and two eggs well beaten. The batter should be moderately thick. Stir in a teaspoonful of soda just before frying.

Griddle Cakes. No. 1.

1 pint sour milk.
1 egg.
2 teaspoonfuls soda.
Piece of butter size of a walnut.
Flour enough to make smooth batter.

Stale bread can be used by soaking until soft, in either milk or water, several hours. Less flour will be needed if the bread is used.

GRIDDLE CAKES. NO. 2.

1 quart sweet milk.
2 eggs.
1 teaspoonful salt.
1 tablespoonful butter, melted in the milk.
1 gill yeast.
Flour enough to make a smooth batter. Make in the morning, and they will be light for tea.

RISEN WAFFLES.

1 quart milk.
1 heaping quart flour.
5 tablespoonfuls yeast.
2 eggs.
1 tablespoonful melted butter.
1 teaspoonful salt.
Set the mixture—without the eggs and butter—over night as a sponge; Add these in the morning; bake in waffle irons.

RICE WAFFLES.

1 cup boiled rice.
1 pint milk.
2 eggs.
Piece of lard, size of a walnut.
½ teaspoonful soda.
1 teaspoonful cream tartar.
1 teaspoonful salt.
Enough flour for a thin batter.

QUICK WAFFLES.

1 pint milk.
3 eggs beaten very lightly.
1 tablespoonful melted butter.

1 teaspoonful cream tartar sifted in the flour.
½ teaspoonful soda.
1 teaspoonful salt.
1 pint flour, or enough to make a soft batter.

FRITTERS.

FRITTERS.

2 eggs well beaten.
2 tablespoonfuls melted lard.
⅔ cup sweet milk.
1 heaping teaspoonful baking powder.
A little salt.
Flour to make a stiff batter.

Drop from spoon into hot lard; turn two or three times while cooking to prevent too much browning. To be eaten warm with maple or sugar syrup.

SNOW FRITTERS.

Stir together enough milk, flour and a little salt to make a thick batter; add new fallen snow in the proportion of a teacupful to a pint of milk. Have the fat ready hot, at the time you stir in the snow, and drop the batter into it with a spoon. These are preferred by some to those made with eggs.

EGG PLANT FRITTERS.

Take a large sized egg plant, leave the stem and skin on, and boil it in a porcelain kettle until very soft, just so you can get it out with the aid of a fork or spoon; take off all the skin and mash very fine in an earthen bowl. When cold, add a teaspoon of salt, plenty of pepper, a large iron spoonful of flour, a half teacupful of cream or milk, and three eggs. This forms a nice batter. Have lard hot, drop the batter in as you would fritters, and brown them nicely on each side.

Fritters or Pancakes.

1 pint milk.
3 eggs.
A little salt.
Flour enough to make quite a thick batter. Beat well, then drop with a spoon into hot fat and fry like doughnuts. To be eaten with syrup.

VEGETABLE MAXIMS.

To beat mashed potatoes with a fork, improves them as much as to beat the eggs for a cake.

Sweet potatoes are best steamed until tender and then baked.

Potatoes fried in boiling lard, like fritters, are very nice, and do not soak fat if the grease is hot enough.

Three hours is short time enough to cook oat meal.

It is a rare thing to see any kind of farinaceous food, —either of oat, corn, barley, rice or wheat—sufficiently cooked.

Any kind of mush cooks more quickly and is nicer, not to be salted till nearly done.

Many people think tomatoes equal to peaches when eaten with cream and sugar.

Tomatoes are preserved with salt the same as cucumbers.

Vegetables which are eaten without cooking, as radishes and celery, should be kept cold till they are eaten.

No vegetable is nice if it wilts before it is cooked.

Bread mixed with water will keep moist longer than if mixed with milk.

To warm over gems, rolls, etc., dip them in cold water for an instant, and put them into a hot oven.

To freshen stale crackers, put them into a hot oven dry.

Fried cakes can be freshened in the same way as crackers.

Cold griddle cakes soaked soft and stirred into fresh batter are fully equal to bread crumbs.

Chocolate is never nice warmed up after it has cooled. It should be kept hot.

Use boiling milk in coffee and chocolate.

Unused tea may be saved by pouring it off the **grounds** and heating the liquid over.

HYGIENIC EFFECT OF VEGETABLES.

WHEAT.

Wheat contains all of the elements necessary to health in the best proportions for a moderate climate, when cooked by boiling, or as cracked wheat, or Graham flour. The common superfine flour, however, contains, little except starchy matter which serves as fuel.

INDIAN CORN.

Indian corn contains a great amount of oil, and so possesses remarkable fattening qualities, and is likewise remarkable as a heat producer.

OATS

are very rich in nutriment for the brain and muscles.

RICE

will keep a person fat, but lacks the elements which produce muscle or brain.

POTATOES.

Both Irish and sweet potatoes are very poor food for brain and muscle, but they contain a great amount of waste matter, and they are the best of anything to mix with strong foods like most meats.

TURNIPS, CARROTS, SQUASHES, PARSNIPS, ETC.,

are nearly all water and are dear at any price except in hot weather, when we need to flood the system and take very little strong food.

BUCKWHEAT

is only good for a ride in the cold, having but little material for muscle or brain, but over 75 per cent. of heating matter. It should never be eaten except in winter.

RYE

is excellent food for persons inclined to constipation and with corn meal makes good bread, nourishing and digestible.

BEANS AND PEAS.

These contain double the amount of muscle and brain matter, and treble the waste material necessary, but lack in heating material. The are appropriately used with pork or butter to supply the requisite carbonates. Being hard of digestion they are good for active persons of strong digestion.

FRUITS.

Fruits are necessary to people of sedentary habits. Their acids are needed every day to eliminate effete matter which clogs the system, causing jaundice, sleeplessness, scurvy and troublesome diseases of the skin. Their solid matter also is of great value as it is mostly woody fibre and indigestible, so remedying constipation. Apples compared with wheat contain twice as much food for muscle, and four times as much for brain.

SUGAR.

The sap and juices of all plants and fruits contain sugar. Those plants and fruits which contain sour or acid juice yield grape sugar; while those which contain little or no acid in their saps, contain generally cane sugar.

Grape Sugar consists of twelve parts of carbon to fourteen parts of water; while cane sugar contains twelve parts of carbon to eleven parts of water. Two pounds of cane sugar will sweeten as much as five pounds of grape sugar. Grape sugar may be produced by art, while cane sugar cannot. Eleven-twelfths of all the sugar of commerce is made from sugar cane. This is sold in the forms of raw, or muscovado, or is commonly called *brown sugar*, molasses, refined sugars, sugar-house molasses, and syrups.

Cane-Juice contains vegetable albumen, a substance which has a strong tendency to fermentation, hence when left to itself is rapidly changed; the acid of vinegar being generated. To neutralize this acid, lime is added and it is boiled until a syrup is produced. The liquid is then drawn off into shallow vessels and stirred. As it cools, the sugar granulates or appears in the form of grains or crystals. Part of the syrup will be changed by the boiling so that it will not granulate, and this will keep the remainder from becoming solid. The product is then placed where it can drain and a large part of this syrup flows away, and is collected in separate vessels and is known as molasses. This sugar is muscovado, or more commonly called brown sugar.

This brown sugar contains more or less vegetable albumen; this albumen has a great tendency to decomposition by which process the cane sugar is changed to grape sugar. This change, of course, lessens its sweetening properties, and lowers its value.

The vegetable albumen in this raw sugar offers nourishment to a minute insect called the sugar-mite. This sugar is seldom found without this disgusting insect. The refined sugars contain no albumen, and consequently offer no nourishment to them. Their presence can be detected by dissolving two or three tablespoonfuls of sugar in a wine-glass of tepid water. Let it stand an hour or two, and the animalculæ will be found on the surface. The mite is visible to the naked eye as a mere speck, but can be easily seen with the microscope.

The molasses which flows away from the sugar consists of the saccharine, or sugary matter combined with the lime used in its manufacture; also with small quantities of alkalies.

Molasses itself is also aciduous. On this account it cannot be used with yeast. But the molasses takes effect upon saleratus (or soda) and sets free carbonate acid gas. Carbonate of magnesia and tartaric acid may be used instead of saleratus with molasses, and it is more agreeable, as well as more wholesome. The peculiar strong taste of molasses may be removed by boiling for half an hour with pulverized charcoal. Crude sugar is refined to cleanse it of its impurities, and improve its color and taste; this is done, by first melting it, and mixing with it a small portion of animal albumen (ox blood), which clears it of mechanical contaminations. The syrup is then filtered through a bed of animal charcoal (burnt bones crushed), by which it is decolorized. It is then crystallized by boiling at a low temperature in vacuum pans in which the atmospheric pressure is removed.

Sugar-house Molasses and Syrups are the residue which remain uncrystallized in purifying and refining brown sugars. These are much more cleanly and pure than common molasses and consequently are less used for cooking. Part of the sugar taken into the system is absolved through the veins and burned away to produce heat. Another part is turned into lactic acid, and assists in digestion; and a part is converted into fat in the body. There is an old opinion that sugar when eaten freely, attacks the teeth, corrupting them and spoiling their color, but good authority, including Dr. Pereira, declares this opinion totally unfounded. No people have finer teeth than the negroes of Jamaica, and none, perhaps, use sugar more liberally.

Nature evidently intended children to have sugar, as a fondness for it seems a common instinct; and besides it is very plenty in their first food—milk.

CAKE.

Use none but the best materials for cake making. Have all your materials ready for use before you begin mixing the ingredients; butter your pans beforehand, for cake is injured by standing. Cake is better made in earthen than in tin. All kinds of cake are better if the whites and yolks are beaten separately; be careful in separating that none of the yolk gets in the white, as it may prevent their frothing well. Eggs beat more quickly that have been laid two or three days, than when laid the same day. In warm weather if the eggs are placed in cold water or on ice some time before using, they will cut into a much finer froth. Much time can be saved by using an egg-beater, and we would recommend the "Dover" as being the best in use for this purpose. The whites are perfectly beaten when they will remain on the upturned vessel in which they were beaten without slipping; the yolks are light with no stringy appearance, when perfectly beaten; it takes as long, if not longer to beat the yolks than the whites. The whites make the cake lighter and the yolks enrich it. For very nice cake the yolks should be strained after beating. Do not use fresh and stale milk in the same cake. Sour milk makes a spongy cake; sweet milk one closer in grain. Except for molasses cake use none but white sugar, and many prefer the powdered to the granulated. Be careful in your weights and measures. Beat the butter and sugar together, until they look like cream. When cream or sour milk is used, half of it should be added when half the flour is, and the rest of the flour, milk and soda stirred in last. When fruit is used it should be dredged in the flour, as it prevents it settling to the bottom. In winter *soften*, but do not melt the butter. In summer do not stir the cake with your hands as the warmth makes it less light. If the butter is from a firkin, wash it to remove the salt. Streaks in cake are caused by unskilful mixing, too rapid baking, or sudden decrease in heat while baking. If necessary to move the cake while in the oven, do so very carefully as a slight jar may cause it to fall; if it hardens too quickly on top, cover with paper. It should rise to its full height before the crust forms. Sift your flour before measuring, as all recipes are for sifted flour. It is better to line the pans with paper, which can be buttered; in buttering the pans melt the butter to extract the salt. Keep the cake in a tin box or stone jar.

Molasses Cakes should be made of *real* West India molasses, syrup will not do. They should be put in the oven immediately after adding the soda; bake in a quick but not hot oven, without burning, until well done. They must be used fresh unless made hard; when thus made they will keep some time. If shortened with lard, salt must be added. Alum makes hard gingerbread more brittle, but should be used in small quantities, and when used more soda is needed. If eaten warm, break instead of cutting. Bake in shallow pans, as most people prefer the crust to soft gingerbread. Warm gingerbread baked in deeper pans, and eaten with sauce makes a good dessert for dinner.

ORANGE CAKE. NO. 1.

1 cup white sugar.
½ cup butter.
¼ cup of milk.
4 eggs.
1 heaping tablespoonful baking powder.
2 cups sifted flour.
1 orange (grated peel).
Beat the butter and sugar to a cream, then add the eggs

well beaten, and the milk. Stir the baking powder into the flour, and add lastly. Grate the orange peel into the cake. This is sufficient for four layers. Bake in jelly cake tins.

Icing for the Same.

Whites of 2 eggs.
1 heaping coffee-cup pulverized sugar.
Juice of one orange.
Beat the whites of the eggs and sugar until it creams; then add the orange juice. Spread between the layers of cake when cold. Reserve a little for frosting on top layer.

Lemon Cake.

Make the same as orange, only substituting one lemon for the orange, and using in the same manner.

Orange Cake. No. 2.

Yolks of 5 eggs.
2 cups of sugar.
4 tablespoonfuls butter.
½ cup sweet milk.
2½ cups of flour.
1½ teaspoonfuls baking powder.
Juice of one orange.
Bake in four cakes. Make icing as in the first recipe using the whites of the five eggs, and spread between the layers, sprinkling the grated peel over it. Frost the top.

Sea Foam Cake.

Whites of 10 eggs.
1½ teacups pulverized sugar.
1 rounding cup of flour.
½ teaspoonful cream tartar mixed in the flour.
Flavor with lemon.
Beat the whites to a stiff froth, sift the sugar in, then add the flour in which the cream tartar has been mixed,

stir lightly, just enough to mix the flour. Bake one hour When the sizzling sound ceases, the cake is done.

Ribbon Cake. (*White Part.*)

Whites of 6 eggs.
1 cup sugar.
½ cup of butter.
½ cup of milk.
1 teaspoonful baking powder.
2 cups of flour.
Flavor with lemon.

Beat the sugar and butter to a cream, and the whites to a stiff froth. Bake in jelly cake tins. This will make two layers, which will be an inch thick when done.

Dark Part.

¼ cup molasses.
¼ cup of sugar.
1 egg.
¼ cup of butter.
1 cup of seeded raisins.
½ cup of currants.
1 cup flour.
¼ cup hot water or coffee.
½ teaspoonful saleratus.
¼ teaspoonful cloves, and same of cinnamon.

A little nutmeg, and small piece of citron chopped *very* fine.

Beat the sugar, molasses and butter together; then add the egg well beaten. Rub the fruit in the flour, so all will mix well. Dissolve the saleratus in the hot water. Mix together. This is sufficient for one layer. When the cake is done, place a layer of white on a plate, and spread with jelly of some kind; then put the dark cake on, and spread this with jelly also; then put the layer of white on, and frost the top.

Silver Cake.

Whites of 5 eggs.
2 cups white sugar.
1 cup butter.
1 cup milk.
2½ cups sifted flour.
1 cup cornstarch.
2 teaspoonfuls baking powder.
Flavor with lemon.

Cream the butter and sugar; add next the whites of the eggs well beaten, then the cornstarch and flour into which the baking powder has been sifted; lastly the flavoring.

Gold Cake.

Make in the same manner as silver cake, only using the yolks instead of whites, and flavor with vanilla.

Feather Cake.

1 cup of sugar.
1 cup of milk.
1 tablespoonful of butter.
1 egg.
2½ cups of flour.
2 teaspoonfuls cream tartar.
1 teaspoonful soda.
Flavor with nutmeg or lemon.   Bake in loaf.

Tri-Color Cake.

1 coffee cup of white sugar.
1 tablespoonful butter.
Whites of 4 eggs.
⅔ cup of sweet cream.
1 cup of flour.
½ teaspoonful soda.
1 teaspoonful cream tartar.

Make another cake the same way, using the yolks; then another, using one-half cup of red sand sugar, and one-half cup white sugar, in place of the white sugar. Bake in sheets having each about three-quarters of an inch in thickness. Lay the three sheets one above another thus: the yellow underneath, the red in the center, and the white above. Put them together while warm, and brush with the beaten white of an egg, to make them adhere. Put icing on the top.

CITRON CAKE.

Yolks of 6 eggs.
1 cup of sugar.
½ cup of butter.
1½ cups of sifted flour.
½ cup of cornstarch.
¼ cup of milk.
1 teaspoonful baking powder.
¼ pound citron.
Flavor with vanilla.

Mix according to previous directions for cake. The citron must be shaved in very thin pieces, and rolled in flour to prevent settling to the bottom of the cake. Bake in a loaf.

For the Frosting.

White of 1 egg.
½ cup of pulverized sugar beaten together and flavored with vanilla.

DELICATE CAKE.

Whites of 4 eggs.
1½ cups of sugar.
½ cup of butter.
½ cup sweet milk.
½ teaspoonful soda, dissolved in the milk.
1 teaspoonful cream tartar.
2 teacupfuls flour.
Bake in a loaf.

CHOCOLATE CAKE.

1 cup of butter.
2 cups of sugar.

3 cups of flour.
4 eggs.
1 cup of milk.
2 teaspoonfuls baking powder mixed in flour.
Bake in jelly cake tins.

Filling.

Whites of two eggs beaten to a froth.
1 cup of powdered sugar.
¼ pound grated chocolate, wet in
1 tablespoonful of cream.
1 teaspoonful of vanilla.

Beat the sugar into the whipped whites; then the chocolate. Whisk all together hard for three minutes before adding the vanilla. Let the cake get quite cold before you spread it. Reserve a little of the mixture for the top, and beat more sugar into this to form a firm icing.

WATER MELON CAKE. (*White Part.*)

Whites of 6 eggs.
2 cups of white sugar.
1 cup of butter.
1 cup of milk.
4 even cups of flour.
2 teaspoonfuls baking powder.
Flavored with lemon.

Red Part.

Whites of 2 eggs.
¾ cup red sugar sand.
½ cup butter.
½ cup milk.
2 cups flour.
1 teaspoonful baking powder.

Beat the sugar and butter to a cream, and the eggs to a stiff froth. Take one-half the quantity of the white mixture, for the bottom layer; then put the red mixture on, and put on two rows of seeded raisins so they will be an inch apart. Then the rest of the white for top layer.

Bake in loaf tins. The raisins represent the seeds of water melons, so only a few are necessary.

CREAM CAKE.

1 cup of sugar.
2 eggs.
½ cup of milk.
½ teaspoonful soda.
1 teaspoonful cream tartar.
1½ cups of flour.

Cream for Filling.

2 eggs.
1 cup of sugar.
½ cup of flour.
1 pint of milk.

Boil as a custard in a vessel set within another of boiling water. When cold, flavor with vanilla. Bake the cake in two jelly cake tins. When cold, split them, and spread the cream on the lower crust of each, and then place the top on.

ICE CREAM CAKE.

Whites of 6 eggs.
2 cups of sugar.
2 cups of sifted flour.
1 cup of cornstarch.
1 cup of butter.
1 cup of milk.
2 teaspoonfuls baking powder, or 1 teaspoonful soda, and two of cream tartar.
Bake in jelly cake tins.

Icing to put Between the Layers.

Whites of 4 eggs.
4 cups pulverized sugar.

Pour a pint of boiling water over the sugar, boil hard until clear and strings from the spoon; then pour the boiling hot sugar over the beaten whites of the eggs, stirring hard all the time until a stiff cream or foam. Then add a half teaspoonful of citric acid, and flavor to taste with vanilla. Spread between each layer, and on the top.

HICKORY NUT CAKE. NO. 1.

2 cups of sugar.
¾ cup of butter.
¼ cup sweet milk.
2¾ cups flour.
1 coffee cup of hickory nuts.
½ teaspoonful soda.
1 teaspoonful cream tartar.
Whites of 3 eggs.

HICKORY NUT CAKE. NO. 2.

1½ cups of sugar.
½ cup of butter.
2 cups of flour.
¾ cup sweet milk.
2 eggs.
1½ teaspoonfuls baking powder.
1 cup hickory nuts, chopped.

If soda and cream tartar are used, take 1 teaspoonful cream tartar, and ½ teaspoonful of soda.

"ONE, TWO, THREE, FOUR" CAKE.

1 cup of butter.
2 cups of sugar.
3 cups of flour.
4 eggs.
½ cup of milk.
2 teaspoonfuls baking powder.
A little vanilla.

Beat the sugar and butter to a cream, then add the eggs, well beaten, then the flour into which the baking powder has been sifted, then the milk, and last the flavoring.

CAKE.

ALMOND CAKE.

1 cup of butter.
2 cups of sugar.
2 cups of flour.
6 eggs.
A little baking powder.
1 teaspoonful almond extract.
Split almonds in halves and put over the top. Bake in shallow tins.

COFFEE CAKE.

1 cup of sugar.
2 cups of flour.
½ cup butter.
½ cup molasses.
½ cup cold coffee.
1 cup raisins seeded.
2 eggs.
1 teaspoonful cinnamon.
1 teaspoonful mace.
1 teaspoonful cloves.
1 teaspoonful soda, dissolved in the coffee.
Mix together, adding the flour last.

POUND CAKE.

1 pound of sugar.
¾ pound butter, worked free from salt.
1 pound flour, sifted.
8 eggs.
Beat the sugar and butter to a cream, and add the yolks well beaten. Beat the whites to a stiff froth, and add them in alternate spoonfuls with the flour. Beat a long time and bake in round basins. It should be three days old before cutting. A glass of wine or brandy improves it. Flavor or not as you please.

EVERY DAY FRUIT CAKE.

1 cup of sour milk.
1 cup of butter.

2 cups of sugar.
4 cups of flour.
4 eggs.
2 cups of raisins.
1 teaspoonful soda.
Salt, cinnamon, cloves, citron, and wine or brandy to taste.

Beat butter and sugar to a cream; then add the milk, spices, and raisins, after stirring these together, add the yolks of eggs well beaten. Beat the whites to a froth, and stir in with the flour. Dissolve the soda in a little water and add it last. This will make two loaves.

WEDDING CAKE.

1 pound of powdered sugar.
1 pound of butter.
1 pound of flour.
12 eggs.
1 pound of currants, well washed and dredged.
1 pound of raisins, seeded and chopped.
½ pound of citron, cut into slips.
1 tablespoonful cinnamon.
2 teaspoonfuls nutmeg.
1 teaspoonful cloves.
1 wineglass of boiled cider.

Cream the butter and sugar, then add the yolks of the eggs well beaten, and stir *well* together; then put in half of the flour. The spice should come next, then the whipped whites stirred in alternately with the rest of the flour; lastly the cider. This is sufficient for two large cakes. Line deep tins with well buttered paper, and bake at least two hours. The icing should be laid on stiff and thickly. Be sure your cake is entirely done before taking from the oven.

FRUIT CAKE.

1 pound powdered sugar.
1 pound of flour.

¾ pound of butter.
7 eggs.
½ pound currants, picked over and dredged.
½ pound of raisins, seeded and chopped, then dredged.
¼ pound citron, cut into slips.
1 teaspoonful of nutmeg.
1 teaspoonful cinnamon.
1 glass of boiled cider.

Beat the sugar and butter to a cream; add the yolks well beaten, then the spice and the whipped whites alternately with the flour; fruit and brandy last.

Farmer's Fruit Cake.

2 cups dried apples.
2 cups molasses.
2 eggs.
1 cup of butter.
1 teaspoonful each of cloves, cinnamon and nutmeg.
3½ cups of flour.
1 teaspoonful of soda.

Soak the apples over night in cold water, then chop them the size of raisins; put them in the molasses and simmer slowly two hours. Add the other ingredients, mix well and bake.

Fruit and Nut Cake.

4 cups of flour.
2 cups of sugar.
1 cup of butter.
3 eggs, whites and yolks separated.
1 cup cold water.
1 coffee cup full of hickory nut kernels.
½ pound raisins, seeded, chopped and dredged with flour.
1 teaspoonful soda, dissolved in hot water.
2 teaspoonfuls cream tartar, sifted in the flour.
1 teaspoonful mixed nutmeg and cinnamon.

Rub butter and sugar together to a smooth cream; put

in the yolks, then the water, spice, soda; next the whites and flour. The fruit and nuts, stirred together and dredged, should go in last. Mix thoroughly and bake in two loaves.

Sponge Cake. No. 1.

1 teacup powdered sugar.
3 eggs.
½ teaspoonful cream tartar.
¼ teaspoonful soda.
1 teacupful flour.
Flavor with lemon, half the juice and half the rind of one.
Bake twenty minutes in shallow tins.

Sponge Cake. No. 2.

3 eggs.
1½ cups sugar.
2 even cups sifted flour.
1 teaspoonful cream tartar.
½ teaspoonful soda.
½ cup cold water.
Juice of half a lemon.
A little salt.
Beat eggs altogether, then add one cup of flour with the cream tartar mixed in it. Beat again, then add the soda in the water, then the lemon, and lastly one cup of flour. Stir and bake quickly.

Plain Cake.

3 eggs.
2 cups of sugar.
½ cup of butter.
¾ cup of sweet milk.
1 teaspoonful cream tartar.
½ teaspoonful soda.
Flavor with lemon or vanilla.
Flour enough to make it of proper consistency.

COCOANUT CAKE.

2 eggs.
1 cup of sugar.
⅔ cup of milk.
½ cup of butter.
2 cups of flour.
2 heaping teaspoonfuls baking powder.
Bake in jelly cake tins.

Frosting.

Whites of 2 eggs.
8 teaspoonfuls sugar.
Flavor to suit.

Spread each cake with a thin layer of frosting, sprinkled with prepared cocoanut, and frost the top, which should be thickly sprinkled with the cocoanut.

MYRTLE'S CAKE.

5 eggs, beaten light and yolks strained.
3 cups of powdered sugar.
1 cup of butter creamed with the sugar.
1 cup sweet milk.
4 cups of sifted flour.
Juice of 1 lemon, and half the grated peel.
A little nutmeg.
Bake in two loaves. Cover with lemon frosting.

SPICE CAKE.

4 eggs.
1 cup of butter.
2 cups of brown sugar.
1 cup of sweet milk.
3 cups of flour.
1 nutmeg.
1 teaspoonful of cloves.
2 teaspoonfuls of cinnamon.
1½ teaspoonfuls of baking powder, or
½ teaspoonful of soda and 1 teaspoonful cream tartar.

White Cake.

2 cups of sugar.
1 cup of butter.
3 cups of flour.
Whites of 4 eggs.
1 even teaspoonful of soda.
1 cup sour cream.

Beat butter and sugar to a cream; add the eggs well beaten, stir in the flour, and then the soda dissolved and strained; lastly add the cream. Bake immediately.

Currant Cake.

1 cup of butter.
2 cups of powdered sugar.
3 cups of sifted flour.
4 eggs.
½ cup sweet milk.
½ pound currants, washed, dried and dredged.
½ grated nutmeg.

Beat the sugar and butter to a cream. Put the fruit in last. Bake in cups or small pans.

Jelly Cake.

1 cup of sugar.
1 cup of flour.
3 eggs.
Butter the size of an egg.
1 teaspoonful cream tartar, sifted in the flour.
½ teaspoonful soda, dissolved in a tablespoonful of milk.

Bake in jelly cake tins, and when cold spread with fruit jelly.

Marble Cake. No. 1.

1 cup butter.
2 cups powdered sugar.
3 cups flour.
2 eggs.

1 cup sweet milk.
½ teaspoonful soda.
1 teaspoonful cream tartar, sifted with the flour.

After the cake is mixed take out about a teacupful of the batter, and stir into this a great spoonful of grated chocolate, wet with a *scant* tablespoonful of milk. Fill your tin about an inch deep with the yellow batter, and drop upon this, in two or three places, a spoonful of the dark mixture. Give to the brown spots a slight stir with the tip of your spoon, spreading it in broken circles upon the lighter surface. Pour in more yellow batter, then drop in the brown as before, proceeding in this order, until all is used up.

Marble Cake. No. 2.

1½ cups of white sugar.
¼ cup of butter.
½ cup of sweet milk.
½ teaspoonful soda dissolved in the milk.
1 teaspoonful cream tartar mixed with the flour.
2½ cups of flour.
Whites of 4 eggs beat to a stiff froth.
Flavor with lemon.

For the Dark Cake, take

1 cup of nice coffee sugar.
1 tablespoonful of molasses.
½ cup of butter.
½ cup of sour milk.
½ teaspoonful soda dissolved in the milk.
2½ cups of flour.
Yolks of 4 eggs, well beaten.
1 teaspoonful of clove.
A little allspice, cinnamon and nutmeg.

Put a layer of the light cake in your pan, and mix in some of the dark, then more of the light, and so on until your pan is a little more than half full.

Corn Starch Cake.

½ cup of butter.
2 cups of sugar.
Whites of 3 eggs well beaten.
1 cup of milk.
Juice of ½ lemon.
2 cups sifted flour.
2 teaspoonfuls cream tartar in the flour.
1 teaspoonful soda.
1 cup cornstarch dissolved in the milk.

Beat sugar and butter to a cream; then add the other ingredients, and lastly the cornstarch. Bake immediately in a moderate oven. One tablespoonful of baking powder can be used instead of soda and cream tartar.

Pork Cake.

1 pound salt pork, chopped fine.
1 pint boiling water poured on the pork.
2 cups of sugar.
1 cup of molasses.
1 tablespoonful of cloves.
1 tablespoonful cinnamon.
1 pound of raisins.
2 teaspoonfuls saleratus.

Flour enough to make it rather thick but not too stiff. Bake in two cakes.

Snow Drift Cake.

2 cups powdered sugar.
1 heaping cup sifted flour.
Whites of 6 eggs, whipped stiff.
Juice of 1 lemon and half the grated peel.
A little salt.

Whip the eggs stiff, beat in the sugar, lemon, salt, and finally the flour. Stir in very lightly and quickly and bake at once in two loaves. Or, it may be baked as jelly cake, and spread with this

Filling.

Whites of 3 eggs.
1 heaping cup of powdered sugar.
Juice of 1 orange and half the peel.
Juice of ½ lemon.
Whip to a good meringue and put between the layers, adding more sugar for the frosting on the top.

Tea Cake.

1½ cups of white sugar.
½ cup of butter.
⅔ cup of milk.
3 eggs.
2 cups of flour.
1 teaspoonful of soda.
2 teaspoonfuls of cream tartar. Flavoring.
Mix according to previous directions, and bake quickly.

Raspberry Rolls.

3 eggs.
1 cup of white sugar.
1 cup of flour.
1 teaspoonful cream tartar.
½ teaspoonful soda.
Flavor with lemon.

Beat the eggs, yolks and whites together, for one or two minutes; then add the sugar, and beat a few minutes more, next the flour with the cream tartar mixed in it. Dissolve the soda in as little hot water as possible, and stir in thoroughly; add the flavoring, and beat well for a few minutes. Bake in two rather wide, shallow tins. When done turn the cake upon a sieve, and, while warm, spread a little raspberry or strawberry jam over it; roll up the cake and sift sugar over. This should be done carefully. Cut in slices, when cold.

Icing. No. 1.

Whites of 2 eggs.
½ pound powdered white sugar.

Lemon, vanilla, or other flavoring.

Break the whites into a broad, clean, cool dish. Throw a small handful of sugar upon them, and whip it in with long, even strokes of the beater. In a few minutes throw in more sugar, and keep doing so, until it is all used up. Beat steadily, always with a regular, sweeping movement, until the icing is of a smooth, fine, and firm texture. Half an hour's beating should be sufficient, if done well. If not stiff enough, put in more sugar. If seasoned with lemon juice, allow, in measuring your sugar, for the additional liquid. Lemon juice or tartaric acid whitens the icing. Use at least a quarter of a pound of sugar for each egg. In spreading the icing, use a broad-bladed knife, dipped in cold water. It is better to dry it in a sunny window, where no dust can reach it; but it may be set in a moderate oven for two or three minutes. Icing may be colored yellow, by putting the grated peel of a lemon or orange in a thin muslin bag, straining a little juice through it, and squeezing it hard into the egg and sugar. Strawberry juice colors a pretty pink, as does also cranberry syrup.

Icing. No. 2.

20 teaspoonfuls powdered sugar.
Whites of 2 eggs.
½ teaspoonful cornstarch.

Beat the whites until they will adhere to the plate when turned up; then add sugar and cornstarch. Rub the cake when warm, with a little flour, and the icing will remain in place better. Many persons prefer this way of making icing, but the directions given in recipe No. 1. are recommended as being preferable.

Rich Cookies.

1 teacupful of butter.
2 teacupfuls of sugar.
2 eggs.
½ teaspoonful of soda.
1 teaspoonful of cream tartar.

Work the butter and sugar together. Beat the eggs separately and stir in, first the yolk, and then the white. Mix the cream tartar with the flour, and dissolve the soda in a very little hot water. Mix in a little flour before the soda is put in, and then add flour enough to knead soft. Spread granulated sugar on the paste board, and roll the dough on it, instead of flour, and after it is rolled thin enough sift sugar over the dough and pass the rolling-pin lightly over. Be as quick as possible in getting the cakes into the oven after the cream tartar and flour are added; bake quickly on buttered papers in the pans. If there is danger of scorching, cover with papers. Let them cool a little, and then lift the paper with the cakes; do not remove the cakes from the paper until they are cool.

COOKIES.

2 coffee cups of coffee sugar.
1 coffee cup of butter.
1 coffee cup of sour milk.
2 eggs.
1 teaspoonful saleratus.
Spice, or seeds, as you please.
Flour to make batter just stiff enough to be moulded.

AMMONIA COOKIES.

1 cup of butter.
2 cups of sugar.
2 eggs.
½ pint of sweet milk.
½ ounce of carbonate of ammonia, dissolved over night in the milk; cover tight. Mix soft, and roll thin.

COCOANUT DROPS.

Grate a cocoanut and weigh it, then add half the weight of powdered sugar, and the white of one egg cut to a stiff froth. Stir the ingredients together, then drop the mixture with a dessert spoon upon buttered white paper, and sift sugar over them. Bake in a slow oven fifteen minutes.

Ring Jumbles.

1 pound of butter.
1 pound of sugar.
4 eggs.
Flour enough to make a soft dough.
Small wine-glass of rose-water.

Cream the butter and sugar, add the beaten yolks, then the rose-water, next half the flour, lastly the whites, stirred in very lightly, alternately with the remaining flour. Have a broad and shallow pan ready, lined on the bottom with buttered paper. With a tablespoon form regular rings of the dough upon this, leaving a hole in the center of each. Bake quickly, and sift fine sugar over them as soon as they are done. Lemon or vanilla may be substituted for the rose-water.

Macaroons.

½ pound of sweet almonds.
Whites of 3 eggs.
½ pound of powdered sugar.

Prepare the almonds the day before you make the cakes by blanching them in boiling water, stripping off the skins and pounding them, when perfectly cold, a few at a time, and adding from time to time a little rose-water, or orange-flower water. Beat the eggs very stiff and stir in the sugar. Mix well, and then add the almonds. Drop with a teaspoon upon buttered tin sheets, sift fine sugar over, and bake in a slack oven.

Kisses.

Whites of 3 eggs.
5 tablespoonfuls of finest white sugar.
Flavor with lemon.

Beat the eggs to a stiff froth, then add the sugar and lemon. Have ready a nice pan, buttered, in which lay white paper, and drop them on it with a teaspoon, and sift sugar over them. Bake in a slow oven half an hour. This measure will make a cake-basket full.

SUGAR GINGERBREAD.

1 cup butter.
2 cups sugar.
½ cup sour milk.
2 eggs.
1 small teaspoonful soda.
A little ginger.
Flour to make a stiff batter; bake as soon as mixed.

HARD GINGERBREAD.

¾ cup of shortening.
1 cup of molasses.
1 cup of sugar.
¾ cup hot water.
1 teaspoonful of salt.
1 tablespoonful of ginger.
A piece of alum, the size of a hazelnut, dissolved in the water.
A dessert spoonful of soda, dissolved in the molasses.

Mix the ingredients, and add flour enough to make a stiff batter; it must not be quite stiff enough to roll out. Put it in square pans, pat it smooth, and mark it in strips.

SOFT GINGERBREAD.

1 cup of butter.
1 cup of sugar.
1 cup of molasses.
1 cup sour or buttermilk.
1 teaspoonful of soda dissolved in boiling water.
1 teaspoonful of cinnamon.
1 tablespoonful of ginger.
2 eggs.

Enough flour to make it as thick as the batter for cup cake, add the flour, working it in gradually; it will take nearly five cups. Stir the butter, sugar, molasses, and spice together to a light cream, set them on the stove until slightly warmed; add the milk to the warmed mixture, then the eggs (beaten light), the soda, and lastly the flour. Beat very hard ten minutes, and bake at once.

Sponge Gingerbread. (*Without Eggs.*)

5 cups of flour.
1 heaping tablespoonful of butter.
1 cup of molasses.
1 cup of sugar.
1 cup of milk (sour is best).
2 teaspoonfuls saleratus, dissolved in hot water
2 teaspoonfuls ginger.
1 teaspoonful of cinnamon.

Mix the molasses, sugar, butter, and spice together; warm them slightly, and beat until they are several degrees lighter than when you began. Add the milk, then the soda, and when all are mixed well, put in the flour. Beat hard five minutes, and bake in a broad shallow pan.

Ginger Snaps. No. 1.

1 cup of brown sugar.
1 cup of molasses.
1 cup of butter.
1 teaspoonful of soda.
2 teaspoonfuls of ginger.

Boil the sugar, molasses and butter together, then add the soda and ginger while warm. Add flour enough to mix stiff; and roll very thin.

Ginger Snaps. No. 2.

1 large cup butter and lard mixed.
1 coffee cup sugar.
1 cup of molasses.
½ cup of water.
1 tablespoonful of ginger.
1 teaspoonful of soda dissolved in hot water.
Flour for pretty stiff dough.
Roll out thin, and bake quickly.

Breakfast Cookies.

1 cup of sugar.
1 cup of molasses.
½ cup of butter.
½ cup of lard.
1 egg.
4 tablespoonfuls warm water.
4 even teaspoonfuls of soda, dissolved in the water.
1 even teaspoonful of ginger.
1 even teaspoonful of grated alum.
Flour enough to make batter just stiff enough to be moulded.

Doughnuts. No. 1.

1 cup of sour milk.
1½ cups of sugar.
1 teaspoonful soda.
1 egg.
1 tablespoonful melted lard.
A little salt.
Beat the eggs, and mix with sugar and lard. Dissolve the soda in the milk, and stir into the above mixture as rapidly as possible, stirring in flour at the same time.
Knead soft.

Doughnuts. (*Very Nice.*) No. 2.

1 cup white sugar (scant).
2 eggs.
1 tablespoonful of cream, or small piece of butter melted, the size of a walnut.
1 cup of milk.
2 teaspoonfuls of baking powder.
Beat the eggs and sugar together one-half hour, before putting in the flour; this beating will make them very white. Add flour to make them about the same consistency of cookies.

Raised Doughnuts.

1 pint of milk.
½ teacupful of yeast.
2 teacupfuls of sugar.
½ teacupful of lard.
2 eggs.
1 teaspoonful of soda.
Nutmeg or cinnamon to taste.

Put yeast in the milk, stir in the flour, and let it rise over night; in the morning add the other ingredients; work in more flour, and let it rise very light. Fry in hot lard.

Crullers. No. 1.

2 cups of sugar.
1 cup of butter.
2 eggs.
2 cups sour milk.
1 teaspoonful soda dissolved in hot water.

Flour to roll out tolerably stiff. Roll thin, cut into small cakes, and fry in a plenty of hot lard.

SWEET-MEAT MAXIMS.

Cake without butter should never be beaten, as it is sure to make it tough and leathery. Put the materials together as lightly as possible, stirring it on the top, not from the bottom. Remember this in sponge cake, and save yourself trouble.

To keep fruit cake, change it occasionally from a dry to a damp and from a damp to a dry place.

As a rule, eggs having a dark shell beat up nicer than those with a light shell.

All kinds of cake are better for having the whites and yolks beaten separately.

It is hard to whip whites stiff in a warm room.

Stir butter and sugar to a cream.

Never use fresh and old milk in the same cake.

Remember soda will not take the place of eggs.

A cake should not be moved while baking.

Cake is best kept in a tight can or jar.

Do not cut more at a time than you expect to use.

None but the best butter will do in pastry.

In making pastry everything should be kept as cool as possible.

If the shortening is soft, the crust will be heavy and solid.

Good pastry has no resemblance to putty or leather.

"Pork fat and pies kill more people yearly in the United States than do liquor and tobacco."

Batter puddings and custards should be baked as soon as mixed.

For baked puddings and custards beat the eggs but little.

A Dover egg beater is worth a good many times its cost to a cake or pastry cook.

Flour is equal to cornstarch for blanc-mange.

A little cream tartar will keep jellies and rich preserves from candying.

To boil a pudding takes twice as long as to bake it.

Creams and custards which are to be frozen should have one-third more sugar than those which are not to be frozen.

Do not cook a dish of custard on the stove, but in a dish of boiling water.

To retain the color of fruit in glass cans, wrap them in something to exclude the light.

MEASURES.

One common sized tumbler equals half a pint or two gills.

A quart of sifted flour, heaped, a quart of sifted sugar, and a quart of softened butter, each weigh about a pound, and so nearly that measuring is as good as weighing.

Water is heavier, and a pint of water weighs nearly a pound.

Ten eggs weigh about a pound.

A common sized wine glass holds half a gill.

Four ordinary teacups of liquid are equal to one quart.

ADDITIONAL RECIPES.

ADDITIONAL RECIPES.

ADDITIONAL RECIPES.

ADDITIONAL RECIPES.

ADDITIONAL RECIPES.

ADDITIONAL RECIPES.

PIES.

The flour should be sifted. Lard can be mixed with butter for shortening; use none but good butter for pastry; but which ever you use rub it into the flour; do not rub out every lump, the less the hands are used, the better. Add cold water in winter, ice-water in summer. If lard is used, salt must be added. Stir the mixture quickly with a knife, after the water is added. Do not mould it, as it makes it tough. The thickness of the crust depends on the filling. If juicy fruit is used, such as cherries, plums and berries, the crust should be thicker than for apple, peach and pumpkin. In making pies from juicy fruit, use deep dishes. Sprinkle a little flour in such pies to absorb the juice. Most pies require an hour to cook. Much depends on the kind of oven used.

PIE CRUST. NO. 1.

2½ cups of flour.
¼ cup of butter.
½ cup of lard.
½ cup of water.
A little salt.

Mix with a *sharp knife;* do not use the hand. The above is sufficient for two pies.

PIE CRUST. NO. 2.

To 1 quart flour, take
1 cup butter or lard.

If lard is used, salt must be added. Stir or chop the flour and butter together. Soften this with ice water, if in summer, and cold water in winter. Prepare the lower crust and fill with whatever filling you may use. Take out from the crust as much as you may need for the upper crust. Roll the top crust out, and spread evenly over it a small quantity of butter, and dredge well with flour. Cut the air holes and cover the pie. Take it in your left hand, hold it slightly inclined, and quickly pour over it enough cold water to nearly wash off the flour. The butter and the flour which remain will make a more flaky crust than by the old fashioned way of rolling the crust repeatedly.

French Puff-Paste.

1 pound of flour.
¾ pound of butter.
1 egg; the yolk only.
Ice water.

Chop half the butter into the flour; stir the beaten egg into half a cup of ice water, and work the flour into a stiff dough; roll out thin; baste with one-third the remaining butter, fold closely, roll out again, and so on until the butter is used up. Roll very thin, and set the last folded roll in a very cold place ten or fifteen minutes before making out the crust. Wash with beaten egg while hot. This paste is very nice for fruit pies, and oyster *pâtés*.

Mince Pies.

2 pounds lean fresh beef, boiled, and, when cold, chopped fine.
¾ pound beef suet, chopped very fine.
4 pounds of apples, pared and chopped.
1½ pounds of raisins.
1 pound of currants, well washed.
¾ pound citron, shaved fine.
Cinnamon, nutmeg, mace, cloves, allspice, sugar and salt to taste.
1 pint boiled cider, or syrup of canned fruit.

Mix thoroughly, using enough of the liquor in which

the meat was boiled, to moisten it. Heat all together, and when done, pour in a stone jar. Keep closely covered in a cool, dry place.

Mock Mince Pie.

4 large crackers, rolled fine.
½ cup sugar.
½ cup molasses.
1 cup water (more if necessary).
½ cup vinegar.
1 egg.
1 cup chopped raisins.
½ cup currants.
¼ cup butter.
Spices and salt to taste.

Apple Pie. No. 1.

Pare, core and slice, ripe, tart, winter apples; line your dish with a good crust, put in a layer of fruit, then sprinkle light brown sugar thickly over it, lay on more apples, and so on until the dish is well filled. Lay on two or three thin shavings of butter, and add about two spoonfuls of water. Flavor to taste. Cover with crust immediately, as the under crust will be clammy if it is not put directly in the oven. When done, sift powdered sugar over the top before sending to the table.

Apple Pie. No. 2.

Stew green or ripe apples, after they have been pared and cored. Mash to a smooth mass, sweeten to taste, and while hot, stir in a teaspoonful of butter to each pie. Season with nutmeg. When cool, fill your crust, and either cross-bar the top with strips of paste, or bake without a cover. Eat cold, with powdered sugar strewed over it.

Apple Custard Pie.

3 cups stewed apples.
4 eggs.
1 quart milk.

Mash the apple fine and make very sweet. Beat the yolks light, and mix well with the apple. Season with nutmeg, stir the milk in gradually. Lastly add the whites, well beaten. Fill the crust and bake without cover.

Cherry Pie.

Line the dish with a good crust, and fill with ripe cherries, spread sugar over them, enough to sweeten. Sprinkle a little flour over, cover and bake. Eat cold, with sugar sifted over the top.

Blackberry, Raspberry and Plum Pies,

Are made in the same manner.

Green Currants and Gooseberries.

These require a great deal of sugar, at least two-thirds as much in measure as of fruit. Currant pies should be made in a deep plate, and with an upper crust.

Gooseberries should be stewed like cranberries, sweetened to suit the taste, and laid upon the under crust, with strips placed diagonally across the top.

Rhubarb Pie.

Skin the stalks, and cut in lengths of half an inch; fill the crust with the raw fruit, and sprinkle liberally with sugar. Cover and bake nearly three-quarters of an hour. Brush with egg while hot, and return to the oven to glaze, if you wish. It should be eaten cold, like all fruit pies.

If hot water in which a teaspoonful of soda has been dissolved is poured over the rhubard and allowed to stand a few minutes, it will extract a great deal of its acid.

Sweet Potato Pie.

1 pound mealy sweet potatoes. The firm, yellow ones are best.
½ cup butter.
¾ cup white sugar.
1 tablespoonful cinnamon.
1 teaspoonful nutmeg.
4 eggs, whites and yolks beaten separately.
1 lemon, juice and rind, and glass of brandy.

Parboil the potatoes, and grate them when quite cold. They will be sticky and heavy, if grated hot. Cream the sugar and butter; add the yolk, the spice and lemon; beat the potato in by degrees, and until all is light; then the brandy, and stir in the whites. Bake in dishes lined with good paste, without cover. Cool before eating.

Cocoanut Pie.

1 quart of new milk.
3 eggs.
1 tablespoonful of butter.
2 tablespoonfuls of sugar.
1 pint of grated cocoanut, which should be fresh.

Bake like custard pie.

Custard Pie.

1 quart milk.
5 eggs (if plain, 3).
5 tablespoonfuls sugar.
Flavor with lemon.
A little salt.

Line your plate with pastry, pour in the custard and bake half an hour.

Chocolate Custard Pie.

1 quarter-cake of Baker's chocolate, grated.
1 pint of boiling water.
6 eggs.

1 quart milk.
½ cup white sugar.
2 teaspoonfuls vanilla.

Dissolve the chocolate in a very little milk, stir into the boiling water, and boil three minutes. When nearly cold, beat up the yolks of all the eggs, and the whites of three. Stir this mixture into the milk, season, and pour into shells of good paste. When the custard is "set," but not more than half done, spread over the whites, whipped to a froth, with two tablespoonfuls of sugar. These custards may be baked without paste, in a pudding-dish, or cups set in boiling water.

CORN STARCH PIE.

3 eggs.
1½ pints of milk.
3 tablespoonfuls white sugar.
1 tablespoonful cornstarch.
1 teaspoonful essence bitter almonds or vanilla.

Boil the milk, stir in the cornstarch, wet in a little cold milk, and boil one minute. When nearly cold, stir in the sugar, the yolks of all the eggs, and the whites of two; flavor, and pour into your paste. Whip the remaining whites to a meringue, with two tablespoonfuls white sugar, and a teaspoonful of vanilla. When the custard is just "set," draw your pies to the edge of the oven to spread this over them. Do it quickly, else the custard will fall by exposure to the air.

CRANBERRY PIE.

Take the sauce as prepared to eat with meat; grate a little nutmeg over it, put three or four thin shavings of butter on it, and then lay on the upper crust. Perhaps it may be necessary to add more sugar. Instead of an upper crust you can lay very narrow strips across, diagonally.

CREAM PIE.

1 pint milk.
2 tablespoonfuls of corn starch.

2 eggs (beaten well).
1 cup of sugar.
A little salt.
Juice of 1 lemon.
The crust should be previously baked. Boil nearly the pint of milk, beat the corn starch in the remainder of the milk; and stir it in to the boiled milk; remove from the stove. To this add the other ingredients, and fill the paste. Then take the white of an egg well whipped, sweeten and spread on the top, and put in the oven to brown a little.

LEMON PIE. No, 1.

1 tablespoonful corn starch.
1 cup of sugar.
1 cup of cold water.
3 eggs.
Juice and pulp of 1 lemon.
A little salt.
Cook the corn starch in the water; when cold, add the yolks of the eggs, sugar, lemon and salt. Beat the whites of the eggs to a froth, and stir them in carefully just before putting in the oven.

LEMON PIE. (*With two crusts.*) No. 2.

1 cup sugar.
1 lemon.
1 egg.
Beat the sugar and egg together; then add the lemon which has been peeled and sliced. Spread a small plate with paste and cover. It needs a richer paste than other pies.

LEMON PIE. (*With Frosting.*) No. 3.

Grated rind and juice of 2 lemons.
2 cups sugar.
3 eggs.
A piece of butter as large as an egg.
2 tablespoonfuls of corn starch.

Have ready two cups of boiling water in a saucepan, and stir into it the corn starch (which has been rubbed smooth in cold water) until it looks clear. Then pour into a dish, and add the sugar and butter. When it becomes nearly cool, add the yolks of the three eggs and one of the whites, beaten together, the lemons, and bake in two squash pie plates of medium size, lined with a delicate crust. Beat up the two whites with two spoonfuls of sugar very stiff; spread this over the pies after they are baked; sprinkle with sugar, and brown a few moments in the oven.

Lemon Pie. No. 4.

3 lemons, the juice and grated peel.
3 crackers (grated).
2 cups of sugar.
3 eggs.
1 cup cold water.
This is sufficient for two pies.

Peach Pie.

Peel, stone and slice the peaches. Line a pie plate with a good crust, and lay in your fruit, sprinkling sugar liberally over them in proportion to their sweetness. Very ripe peaches require comparatively little. Allow three peach kernels, chopped fine, to each pie; pour in a very little water, and bake with an upper crust, or with crossbars of paste over the top. If the peaches have been dried, stew in a little water.

Orange Pie.

4 eggs.
1 cup of white sugar.
2 tablespoonfuls butter.
1½ oranges, juice and half the grated rind.
Juice of 1 lemon.
Nutmeg to taste.

Cream the butter and sugar, beating in the orange and lemon until very light; add the beaten yolks, fill two pastry shells and bake. Beat the whites stiff with two tablespoonfuls of powdered sugar, and when the pies are done, spread over them, returning to the oven for three or four minutes.

STRAWBERRY PIE.

Cap and pick over the berries, arrange in layers, sprinkle with a good coating of sugar. Fill the plate very full, as strawberries shrink very much in cooking. Cover with crust and bake.

Huckleberry pie is made in the same way.

PUMPKIN PIE.

1 pint of pumpkin, stewed and strained.
1 quart of milk.
1 cup sugar.
2 eggs.
A little salt.

Flavor with ginger and allspice, or cinnamon and nutmeg, as you prefer. The above mixture will make two pies.

Squash pies may be made in the same way, by using less squash and more eggs.

TARTLETTS.

ORANGE TARTLETTS.

2 fine Havana oranges, juice of both, and grated peel of one.

¾ cup of sugar, ½ cup if the oranges are very sweet.
1 tablespoonful of butter.
½ lemon, juice only, to wet 1 teaspoonful corn starch.

Beat all well together, and bake in tartlet shells without a cover.

LEMON TART FILLING.

The grated rind, pulp and juice of 1 lemon.
1 cup white sugar.

4 eggs.
1 tablespoonful of butter.

Beat all together, put in a tin pail and place in boiling water, stir five minutes, put in tarts.

A nice dish of tarts for the tea-table can be made of scraps of pie crust, that are often wasted: Roll out thin, cut with a small biscuit cutter, bake, arrange on a plate, and place a teaspoonful of jelly on each one just before tea time.

Cream Raspberry Tartletts.

Line a dish with paste. Sweeten the raspberries very sweet with white sugar, and fill the dish. Cover as for a pie, do not press the paste down at the edges very closely. When done, remove the cover and pour over this mixture:

1 cup milk or cream heated to boiling.
Whites of 2 eggs.
1 tablespoonful white sugar.
½ teaspoonful corn starch wet in cold water.

Beat the whites lightly, and stir into the boiling milk, mix the ingredients together and boil three minutes. When cold put them in the tartlet. Replace the cover, and set aside to cool. Sprinkle sugar over the top.

Strawberry cream tartlets can be made in the same manner.

ADDITIONAL RECIPES.

PUDDINGS.

The eggs for all kinds of puddings should be strained and if hot milk is used, stirred in after all the other ingredients. Milk for tapioca, rice, and such, should be boiled, also for bread and cracker, unless the bread is soaked over night. Suet must be chopped fine. In batter pudding stir in the flour gradually. Put berries or cherries in last. In boiling puddings the cloth must be dipped and dredged well with flour, and be sure that the water is boiling hot and do not let it stop boiling. Dip the pudding in cold water when it comes from the kettle and it will turn out easily. A flour pudding is lighter when all the materials are beaten together. If you boil the pudding in a dish it must be well buttered, the same must be done for a baked pudding.

To cut a boiled pudding without making it heavy, lay the knife blade first one side and then the other to warm it. Boiled puddings should be served immediately, as they soon become heavy.

English Plum Pudding. No 1.

1 pound suet, chopped fine.
1 pound fine bread crumbs.
1 pound seeded raisins.
¼ pound citron chopped fine.
1 pound sugar.
½ cup of flour.
10 eggs.
½ pint brandy.
½ teaspoonful salt.

½ teaspoonful saleratus.
Cinnamon, nutmeg, and cloves to taste.

Mix well together; put in a pudding dish, and set it in the steamer, and steam eight hours.

English Plum Pudding. No 2.

1 pound flour.
½ pound finely chopped suet.
1 pound raisins (stoned).
1 pound currants.
½ pound citron (cut in thin strips).
6 well beaten eggs.
Chopped peel of 1 orange or lemon, and its juice.
1 glass brandy or whisky.
Nutmeg, cinnamon, cloves and allspice to taste.
¼ teaspoonful salt.
½ pound sugar.
½ teacupful sweet milk.
A little saleratus.

Mix the solids well together, and add suet to sugar, beat the eggs to a foam, and mix with them; then fruit and spices, next the liquid and lastly the milk and saleratus. Dip the pudding cloth in boiling water, sprinkle it over with flour, turn the pudding in, and tie loosely. Put it in boiling water and boil four hours and a half continually.

Porcupine Pudding.

1 cup molasses.
1 cup sweet milk.
½ cup butter.
3 cups flour.
1 cup raisins.
½ cup of currants.
2 teaspoonfuls cream.
1 teaspoonful soda.
1 teaspoonful cloves.
1 teaspoonful cinnamon.

1 teaspoonful ginger.
Mix together and steam two hours.

QUEEN OF PUDDINGS.

1 pint fine bread crumbs.
1 quart fresh, rich milk (hot).
Yolks of 4 eggs.
1½ cups of white sugar.
1 tablespoonful butter.
½ cup of jelly or jam.

Soak the crumbs in the hot milk; rub the butter and sugar together, and stir in the yolks well beaten. Mix all together with such flavoring as you like, and bake in a deep pudding dish. When done, make a meringue of the whipped whites and half a cup of sugar; cover the pudding with the jelly, and over that place the meringue and brown in the oven. Eat cold with cream. Fresh fruit is very nice instead of the jelly.

BLACK PUDDING.

1 cup of suet (chopped fine).
1 cup of molasses.
1 cup of raisins.
1 cup of milk.
3½ cups of flour.
1½ teaspoonful soda.
A little cinnamon.
Put in a dish and steam three hours.

BAKED PLUM PUDDING.

1¼ pounds of flour.
1 pound of raisins, seeded and dredged **in flour**
½ cup of suet, powdered.
1 cup of sugar.
2 ounces of citron cut in bits.
5 eggs.

1 teaspoonful each, nutmeg, cinnamon and cloves.
2 cups of milk, or enough to make a thick batter of the flour.

Beat yolks and sugar together, add the spice, suet and flour, gradually moistening with the milk, until you can stir with the spoon. Put in the fruit by degrees, and finally stir in the beaten whites. Beat well, and bake in a buttered mould one and one-half hours in a moderate oven. Serve with cream sauce.

Plum Pudding. No. 2.

1 pound bread crumbs, or six pounded crackers.
1 quart milk.
1 large spoonful flour.
1 teacupful sugar.
1 nutmeg.
1 teaspoonful cinnamon.
½ teaspoonful powdered clove.
A piece of butter the size of an egg.
The same quantity of chopped suet.
1 pound raisins.
6 eggs.

Boil the milk. It is well to soak the bread in the milk over night; then the entire crust becomes soft, and mixes well with the other ingredients. Bake one hour and a half. Serve with rich sauce, if eaten warm; but it is excellent cold, cut up like cake. A pudding made in this way will keep several weeks, and when one is to be used, it may be loosened from the dish by a knife passed around it, and a little hot water be poured around the edge. It should then be covered close, and set for half an hour into the stove or oven.

Cracker Pudding.

1 quart milk.
1 cup powdered cracker.
3 eggs.

2 tablespoonfuls melted butter.
½ tablespoonful soda, dissolved in hot water.
Heat the milk slightly, and pouring it over the cracker let them stand together fifteen minutes. Stir into this first the beaten yolks, then the butter and soda; beat all smooth and add the whipped whites.

BIRD'S NEST. (*Apple.*)

1 pint cold milk.
3 eggs.
5 tablespoonfuls flour.
6 medium sized, fair apples.
1 small teaspoonful salt.

Pare the apples and take out the cores; arrange them in a buttered dish that will just receive them (one in the centre and five around it). Wet the flour smooth in part of the milk, then add the eggs and beat all together a few minutes; then put in the salt and the rest of the milk. Stir it well, and pour it into the dish of apples. Bake it an hour and make a melted sauce. For a large family make double measure, but bake it in two dishes, as the centre apples of a large dish will not cook as quickly as those around the edge.

HEN'S NEST PUDDING.

Make a hole at one end of five small eggs and empty them, and wash the interior with pure water, shaken around well in them, then fill with blanc-mange, and when stiff and cold take off the shell; pare the yellow rind very thin from two lemons or oranges, boil them in water till very tender, then cut them in very thin strips to resemble straw; add to them half a cup of sugar and simmer fifteen minutes longer in the syrup. Lay them out upon a dish to cool, taking care not to break them. Fill a small deep dish full of nice jelly, and when it is set put the straw in the form of a nest, and lay the eggs in it. Nice for dessert or supper.

Puddings.

Bread Pudding.

Take nice pieces of light bread, break them up, and put a small pint bowl full into a quart of milk; set it in a tin pail or brown dish on the back part of the stove or range, where it will heat very gradually, and let it stand an hour or more. When the bread is soft enough to be made fine with a spoon, just boil it up; set it off, stir in a large teaspoonful of butter, a little salt, and from two to four beaten eggs. Bake one hour. To be eaten with a sauce. If you wish it without a sauce, put in twice the quantity of butter, beat the eggs with a cup of sugar, a teaspoonful of cinnamon and half as much powdered clove.

Sago Pudding.

1 pint of milk.
1½ tablespoonfuls of pearl sago.
2 eggs.
2 large tablespoonfuls of sugar.
½ a teaspoonful of salt.
Flavor with vanilla or lemon.

Wash the sago in warm but not hot water, twice; then put it with the milk into a pail and set it into a kettle of hot water. Stir it very often, as it swells fast, or it will lie in a compact mass at the bottom. When it has boiled two or three minutes, take the pail from the kettle, add the salt, and the eggs beaten with the sugar. Add the flavoring, put it into a dish, and grate nutmeg over it. Set it immediately into the oven and bake about three-quarters of an hour. If you make a quart of milk, three eggs answer very well. It should then bake an hour. With this number of eggs, the sago settles a little. To have it equally diffused, take five eggs.

Apple and Tapioca Pudding.

1 teacupful tapioca.
6 good-sized, mellow, sour apples.
1 quart water.

1 teaspoonful salt.
1 teacupful sugar.

Pare the apples and remove the core. Cover the tapioca with three cups of lukewarm water, and set it in a tolerably warm place to soak five or six hours, stirring now and then. Wash the apples, butter a deep pudding dish and lay them in with the open end up. Fill the holes in the apples with the sugar, and add a cup of lukewarm water; cover closely and steam in a moderate oven until soft all through, turning them as they cook at the bottom. If the dish is more than a third full of liquid, turn some of it out before you pour the soaked tapioca over all. Bake, after the tapioca goes in, one hour. Eat warm, with sweet, hard sauce. You can make sago pudding in the same way.

Tapioca Pudding.

1 cup tapioca.
1 quart milk.
5 eggs, whites and yolks beaten separately.
2 tablespoonfuls butter, melted.
2 tablespoonfuls sugar.

Soak the tapioca in enough cold water to cover it, two hours; drain off the water if it be not all absorbed; soak two hours longer in the milk, which should be slightly warmed. When the tapioca is quite soft, beat the sugar and butter together; add the yolks, the milk and tapioca, lastly the whites. Stir very well, and bake in a buttered dish. Eat warm with sweet sauce.

Farina Pudding.

2 tablespoonfuls farina.
1 pint milk.
2 eggs.
1 small cup sugar.
½ teaspoonful salt.
Flavor with lemon or nutmeg.

Set the milk in a pail into a kettle of hot water. **When**

the top foams up, stir in the farina gradually, and add the salt. Let it remain ten or fifteen minutes, and stir repeatedly. Take the pail from the kettle, beat the eggs and sugar together, and stir them in; add the essence, and pour the mixture in a buttered dish. Bake half an hour or forty minutes. No sauce is necessary.

Cocoanut Pudding.

½ pound grated cocoanut.
½ cup stale sponge cake, broken up fine.
2 tablespoonfuls butter.
1 cup of sugar.
1 cup of rich milk or cream.
6 eggs.
2 teaspoonfuls vanilla or rose water.

Rub together the butter and sugar, and then add the beaten yolks. Stir in the cocoanut when these are well mixed. Add the milk, cake crumbs, flavoring, and finally the whites of three eggs. Bake the pudding nearly three-quarters of an hour. Make a meringue of the whipped whites of the other three eggs, and three tablespoonfuls of sugar flavored with vanilla spread over the top, and set back in the oven until this is slightly browned.

Berry Pudding.

1 pint of milk.
2 eggs.
1 saltspoonful of salt.
¼ teaspoonful soda, dissolved in hot water.
½ teaspoonful cream tartar, sifted through a cup of flour, and added to enough flour to make a thick batter.
1 pint blackberries, raspberries, currants or huckleberries, well dredged with flour, stirred in at the last. Boil one hour in buttered mould.

Fruit Valise Pudding.

1 quart of flour.
2 tablespoonfuls butter.

1 teaspoonful soda, dissolved in hot water.
2 teaspoonfuls cream tartar mixed with the flour.
½ teaspoonful salt.
2 cups of milk, or enough to make the flour into a soft dough.
1 quart of berries.

Stoned cherries, sliced peaches, oranges or other fruit; jam, preserves, canned fruit or marmalade may be substituted for the berries. Roll the crust into a sheet less than half an inch thick. Cover thickly with the fruit and sprinkle with sugar. Roll the sheet closely, leaving a margin at one end to fold over the roll. Pinch the ends down closely to prevent the escape of the fruit and then sew up in a bag the size and shape of the valise. Dip the bag in hot water, and flour well before putting in the pudding. Boil an hour and a half. Cut the slices crosswise, and serve hot with sauce.

Lemon Pudding.

1 cup of sugar.
4 eggs.
2 tablespoonfuls of corn starch.
2 lemons, juice of both and rind of one.
1 pint milk.
1 tablespoonful butter.

Heat the milk to boiling, and stir in the corn starch, wet with a few spoonfuls of cold water. Boil five minutes, stirring constantly. While hot mix in the butter and set it away to cool. Beat the yolks light, and add the sugar, mixing very thoroughly before putting in the lemon juice and grated rind. Beat this to a stiff cream and add gradually to the corn starch and milk, when the latter is cold. Stir all smooth, put in a buttered dish, and bake Eat cold.

Orange Pudding.

5 sweet oranges.
1 coffee cupful of white sugar.
1 pint milk.

Yolks of 3 eggs.
1 tablespoonful corn starch.

Peel and cut the oranges into thin slices, taking out the seeds; pour over them the sugar; set the milk in a pot of boiling water, and let it get boiling hot; add the yolks of the eggs well beaten, then the corn starch made smooth with a little cold milk; stir all the time; as soon as thickened, pour over the fruit. Beat the whites to a stiff froth, adding a tablespoon of sugar, and spread over the top for frosting; set it in the oven for a few minutes to harden; eat cold or hot (but better cold), for dinner or supper. Berries or peaches can be substituted for oranges.

Boston Lemon Pudding.

2 cups dry bread crumbs.
¾ cup powdered sugar.
½ cup butter (or a little less).
2 lemons, all the juice and half the grated rind.
2 tablespoonfuls sifted flour.
5 eggs, beaten light.

The yolks must be strained. Rub butter and sugar to a cream; add the beaten yolks and lemon. Whip very light; put in handful by handful the bread crumbs, alternately with the stiffened whites; then the flour. Butter the mould, and put in the mixture (remembering to leave room for swelling), and boil two hours steadily.

Boston Orange Pudding

Is made in the same way, substituting oranges for lemons in the pudding, but retaining the lemon in the sauce.

Both of these are excellent desserts. They can be baked as well as boiled.

Rice Pudding. (*Plain.*)

4 tablespoonfuls rice.
2 quarts milk.
8 tablespoonfuls sugar.

1 teaspoonful salt.
Butter the size of an egg, melted.
Nutmeg and cinnamon to taste.

Wash and pick over the rice, and soak in one pint of the milk two hours. Then add the rest of the milk, the sugar, salt, butter, and spice. Bake two hours, and eat cold.

RICE PUDDING WITH EGGS.

1 quart milk.
4 eggs.
½ cup rice.
¾ cup sugar.
1 tablespoonful butter.
Handful of raisins, seeded and cut in two.

Soak the rice for an hour in a pint of milk and then set it on the stove where it will slowly heat to a boil. Remove it in five minutes after boiling, and let it cook. Beat the yolks, add the sugar and rice in the boiled milk, with the unboiled, the beaten whites and lastly the raisins. Grate nutmeg over it, and bake three-fourths of an hour or until the custard is a light brown. Eat cold.

RICE AND TAPIOCA PUDDING.

½ cup rice.
½ cup tapioca.
¾ cup sugar.
3 pints milk.
Cinnamon to taste.

Soak the tapioca in a cup of the milk three hours; wash the rice in several waters, and soak in another cup of milk as long as you do the tapioca. Sweeten the remaining quart of milk; put all the ingredients together, and bake two hours in a slow oven. Eat cold.

BOILED RICE.

1 cup whole rice.
1 quart water (cold).

A little salt.

Pick over and wash the rice, put it in the water and set the vessel in a kettle of boiling water. As it swells, and the water boils away, add more. from the teakettle. It will require an hour or more to cook it. To be eaten with a sauce, or with sugar and cream.

VELVET PUDDING.

5 eggs beaten separately.
1 teacupful of white sugar.
4 tablespoonfuls corn starch dissolved in a little cold milk and added to the yolks and sugar. Boil three pints of sweet milk, and pour into it the yolks and sugar while boiling. Remove from the fire when it has become quite thick. Flavor with vanilla and pour into a baking dish. Beat the whites of the eggs to a stiff froth with half a teacupful of white sugar; then pour it over the top of the pudding, and return it to the stove until it is slightly browned. Eat with sauce.

FOOD PUDDING.

4 eggs, yolks and whites beaten separately.
1 tablespoonful of flour to each egg.
1 pint of milk.
A little salt.
Bake in jelly tins fifteen minutes; and must be eaten as soon as done. Eat with sauce.

PINE APPLE PUDDING.

Prepare ripe pine apples by grating them very fine. Make a custard with cream and egg. Heat the custard over steam until sufficiently hot to congeal the cream. Having previously drained the pine apple free from juice, and sweetened it one hour before, it will be ready to mix with the cream. Pour in a fancy dish (that has been heated, so that it will not break) a layer of the cream, then a layer of the pine apple, alternately, until the whole is in the dish. Beat sweet cream stiff, sweeten with loaf sugar very sweet, and just before the dessert is served add the juice of the fruit, and put the beaten cream on the top of the pudding. The only care in making this dessert, is the danger of the custard and cream becoming sour.

Cocoa pudding can be made in the same way, adding the cocoa milk to the cream.

CORN STARCH PUDDING. (*Boiled.*)

3 tablespoonfuls corn starch.
1 quart milk.
3 eggs.
A little salt.
Flavor with lemon or vanilla.

Mix the corn starch in a little of the milk, add to it the eggs, well beaten, and the salt. Heat the remainder of the milk till near boiling. Add the above preparation and boil four minutes. Stir briskly. Eat warm with sauce or cream and sugar.

CORN STARCH PUDDING. (*Baked.*)

4 tablespoonfuls corn starch
1 quart milk.
4 eggs, whites and yolks separate.
¾ cup sugar.
Nutmeg and cinnamon.
1 tablespoonful butter.

Dissolve the corn starch in a little cold milk, and having heated the rest of the milk to boiling, stir this in and boil three minutes, stirring all the time. Remove from the fire, and while still very hot, put in the butter. Set away until cold; beat the eggs very light, the sugar and seasoning with them, and stir into the corn starch, beating thoroughly to a smooth custard. Turn into a buttered dish, and bake half an hour. Eat cold, with powdered sugar sifted over it.

ARROW ROOT PUDDING.

Is made according to either of the recipes for corn starch, substituting arrow root for corn starch.

German Puffs.

3 cups flour.
3 cups milk.
3 eggs, whites and yolks beaten separately and *very* light.
3 teaspoonfuls melted butter.
1 saltspoonful salt.

Pour in nine well buttered cups of same size as that used for measuring, and bake to a fine brown. Eat as soon as done, with sauce.

Snow Pudding.

½ package of gelatine.
1 pint of boiling water.
2 teacupfuls sugar.
Juice of 1 lemon.
Whites of 3 eggs.

Dissolve the gelatine in a little cold water, then add the boiling water, sugar and lemon juice; strain it, break in whites of three eggs, beat one hour, then pour in moulds. For sauce,

Yolks of 3 eggs.
1 pint of milk.

Make the same as boiled custard, and flavor and sweeten to taste. To be eaten cold.

Cottage Pudding.

2 eggs.
1 cup sweet milk.
1 cup sugar.
3 cups flour or enough to make quite a stiff batter.
1 tablespoonful of butter.
1 teaspoonful cream tartar worked into the flour.
½ teaspoonful soda.
1 teaspoonful salt.

Cream the butter and sugar. Beat in yolks, and then the milk, salt and soda (dissolved in hot water) then the beaten whites and flour, alternately. Bake in buttered mould, cut in slices and eat with liquid sauce.

Delicate Pudding.

1 teacup sweet milk.
1 tablespoonful flour.
4 tablespoonfuls melted butter.
Yolks of 5 eggs.
Sweeten and flavor to taste.

Beat the sugar and eggs together, and stir in the other ingredients. Place on the stove to thicken, not boil. Line a deep dish with pastry and cover the bottom with preserves, jelly or any fruit, pour on the mixture when thick, and bake. Make a frosting of the whites and put on the top and brown slightly. Eat cold.

Apple Dumplings. (*Boiled.*)

Make a paste like cream tartar biscuit, and roll it out large, make the middle one-third of an inch thick, but roll the edges thin. Wring a thick, square cloth in water, flour it well, and lay it in a deep dish; lay the crust into it, and fill with sliced or quartered tart apples. Close the crust together, and draw up the cloth around it; tie with a strong string closely, allowing no room to swell. If the dumpling holds three pints of sliced apples, boil it two hours; when done take it from the pot and plunge for a moment in cold water, then turn into a dish. Eat with sauce.

Apple Dumplings. (*Baked.*)

Make a paste same as above, roll it into a sheet less than half an inch thick, cut it in squares, and lay in the center of each, a juicy tart apple, pared and cored. Bring the corners together and pinch slightly. Lay in buttered pan, the pinched edges downward, and bake to a light brown. Sift powdered sugar over, and serve with a rich, sweet sauce.

Steam Pudding.

2 cups sweet milk.
1 cup sweet butter.

1 cup sugar.
1 cup seedless raisins, or currants or citron.
4 cups flour.
2 teaspoonfuls baking powder.
Cinnamon or nutmeg to taste.
A little salt.

Steam two hours and you will have an excellent pudding.

INDIAN PUDDING.

½ pint of corn meal.
1 quart boiling milk.
1 teaspoonful of salt.
1 cup of chopped suet, or
½ cup of butter.
1 cup of molasses.
1 egg.
A little ginger.

Stir the meal into the boiling milk. When cool add the other ingredients. Bake two hours.

INDIAN SUET PUDDING.

1 teacupful of molasses.
1 teacupful of chopped suet.
2½ cups of Indian meal.
1 cup of boiled milk.
½ cup of cold milk.
1 teaspoonful of salt.

Good without eggs though two or three can be used if preferred. Steam three hours in a pudding pan.

BATTER PUDDING.

1 pint of milk.
4 eggs, whites and yolks beaten separately.
2 even cups of flour.
1 teaspoonful salt.
1 pinch of soda.

Bake in a buttered dish three-quarters of an hour. Serve in the pudding-dish as soon as it is drawn from the oven, and eat with a rich sauce.

Or,

You may boil it in a buttered mould or floured bag, flouring it very thickly. Boil two hours, taking care the boiling does not cease for a moment until the pudding is done.

THANKSGIVING PLUM PUDDING.

1 pound raisins.
1 dozen crackers.
4 eggs, well beaten.
2 cups sugar.
1 teaspoonful salt.
1 teaspoonful each, ground cloves, allspice and cinnamon.
1 grated nutmeg.

Mix together the eggs, sugar, salt and spice.

Open the crackers (Boston crackers are best,) and butter them, soak in milk until quite soft. Half fill a pan (which has been well greased) with alternate layers of crackers and the egg mixture, and good muscatel or box raisins. Fill the pan three-fourths full of milk, if filled full it will swell and run over. It requires two hours to bake. Cover while baking, if likely to burn. Slices of bread can be used instead of crackers. It may be served with or without sauce.

BAKED CUSTARD.

1 quart of milk.
4 eggs, beaten light, whites and yolks separately.
5 tablespoonfuls sugar, mixed with the yolks.
Nutmeg and vanilla.

Scald, but not boil the milk; add gradually the beaten yolks, and when mixed well, stir in the whites. Flavor and pour into a deep dish, or custard-cups. Set these in a pan of hot water, grate nutmeg upon each, and bake until firm. Eat cold from the cups.

Minute Pudding.

1 quart water boiling.
Flour ready sifted.
Add a little salt to the water, and stir in rapidly the flour, dropping it from the hand until it is of proper consistency. If milk is used with the water do not salt it, until the flour is stirred in, as there will be danger of curdling the milk. If the fire is very hot it will make the pudding lumpy.

Cracked Wheat.

Take one or two quarts, according to the size of the family, put it into cold water and after stirring it well, let it settle, then pour off the water and add more, in the proportion of three quarts to a quart of wheat. Let it stand over night, and the next day boil it very moderately two or three hours in a tin pail set into a kettle of boiling water. If it becomes too thick, add more water. The evaporation is more rapid at some times than at others. It should not be quite as thick as hasty pudding. Take it up in dishes wet in cold water.

To brown it for breakfast, grease a tin or dripping-pan, turn the wheat out of the dish upon it, and set it into the stove oven. It will become heated through, and browned in half an hour or forty minutes. Some like it better this way than when first boiled.

Oat Meal Pudding.

Have a pint of water in a sauce-pan. Wet two tablespoonfuls of oat-meal in cold water, with a small teaspoonful of salt. Rub it smooth as you can (it will not rub smooth as flour), then stir it into the boiling water, and boil slowly half an hour. Stir it often. Should it be too thin after it has boiled about twenty minutes, scatter in a little more oat meal dry; if too thick, add more water. eat with sugar and cream. There is much difference in oat meal. Be sure and get fresh, sweet, Scotch oat meal.

GRAHAM PUDDING.

1 cup Graham flour, wet up with cold water.
1 large cup *boiling* water, and same quantity of milk.
Stir the wet flour into the boiling water, slightly salted. Boil ten minutes, stirring almost constantly. Add the milk, and cook, after it has come again to a boil, ten minutes longer. Serve with milk and sugar, for breakfast.

HOMINY. (*Boiled and Fried.*)

Take a pint of hominy, put cold water over it, stir and let it settle; then pour off the water. Do this twice; then put it into a tin pudding pan or pail, in three pints of water to soak over night. In the morning set the pail into a kettle of boiling water; add a little salt; stir it often. If it becomes so thick as not to stir easily, add more water. It should be just thick enough, when done, to settle down almost smooth, in a deep dish. Fine hominy will cook in two hours; the coarse requires three. This is nice eaten with milk.

To fry it for breakfast, slice it about half an inch thick, and lay it on a griddle greased with nice beef drippings or butter. It will require about fifteen minutes to brown both sides. The coarse does not fry as nicely as the fine.

HASTY PUDDING.

Boil in a pot or kettle about six quarts of water, leaving room for the addition of the meal; mix a pint bowl full of Indian meal and cold water, with a small spoonful of salt. When the water boils, stir this into it. After thirty or forty minutes, stir in four or five handfuls of dry meal, and let it boil as much longer; then add more dry meal. Taste to see if it is salt enough. Stir it very often to prevent its burning. Most people make it too thick and do not cook it half long enough. Boil it all together at least two hours. When taken out it should be so soft that it will in a few minutes settle down smooth in a dish. This can be fried in the same manner as hominy.

---o---

PUDDING SAUCES.

Plain Pudding Sauce.

4 large spoonfuls white sugar.
2 spoonfuls butter.
1 spoonful flour.
White of 1 egg, beaten to a stiff froth.

Stir the flour, sugar and butter together, then add the white of the egg; pour into this a gill of boiling water, stirring the mixture very fast. Add essence of lemon or rose, or grate nutmeg over the top.

Hard Sauce.

1 teacupful of sugar.
½ teacupful butter.

Stir together until light; flavor with nutmeg or essence of lemon. Smooth the top with a knife, and grate nutmeg over it.

Lemon Sauce.

1 *large* cup of sugar.
Nearly half a cup of butter.
1 egg.

1 lemon, all the juice and half the grated peel.
1 teaspoonful nutmeg.
3 tablespoonfuls boiling water.

Cream the butter and sugar, and beat in the egg whipped light; then the lemon and nutmeg. Beat hard ten minutes, and add, a spoonful at a time, the boiling water. Put in a tin pail and set within the uncovered top of the tea kettle, which you must keep boiling until the steam heats the sauce very hot, but not to boiling. Stir constantly.

SAUCE FOR VELVET PUDDING.

Yolks of 2 eggs.
1 cup of white sugar.
1 tablespoonful of butter.

Cream the butter and sugar, and add the eggs well beaten; then one cup of boiling milk. Put it over the fire and let it come to a boiling heat. Flavor with vanilla.

JELLY SAUCE.

½ cup currant jelly.
1 tablespoonful butter melted.
½ dessert spoonful arrow root or corn starch, wet with cold water.
3 tablespoonfuls boiling water.

Stir the arrow root into the boiling water and heat, stirring all the time, until it thickens; add the butter, and set aside until almost cool, when beat in, spoonful by spoonful, the jelly to a smooth, pink paste. Stir hard, and heat in a tin vessel, set within another of boiling water, until very hot.

SWEETENED CREAM. (*Cold.*)

1 pint of cream.
4 tablespoonfuls powdered sugar.
1 teaspoonful of nutmeg.
1 teaspoonful of vanilla.

Mix all well together, stirring until the sugar is dissolved.

English Plum Pudding Sauce.

1 cup of sugar.
1 tablespoonful melted butter.
1 tablespoonful corn starch.
1 pint boiling hot water.
Flavoring to taste.

Beat the sugar and butter to a cream; and add the corn starch which has been beaten smoothly with a little cold water. Pour over this the hot water and flavoring, and boil fifteen minutes.

Sauce for all Kinds of Puddings.

1 pint of boiling water.
1 egg.
3 spoonfuls sugar.
2 spoonfuls butter.
2 spoonfuls flour.

Mix the flour smooth in cold water, and stir it into the boiling water and butter, and cook until it thickens, stirring it, that it may not be lumpy; the same as for drawn butter. Beat the egg and sugar together in a bowl, and pour the liquid over them. Season to taste. No farther cooking is necessary.

[We have inserted some wine sauces, as many insist on the use of them; but strawberry, orange or lemon juice may be used instead, and by many is preferred.]

Wine Sauce.

2 teacups of sugar.
1 teacup of butter.
2 eggs.
1 teacupful of wine.

Stir the sugar and butter to a cream; beat the eggs very light, and stir all together, then add the wine. Mix and set on top of a teakettle of boiling water. It must not be put on the stove nor boil.

Foaming Pudding Sauce.

Whites of 3 eggs, well beaten.
1 teacup of sugar.
⅓ cup of water.
1 glass wine.

Melt and boil the sugar in the water; add the wine, and stir in the whites. Serve at once.

ADDITIONAL RECIPES.

ADDITIONAL RECIPES.

ADDITIONAL RECIPES.

ADDITIONAL RECIPES.

FANCY DISHES FOR DESSERT.

GENERAL DIRECTIONS FOR CUSTARD AND BLANC-MANGE.

Creams and custards which are to be frozen should have quite one-third more sugar than those which are not. In heating milk for custards, do not let it quite boil before adding the eggs. A good plan is to take the scalding milk from the fire and slowly pour it over the beaten eggs, beating the eggs and milk all of the time, and return to the fire and boil ten or fifteen minutes, stirring constantly. Always boil the milk in a vessel set in another vessel of boiling water. Custards are better with the whites and yolks beaten separately; and stir the whites in last.

BOILED CUSTARD.

1 quart of milk.
Yolks of five eggs, and whites of seven.
6 tablespoonfuls of sugar.
Flavor with vanilla.

Heat the milk nearly to boiling; beat the yolks light and stir in the sugar. Add the milk; stir in five whites whipped stiff; return to the fire and stir until thick, but not until it breaks. Season with vanilla, and pour into custard cups; whip the whites of two eggs to a stiff froth, and add a heaping tablespoonful of powdered sugar. When the custard is cold, pile a little of this upon the top of each cup. A preserved berry, or a little bright jelly placed upon each improves its looks.

FLOATING ISLAND.

1 quart of milk.
4 eggs, whites and yolks beaten separately.

4 tablespoonfuls white sugar.
2 teaspoonfuls extract vanilla.
½ cup currant jelly.

Beat the yolks well and stir in the sugar. Heat the milk hot and stir in a little at a time; boil until it begins to thicken. Flavor when cool, stir well, and pour into a glass dish. Make a meringue of the whites and beat into it the jelly. Lay on the top bits of jelly cut into any fanciful shape.

WHIPPED SYLLABUBS.

1 pint rich cream.
Whites of 2 eggs.
1 small glass of wine.
1 cup powdered sugar.
Flavor with vanilla or any other extract.

Whip half the sugar into the cream, the rest with the whites of the eggs. Mix these, and add flavoring. Churn in a syllabub churn to a strong froth. Heap in glasses.

RASPBERRY TRIFLE.

Lay in a deep glass dish slices of sponge cake or any delicate cup cake. Pour over some cream or juice of preserved fruit; then add a layer of raspberry or strawberry jam, as thick as your finger. Pour upon this a pint of boiled custard, and beat the whites of three eggs very stiff, and spread over the custard.

MERINGUES.

Whites of 6 eggs.
1 pound powdered sugar.
Flavor with any essence you like.

Cut the whites of the eggs very stiff. Stir in gradually the sugar; beat until thick; add the flavoring. Butter slightly sheets of white paper, and lay upon pieces of hard wood boards. Drop the mixture on the paper, a spoonful at a time, in oval form, rounded, and thick at the top. Bake in a slow oven till the outside is crisp, and of a light brown. Then remove from the paper, and join them by the under side, two by two. The inside will be soft and creamy. Placed singly upon cream in a glass dish, they are a handsome dessert.

Orange Souffle.

4 large oranges.
3 heaping tablespoonfuls powdered sugar.
6 eggs.
3 gills new milk.

Peel, slice, and seed the oranges, put them into the dish you wish to send to the table, sprinkling a heaping tablespoon of sugar over them. Make a custard of the yolks of six eggs, the new milk, and two tablespoonfuls of sugar; set aside to cool, and when cold, pour over the sliced oranges. Beat the whites of the eggs to a stiff froth, add a spoon of powdered sugar, and spread over the pudding, then set in the stove and brown slightly. Excellent for dessert or tea.

Charlotte Russe.

1 pint of milk.
1 pint of cream.
4 eggs.
½ ounce of gelatine.
⅔ cup of sugar.

Flavor with any kind of flavoring desired. Make a custard of the milk, eggs, and sugar, and set away to cool. Dissolve the gelatine in a gill of milk by putting it in a warm place; when it is dissolved pour it into the cream and whip to a froth. When the custard is cold, stir it gently into the cream. Make a mould of sponge cake, by cutting strips from the loaf for the sides, leaving the crust for the bottom in one piece. Pour the mixture in, and set it in a cool place.

Lemon Snow.

Whites of 12 eggs.
½ box of gelatine.
1 pint of hot water.

1 cup of white sugar.
Juice of 2 lemons.
Beat the eggs to a stiff froth. Dissolve the gelatine in the hot water, and add the sugar and lemon juice to it. When it is cooling, add the eggs. Run in moulds.

STAINED FROTH.

Take the whites of three or four eggs, and whip them to a stiff froth, then beat into them the syrup of damsons, or any highly colored preserve. This makes an elegant addition to a dish of soft custard. Some persons, when making custards, lay the white of eggs, cut in this way, upon the top of the boiling milk for a minute or two. This hardens it, and it is taken off upon a dish, and when the custard cups are filled, a piece is laid upon the top of each.

CORN STARCH BLANC MANGE.

1 quart of milk.
4 tablespoonfuls corn starch, wet in a little cold water.
3 eggs, well beaten, whites and yolks separately.
1 cup of sugar.
Vanilla, lemon, or other essence.
One saltspoonful salt.
Heat the milk to boiling; stir in the corn starch and salt, and boil together five minutes, then add the yolks, beaten light, with the sugar; boil two minutes longer, stirring all the while; remove the mixture from the fire, and beat in the whipped whites while it is boiling hot. Pour into a mould wet with cold water, and set in a cold place. Eat with sugar and cream.

VELVET BLANC MANGE.

2 cups sweet cream.
½ ounce Cooper's gelatine, soaked in a little cold water one hour.
½ cup powdered white sugar.
1 teaspoonful extract of bitter almonds.

1 glass white wine.

Heat the cream to boiling, stir in the gelatine and sugar, as soon as they are dissolved, take from the fire. Beat ten minutes, or churn in a syllabub churn until very light; flavor, and add by degrees the wine, mixing it in well. Put in moulds wet with cold water.

Moss Blanc Mange.

In making this blanc mange as little moss should be used as will suffice to harden the milk. If the moss is old, more is necessary than if it is fresh. Allow half a teacupful for a quart of milk. Wash it and put it in soak over night; in the morning tie it up in a piece of muslin, and boil it in the milk gently twenty minutes or half an hour. Then put in half a saltspoonful of salt, strain it upon a large spoonful of crushed sugar, and put it into a mould immediately, as it soon begins to harden. Eat it with sugar and cream.

Lemon Cream.

Whites of 9 eggs.
1 quart of cream.
Juice of 1 large lemon.

Beat the eggs well; put the cream over the fire, and when it comes to the boil stir it swiftly into the eggs, as in making boiled custard, and set the cream back on the fire, and stir slowly until it thickens somewhat. Take it from the fire and put in the lemon juice, stirring constantly all the time until it becomes cool enough not to send off any steam; place on ice. This makes a solid blanc mange, and is quite as good as ice cream.

Tapioca Cream.

3 tablespoonfuls tapioca.
3 eggs.
1 quart of milk.
Sugar and flavor to taste.
A little salt if you like.

Soak the tapioca in a little water for an hour, or until soft. Beat the yolks and the whites of the eggs separately. Boil a quart of new milk; while boiling add the yolks, tapioca and sugar, stirring gradually until thickened. When nearly cold, add the whites beaten to a froth, and flavor. This makes a very nice dish for tea, as well as dessert.

SPANISH CREAM.

½ box of gelatine.
1 small cup of sugar.
Yolks of 3 eggs.
1 quart of milk.

Soak the gelatine in the milk for one hour, then put it on the fire, and as it warms, stir it well. Beat the yolks very light, and stir in the sugar, and add to the scalding milk. Heat to boiling, stirring all the time. Flavor with lemon or vanilla. Strain through thin muslin or tarlatan, and when nearly cold, wet the mould in cold water and pour in the cream.

WINE JELLY.

2 pounds sugar.
1 pint of wine (white, or pale sherry).
1 pint cold water.
1 package Coxe's gelatine.
Juice of two lemons and grated peel of one.
1 quart of boiling water.
Little bit of ground cinnamon.

Soak the gelatine in the cold water one hour, and then add to the water, sugar, lemons and cinnamon. Pour over the mixture the boiling water and stir until the gelatine is thoroughly dissolved. Lastly put in the wine and strain the whole through a flannel bag. Do not squeeze the bag. Wet the jelly moulds with cold water and set the jelly away in them to cool.

FANCY DISHES FOR DESSERT. 241

Orange Jelly.

2 oranges, juice of both and grated peel of one.
1 lemon, juice and peel.
1 package Coxe's gelatine.
1 pint boiling water.
1½ cups sugar.
1 small cup of wine.
Little bit of ground cinnamon.
Soak the gelatine in very little water, one hour.

Squeeze the juice of the oranges and lemons into a bowl, and put with them the grated peel and the cinnamon. Pour over this the boiling water, cover tight and let it stand half an hour. Strain and add the sugar. Let it come to a boil and stir in the gelatine; when this is well dissolved, take it off from the fire. Strain through jelly bag into the moulds.

Calf's Foot Jelly.

4 calf's feet (cleaned).
4 quarts water.
1 pint wine.
3 cups sugar.
Whites of 3 eggs (well beaten).
1 teaspoonful nutmeg,
Juice of 1 lemon and half the grated peel.

Boil the feet in the water until it is reduced one-half. Strain the liquor and let it stand ten or twelve hours. Be careful to remove all the fat and dregs. Melt slowly in the preserving kettle, and add the seasoning, sugar, and the whipped whites of the eggs; boil fast ten minutes; skim well. Strain through the jelly bag. Do not squeeze the bag until it ceases to run freely, then gently squeeze the remainder into another bowl, as it will discolor the clear jelly; the second lot will taste as well as the first. Set away in moulds, which have been wet, in a cool place.

31

Lemon Jelly.

3 sheets American isinglass.
2 pints cold water.
1 cup white sugar.
Juice and grated peel of 1 lemon.

Break the isinglass in small pieces and soak half an hour in one pint of cold water, dissolve in this water the sugar and lemon. Boil in one pint of water two or three cloves for a few minutes, and stir into it the water containing the isinglass, and strain into a mould. Wet the moulds. Let it set till the next day.

ADDITIONAL RECIPES.

ADDITIONAL RECIPES.

ICE-CREAM.

DIRECTIONS FOR SELF-FREEZING.

Have ready a quantity of ice, cracked in small pieces, the smaller the better. This can be done by laying a great lump of ice between two folds of coarse sacking or an old carpet, tucking it in snugly, and beating it, through the cloth, with an ax or mallet, until fine enough. There is no waste of ice; gather up the corners of the cloth and slide as much as you want into the outer vessel. Use an ordinary upright freezer, set in a deep pail; pack around it closely, first, a layer of pounded ice, then one of rock salt—*common salt will not do*. In this order fill the pail; but before covering the freezer-lid, remove it carefully, that none of the salt may get in, and, with a long wooden ladle or flat stick, beat the custard steadily for five minutes. Replace the lid, pack the ice and salt upon it, patting it down hard on top; cover all with several folds of blanket or carpet, and leave it for one hour. Then remove the cover of the freezer, when you have wiped it carefully outside. With your ladle scrape off all the frozen custard which has gathered upon the bottom and sides. Beat again until the custard is a smooth, half congealed paste. The smoothness of the ice cream depends upon your action at this point. Put on the cover, pack in more ice and salt, and turn off the brine. Spread the double carpet over all once more, having buried the freezer out of sight in ice, and leave it for three or four hours. If the ice melts so that there is a quantity of water in the pail, pour it off, but do not open the freezer. In two hours more it will be ready for use. Should the ice melt very fast, you may have to turn the water off more than twice; but this will seldom happen except in very hot weather. You need not devote fifteen minutes in all to the business after the custard is made. If you do not own a freezer, a wooden or tin pail, holding ten or twelve quarts, can be used for the ice and salt, and a three quart pail for the cream, when only a small quantity is required.

Ice Cream. No. 1.

1 quart rich milk.
6 eggs, whites and yolks beaten separately.
4 cups of sugar.
3 pints of rich cream.
5 teaspoonfuls vanilla or other flavoring.

Heat the milk nearly to boiling. Beat the yolks light and stir in the sugar. Pour the hot milk on this gradually, beating all the while. Put in the frothed whites and set the vessel inside another containing hot water. Stir the custard steadily for fifteen minutes, or until as thick as boiled custard. When quite cool, beat in the cream and flavoring, and freeze.

Ice Cream. No. 2.

1 quart rich milk.
3 eggs.
1 coffee cup granulated sugar.
1 large spoonful of corn starch.

Put the milk in a tin pail, and set it in a kettle of hot water to boil; rub the corn starch smooth in a little cold milk, add to it the sugar and the eggs. Beat these well together and stir into the boiling milk. Remove from the fire in a minute or two, and set it to cool. When perfectly cold, add vanilla or lemon, and put it into the freezer.

Chocolate Ice Cream.

1 quart of cream.
1 pint new milk.
2 cups sugar.

2 eggs beaten very light.
5 tablespoonfuls chocolate rubbed smooth in a little milk.

Heat the milk nearly to boiling, and pour slowly in with the beaten egg and sugar. Stir in the chocolate, beat well three minutes, and return to the inner kettle. Heat until it thickens well, stirring constantly; take from the fire and set aside to cool, When the custard is cold, beat in the cream and freeze.

Pine Apple Ice Cream.

1 large, ripe pine apple.
1 pound powdered sugar.
1 quart of cream.

The pine apple must be sliced thin, and the sugar scattered between the slices; cover, and let the fruit steep three hours. Then cut it up in the syrup, and strain it through a hair sieve or bag of coarse lace. Beat gradually into the cream, and freeze as rapidly as possible. A few pieces of pine apple, unsugared, may be reserved, cut into square bits, and stirred through the cream when it is half frozen.

Orange Ice Cream.

2 oranges, the juice of one, and the grated peel of one and a half.
2 cups of sugar.
1 quart of cream.

Sweeten the cream, beat the orange gradually into it, and put at once into the freezer. Freeze rapidly in a pattent freezer, as the acid is apt to turn the cream.

Lemon ice cream may be made in the same way.

Strawberry or Raspberry Ice Cream.

1 quart fresh cream.
1 pound of sugar.
1 quart ripe, sweet berries.

Sprinkle over the berries half the sugar and let them stand three hours, then press, mash, and strain through a thin muslin bag. Add the rest of the sugar and beat in the cream little by little. Freeze quickly; open the freezer and stir several times. This is improved by adding, when the cream is stiff, a pint of whole berries, unsugared. If these are added, a cup more of sugar must be added to the prepared berries.

ICES.

Strawberry Ice.

1 box of strawberries.
1 pint of water.
1 lemon, juice only.
2 cups of white sugar.

Crush the strawberries, then add the water and lemon juice. Let it stand for a few hours, then strain through a bag or cloth upon the sugar. Squeeze out all the juice possible, and stir until the sugar is entirely dissolved. Make it sweeter if desired. Put it in the freezer for an hour.

Lemon Ice.

6 lemons, juice of all, and grated peel of 3.
1 large, sweet orange, juice and grated peel.
1 pint of water.
1 pint of sugar.

Squeeze out all the juice and put into it the grated peels; let them lay or steep in it one hour. Strain, squeezing through a bag. Mix in the sugar and then the water. Stir until the sugar is dissolved, then put in the freezer. Beat all together two or three times while freezing.

Orange Ice

May be made in the same manner as lemon ice, only using six oranges and the juice of two lemons.

Currant and Raspberry Ice.

1 pint of raspberries.
1 quart red currants.
1½ pints of sugar.
1 pint of water.

Squeeze out the juice, mix in the sugar and water and freeze.

SAUCE, PRESERVES AND FRUIT JELLIES.

Porcelain kettles are best for preserving. If bell metal is used, have it thoroughly cleaned, which is done by pouring into it a cupful of vinegar, and a handful of salt, heat this and faithfully scour every part of the inside. Do not let your preserves stand in it a moment after being taken from the stove. If you wish to use again in a few minutes even, wash the kettle, as all acids produce a chemical action on bell-metal which is poisonous. Use only fine sugar for nice preserves, for, like every thing else, the better the material used, the more satisfactory the result. Moist or dark sugar can not be used with the same result as white sugar.

If you are desirous of having very nice preserves or jellies, the sugar can be clarified according to directions given for clarifying sugar for candy. Do not hurry in the process of preserving. Weigh accurately. Put up your preserves in small jars in preference to larger ones, and if many kinds are made, label each jar to prevent mistakes. Keep them in a cool, dark place, that is perfectly dry. If care is taken in weighing and cooking, preserves ought never to require cooking the second time. This trouble may arise if they can not be kept in a dry, cool place, and if so they must be looked after often, as fermentation is quite rapid and will generally show itself soon after they are made, say in a month or six weeks. If they do need attention from that cause, make a little syrup and heat, but do not cook as in the first process.

Cover jellies and jams with tissue paper, double, and

wet with brandy, pressed close to the conserve before you put on the lid. If the jellies are not as firm, after six or eight hours, as you like them to be, set them in the sun with pieces of window glass over them. Remove the glass at night and wipe off the moisture which will collect on the under side. This will be found to be a much better way than boiling, as that injures the flavor and color of jellies.

CITRON PRESERVES.

Cut the citron in thin slices, boil in water with a small piece of alum until clear and tender, then rinse in cold water. Make a syrup of three-fourths pound sugar to one pound citron; boil a piece of ginger in the syrup; then pour the citron in and let it boil a few minutes. Put in one lemon to five citrons.

PRESERVED PEACHES.

Select ripe, but not soft peaches. If they are freestones, pour boiling water on them and let them stand for five minutes, then pour off, and their skins can easily be pulled off; cling-stones must be pared. Extract the stones and weigh the peaches, allowing equal weight of sugar for the same of peaches. Put in the kettle, alternately, a layer of sugar, and then of fruit; set it where the sugar will slowly melt. Crack one quarter of the stones and extract the kernels, break them in pieces and boil in just water enough to cover. When the fruit is well heated through, put in the strained kernel water and boil the fruit until tender, take it out and boil the syrup fast until clear, skimming off all the scum. Place the fruit in a jar, and pour over it the boiling syrup. When cold, cover closely, and set in a dry, cool place.

PRESERVED PEARS

Are put up precisely as are peaches, but are only **pared**, not divided. Leave the stems on.

Preserved Apples.

Firm, well flavored pippins or bell-flower apples make an excellent preserve, prepared in the same manner as quinces. A few quinces cut up among them, or the juice of two lemons to every three pounds of fruit improves them.

Steamed Apples.

Wash rich flavored apples, take out the cores and leave the fruit whole. Steam them in a steamer, until perfectly tender, take them out and serve with cream and sugar.

Baked Pears.

Take a stone jar and fill it with alternate layers of pears (without paring) and sugar, until the jar is full, then pour in as much water as the jar will hold. Bake them in an oven three hours. They are very nice.

Preserved Pine Apple.

Pare, cut into slices, and take out the core of each. Allow equal weight of sugar for the same weight of pine apples. Put in alternate layers the sugar and fruit in the preserving kettle, allowing a teacupful of water for every pound of sugar. Heat to a boil, then remove the apple. Boil and skim the syrup for half an hour. Put the pine apple back in the kettle and boil again fifteen miuutes. Pack in wide-mouthed jars, and pour over the hot syrup. Cover and when cold, tie up tightly.

Preserved Cherries.

Stone the cherries and save all the juice. Weigh the fruit and allow pound for pound. Put in the kettle alternate layers of sugar and fruit, pour over this the juice and boil until the syrup thickens. The short stem red cherries, or the Morellas are the best for this purpose. The sweet cherries are unfit for preserves.

Dried Cherries.

Pit the cherries and stew gently with a little sugar, after which spread them on tins and dry gently in the oven. While drying boil down the syrup and pour it over the fruit each day, a little at a time. When dry, pack in jars and paste paper over the top.

Preserved Crab Apples.

The red Siberian crab is the best for preserving. Pick out those that are nearly perfect, *leaving the stems on*, and put into a preserving kettle with enough warm water to cover them. Heat this to boiling, slowly, and simmer until the skins break. Drain and skin them; then, with a pen-knife, extract the cores through the blossom ends. Weigh them; allow a pound and a quarter of sugar and a teacupful of water to every pound of fruit. Boil the water and sugar together until the scum ceases to rise; put in the fruit, cover the kettle, and simmer until the apples are a clear red, and tender. Take out with a skimmer, spread upon dishes to cool and harden; add to the syrup the juice of one lemon to three pounds of fruit, and boil until clear and rich. Fill your jars three-quarters full of apples, pour the syrup in, and when cool, tie up.

Cranberry Sauce.

Wash and pick a quart of ripe cranberries, and put into a sauce-pan with a teacupful of water. Stew slowly, stirring often until they are thick as marmalade. Cook at least an hour and a half. When done, sweeten abundantly with white sugar. If sweetened while cooking, the color will be bad. Put them into a mould and set aside to get cold.

Cider Apple Sauce.

If you wish very sweet sauce, take only sweet apples if not, one-third sour and two-thirds sweet. Peel, quarter and core the apples; lay them in the sun two or three days to prevent the fruit breaking. To every pailful of apples, put one quart of boiled cider. Boil slowly until the fruit becomes a dark mahogany color. To those who like the flavor of quinces, two to each pailful, cut fine, will be an addition.

Cherry Sauce.

Take thoroughly ripe and stoned cherries; pour over them melted sugar while boiling hot, in the proportion of half a pound of sugar to a pound of cherries. Put them on ice until cold, when the sauce is ready for the table.

Currants.

Strip them from the stems, and allow a pound of sugar to a pound of fruit. Boil together ten minutes. Take them from the syrup and let the syrup boil twenty minutes and pour it on the fruit. Put them in small jars or tumblers and let them stand a few days.

Preserved Strawberries.

Pound for pound. Put them in a preserving kettle over a slow fire until the sugar melts. Boil twenty-five minutes, fast. Take out the fruit in a perforated skimmer and fill a number of small cans three-quarters full. Boil and skim the syrup five minutes longer, fill up the jars, and seal while hot. Keep in a cool, dry place.

Ripe Tomatoes.

Peel the tomatoes and allow equal quantities of fruit and sugar. Let them stand together over night; in the morning drain off the syrup and boil, skimming well. Put in the tomatoes and boil gently twenty minutes. Remove the tomatoes, and boil the syrup until it thickens, add to it the juice of one lemon for every four pounds of fruit. When ready to put in jars, lay in between the fruit, slices of lemon and pour over it the hot syrup. Cover closely.

EGG PLUMS.

Take the plums ripe, but not very ripe. The skin can usually be pulled off, if not easily, pour on boiling water, and instantly turn it off. Allow equal quantities of fruit and sugar, and make the syrup in the usual way. Then lay in a few plums at a time, and boil gently five minutes; lay them into a jar as you take them from the kettle, and when all are done, pour the boiling syrup over them, After two days, drain off the syrup, boil it, and pour it upon them again; do this every two or three days till they look clear. Then if you wish the syrup to be very thick, boil it half an hour, and when cold, pour it upon the plums.

PRESERVED GREEN GAGES AND LARGE PURPLE PLUMS.

Weigh the fruit and scald in boiling water to make the skins come off easily. Let them stand in a large bowl an hour after they are peeled, that the juice may exude. Drain this off, lay the plums in the kettle, alternately with layers of sugar, allowing pound for pound; pour the juice over the top and heat slowly to a boil. Take out the plums at this point, very carefully, with a perforated skimmer, draining them well through it, and spread upon broad dishes in the sun. Boil the syrup until thick and clear, skimming it faithfully. Return the plums to this, and boil ten minutes. Spread out again until cool and firm; keeping the syrup hot on the fire, fill your jars three-quarters full with the fruit; pour on the scalding syrup, cover to keep in the heat, and, when cold, tie up.

If you do not care to take the trouble of peeling the fruit, prick it in several places with a needle, and proceed as directed.

DAMSONS,

Are put up in the same manner as plums, but pricked instead of skinned.

Preserved Figs.

The weight of ripe figs in sugar.
Peel of one lemon and juice of two.
A little ginger.
Cover the figs with cold water for twelve hours. Then simmer in water enough to cover them until tender, and spread out upon a sieve to cool and harden. Make a syrup of the sugar, and a cup of cold water for every pound. Boil until clear of scum; put in the figs and simmer ten minutes. Take them out and spread upon dishes in the sun. Add the lemons and ginger; boil the syrup thick; give the figs another boil of fifteen minutes, and fill the jars three-quarters of the way to the top. Fill up with boiling syrup, cover, and when cold, seal up.

Preserved Orange Peel.

Weigh the oranges whole, and allow pound for pound. Peel the fruit neatly, and cut the rind into narrow strips. Boil until tender, changing the water twice, and replenishing with hot from the kettle. Squeeze the strained juice of the oranges over the sugar; let this heat to a boil; put in the strips and boil twenty minutes.

Lemon peel can be preserved in the same way, allowing more sugar.

Peach Butter.

Select very ripe peaches, peel, remove the pits, and mash them; have ready rich, sweet cider, reduced by boiling to the consistency of molasses (or four gallons to one); add to each gallon, after boiling, one pound of sugar; simmer the peaches in the cider and sugar until the whole is reduced to paste; allow a pint of the molasses and sugar, to three quarts of the mashed fruit. This is a southern mode of preserving peaches, and is very excellent; it is used in the same manner as cider apple sauce.

SAUCE, PRESERVES AND FRUIT JELLIES.

Apple Butter.

Boil down a kettleful of sweet cider to two-thirds the original quantity. Pare, core and slice juicy apples, and put as many into the cider as it will cover. Boil slowly, stirring often with a flat stick, and when the apples are tender to breaking, take them out with a perforated skimmer, draining well against the sides of the kettle. Put in some more apples, as many as the cider will hold, and stew them soft. Take from the fire, pour all together into a tub or large crock; cover and let it stand twelve hours. Then return to the kettle and boil down, stirring all the while, until it is the consistency of soft soap and brown in color; spice with cloves, allspice and cinnamon, if it is agreeable, being careful not to have one spice predominate over the others. Keep in stone jars, in a dry, cool place.

Preserved Watermelon Rinds.

Peel the melon, and boil in just enough water to cover it till it is soft, trying with a fork. (If you wish it green, put green vine leaves above and below each layer, and scatter powdered alum, less than ½ teaspoonful to each pound). Allow a pound of sugar to each pound of rind, made into a syrup; simmer the rinds two hours in this syrup, and flavor with lemon peel tied in a bag. Put the rinds in a dish, and boil the syrup till it looks thick, and pour over the rinds. Next day give the syrup another boiling, and add juice of one lemon, to each quart of syrup. Take care not to make it bitter by too much of the peel.

Citrons can be preserved in the same way. Both these keep through the hot weather with very little care in sealing and keeping.

Preserved Quinces and Sweet Apples.

Equal parts quinces and apples.
¾ of a pound of sugar to one of fruit.
Pare, quarter and core both quinces and apples. Cook

the quince (and apple if you wish) parings and cores in water sufficient to dissolve the sugar. Steam in a steamer the fruit, a little at a time, until it can be pierced with a straw. The quince will need much longer steaming than the apple, as it is very hard. When the syrup is scalding (not boiling), put the steamed fruit in it and let it remain till the next lot is ready and then put in the jar. It is better to put alternate layers of apple and quince. When the fruit is all scalded, pour over the syrup.

Blackberry Jam.

Boil and strain one-third of the berries you expect to use; add to this juice as many pints of sugar as you have pints of fruit remaining, and let it dissolve over the fire; put in the berries and let it cook until the juice is a jelly; mash the berries and take off; seal up in cans.

Raspberry Jam.

¾ pound of sugar to every pound of fruit.

Put the fruit on alone, or with the addition of a pint of currant juice to every four pounds of fruit. Boil half an hour, mashing and stirring well. Add the sugar, and cook twenty minutes more.

Strawberry Jam.

For every pound of fruit three-quarters of a pound of sugar.

1 pint red currant juice to every 4 pounds of strawberries.

Boil the juice of the currants with the strawberries half an hour, stirring all the time. Add the sugar, and boil up rapidly for about twenty minutes, skimming carefully. Put in small jars, with brandied tissue-paper over the top. The currant juice can be omitted, but the flavor will not be so fine.

SAUCE, PRESERVES AND FRUIT JELLIES.

GRAPE JAM.

Separate the skins from the pulp, keeping them in separate dishes; heat the pulp in a preserving kettle with a teacup of water; when heated through, press them through a colander to separate the seeds, add the skins to the pulp, and weigh; to each pound of fruit add three-fourths of a pound of sugar, and just enough water to keep from burning; cook slowly for three-quarters of an hour.

GOOSEBERRY JAM

Is made in the same manner as raspberry, only the currant juice is omitted, and the gooseberries are boiled one hour without the sugar, and another after it is put in. The fruit must be ripe.

CURRANT, BLACKBERRY, STRAWBERRY, ETC.

Put the fruit in a stone jar and set the jar in a kettle of tepid water over the fire. Keep it closely covered, and boil till the fruit is broken in pieces. Then strain, by pressing it through a stout coarse bag; do not put in but a few handfuls of fruit at a time, turn out the pulp, skins and seeds between each squeezing. To each pint of juice allow a pound of sugar. Set the juice on *alone* to boil, and while it is warming, put the sugar in shallow pans in the oven to heat; stir the sugar often to prevent burning. Boil the juice *twenty minutes* from the time it begins to boil. Throw the hot sugar into the boiling juice stirring rapidly. The sugar will "hiss" as it falls in and will quickly melt. If the sugar should be burned about the edges, it will form lumps which can easily be taken out. Take out the spoon when the sugar has dissolved. Let the jelly come to a boil, and take instantly from the fire. Roll your glass or cups in hot water, and fill with the hot liquid. If the jellies do not harden as well as you like, follow directions given in general directions for preserves and fruit jellies. Strawberry jelly should have a little lemon juice added to that of the fruit. Strawberry, raspberry and blackberry jellies are apt to be less firm than those made from more acid fruit, but do not boil.

Quince Jelly.

Pare and slice the quinces, and add for every five pounds of fruit a cup of water. Put peelings, cores, and all into a stone jar; set this in a pot of boiling water, and when the fruit is soft and broken, proceed as with other jellies.

Crab Apple Jelly.

Siberian crab apples are the best for jelly. Cut into pieces without paring or removing the seeds, as the latter give a pleasant flavor to the fruit. Put in a jar with very little water and place the jar in a kettle of hot water; let it boil eight hours. Leave in the jar over night closely covered; in the morning squeeze out the juice allowing for every pint of juice a pound of sugar, then proceed as with other jelly.

Currant Jelly.

Take ripe currants (gathered if possible when the weather has been dry a week), remove leaves and imperfect fruit without picking the currants off the stems, mash thoroughly, and strain through a strong cloth or jelly bag (much depends upon pressing out all the juice, as that which is expressed with the greatest difficulty is the best, and helps most in forming the jelly). To each pint of juice take one pound of sugar; put the juice into a porcelain kettle over the fire, and at the same time set the sugar into a not too hot oven to dry and heat; it should be stirred often to prevent browning. Heat the juice slowly, let it boil five minutes, and then stir in the hot sugar and boil together just one minute; remove from the fire and fill the glasses and bowls immediately, or the jelly will form before they can be filled.

Raspberry and Currant Jelly.

To four quarts red, or black raspberries, put two quarts of red currants; then proceed as with any other berry jelly. The flavor is delicious.

Green Grape Jelly

Is made like currant jelly, only allowing a pound and a half of sugar to a pint of juice.

Ripe grapes require but a pound for a pint.

Apple Jelly.

Take nice, green apples that will cook nicely; quarter the apples without paring, put them in a pan or kettle and cover over with water, and keep them covered; let them boil slowly until entirely done; then put in a bag and drain (not squeeze) them. Allow a pound of sugar to a pint of juice. This is very easily made in the winter.

Wild Plum Jelly.

Boil one gallon of plums in a quart of water, until they break open, then proceed as with other fruit. Allow one pound of sugar for one pint of juice. Boil the juice about fifteen minutes, then add the heated sugar and boil up.

Crab Apple Marmalade.

Stew the apples in just enough water to prevent them from burning. Rub them through a sieve as soon as they are soft, and to each pound of the pulp put a pound of white sugar. Return them to the kettle and stew slowly, stirring all the time until thick. Put a spoonful of the marmalade upon the ice; if it cuts smooth when perfectly cold, it is ready to take up.

Sweet Apple Marmalade.

This is made by boiling sweet apples alone in cider made of sweet apples, and boiled down so as to be very rich. Strain through a very coarse sieve or riddle, and boil again a little while.

WILD PLUM MARMALADE.

Strain the juice and pulp through a wire sieve; add as much sugar as you have strained pulp; boil well, stirring constantly to prevent burning to the kettle.

PEACH MARMALADE.

When the fruit is pared, stoned and weighed, heat slowly to draw out the juice, stirring up often from the bottom. After it is hot, boil quickly, still stirring, three quarters of an hour. Then add the sugar, allowing three-quarters of a pound to each pound of the fruit. Boil well for five minutes, removing every bit of scum. Add the juice of one lemon, for every three pounds of fruit, and the water in which one quarter of the kernels have been boiled and steeped. Stew altogether ten minutes, stirring to a smooth paste, and take from the fire. Spread tissue paper, wet with brandy, over the top of the marmalade.

PEAR MARMALADE.

6 good sized pears boiled to a pulp.
½ their weight in sugar made into a syrup.
Add the pulp and boil a few minutes. Put in four drops of essence of cloves. When cold it is ready for use.

QUINCE MARMALADE.

Peel, core, and slice the quinces, stewing the skins, cores and seeds in a vessel by themselves, with just enough water to cover them. When the flavor has been extracted, and the parings are broken to pieces, strain through a thick cloth. Put the quinces into the preserve kettle; when this water is almost cold pour it over them and boil, stirring and mashing the fruit with a wooden spoon as it becomes soft. Add the juice of two oranges to every three pounds of fruit. When all is reduced to a smooth paste, add a scant three-quarters of a pound of sugar for every pound of fruit; boil ten minutes more, stirring constantly. When cool, put into small jars, with brandied papers over them.

GRAPE MARMALADE.

Take the cooked grapes, rub through a fine colander, measure the pulp, and add the same amount of good coffee sugar. Cook until stiff; turn into cups, and cover with brandied paper.

CANNED FRUITS.

Canned fruits have within a few years taken the place of preserved fruits and are cheaper and much more wholesome and less difficult to prepare. A little attention will soon insure success in the art of canning fruit which for richness of flavor far surpasses the canned fruit which is sent out from the various factories.

If glass cans are used, which are much better for the purpose than tin ones, be careful to see that the rubber bands fit tight, and that there is no crack in the can. If they crack after the fruit is put in, the fruit will not keep; this may be prevented in almost every case by immersing the can in hot water and keeping them in it till you are ready to put the fruit in. When the fruit is sealed, wrap two or three papers round the cans to exclude the light, as the chemical action of light will change the quality and color of the fruit.

If tin cans are used, which are closed with rosin and soldering, they should be heated as glass cans when ready for the fruit, and care should be taken that no rosin drops through the aperture left in the top for the air to escape, as a single drop of rosin will often make the whole can bitter. Be careful in opening cans closed in this way that none of the rosin gets into the can. Cans can be easily closed with cement, the directions for which will be found elsewhere. Keep your cans, if glass or tin, in a cool, dark place. In canning fruit a good rule is to prepare a syrup of sugar and water, in proportion of one quarter of a pound of sugar to a pound of fruit; lay the fruit in, and bring to boiling heat; fill the cans full to overflowing, as the fruit will shrink as it cools, and instantly cover, then remove the cans from the hot water in which they have been standing, and when cool are ready to be packed away. A good way in large fruit, such as apples, pears, etc., is to put them in a steamer, with a cloth in the bottom, and steam until they can be pierced with a fork, have the syrup ready, dip each piece in it, and quickly fill the cans; when through, pour the hot syrup over the fruit and seal quickly, The amount of sugar to be used depends upon the acidity of the fruit. A wide mouthed tunnel and a small dipper with perpendicular handle facilitates all fruit canning very much.

Canned Berries.

Put in a large kettle, and heat slowly to boiling, then add sugar, in the proportion of one tablespoonful to each quart of fruit. If there is much juice in the kettle, dip out the surplus, and leave the berries nearly dry before adding the sugar, for there will be syrup enough. Boil together fifteen minutes, then can. Strawberries, raspberries, cherries, currants, blackberries, grapes, etc., put up in this way, make very nice pies, and are good eaten as preserves.

Canned Pine Apple.

6 pounds of fruit (after being cut).
2½ pounds of sugar.
3 pints of water.

Make a syrup of sugar and water and boil five minutes, and skim or strain if necessary. Then add the fruit, and let it boil up; have cans hot, fill and shut up as soon as possible. As the cans cool, keep tightening them up.

Canned Peaches.

The large free-stones are the best for this purpose. They should be ripe, but not soft. Pare, and extract the stone, breaking the fruit as little as possible. Allow a tablespoonful of sugar, or a little more to a pound of fruit. Put a very little water in the kettle to prevent the fruit from scorching, then fill with the fruit. Be sure that all is well heated through. A few kernels put in each can improves the flavor.

CANNED PLUMS.

Prepare a syrup, allowing a gill of water and one-fourth of a pound of sugar, for every pound of fruit. Dissolve the sugar and put in the plums; prick them to prevent bursting. Heat slowly to a boil. Boil five minutes, then fill the cans, and pour in the hot syrup and seal.

Green gages are nice canned in the same way.

CANNED PEARS.

Make a syrup, allowing a pint of water and a quarter of a pound of sugar to a pound of fruit. Peel the pears, and, if large, quarter and remove the cores, and drop them into water as soon as pared. As soon as the syrup comes to a boil, put in the pears and boil till they can be pierced with a fork, and look clear. Have the cans ready hot, and when filled with fruit, fill them with the hot syrup. If the pears are small and hard, they must be boiled in water until tender, before putting them in the hot syrup.

CANNED TOMATOES.

Pour boiling water over the tomatoes, to loosen the skins. Remove these, strain off all the juice that will come away without pressing hard; put them into a kettle and heat slowly to a boil. Your tomatoes will look much nicer if you remove all the hard parts before putting them on the fire, and rub the pulp soft with your hands. Boil ten minutes, dip out the surplus liquid, pour the tomatoes boiling hot into the cans, and seal. Keep in a cool, dark place.

ADDITIONAL RECIPES.

ADDITIONAL RECIPES.

CONFECTIONERY.

CLARIFICATION OF SUGAR.

Take the white of one egg for brown sugar, and one-half the white for white sugar. Put with the white of the egg one pint of water, and beat it to a froth; then put it in the kettle and turn the sugar on top, so that the water may pass through the sugar in rising. To twelve pounds of sugar take one quart of water. Stir it lightly to loosen the sugar. Put the kettle over the fire and stir once more. As soon as it boils add a little more water, take it from the fire and skim off the froth which will rise. Repeat the boiling and skimming till the froth is colorless.

BOILING SUGAR.

If a pound of refined sugar be dissolved in three gills of water, and clarified as above, it will in boiling pass through the various changes or degrees described in the succeeding part of the directions.

1st *Degree*, is called the *Thread* or *Lisse*. This is ascertained by dipping the finger first in cold water then into the hot sugar and quickly back into the cold water, when the sugar on the finger will stretch into a thread, the length of which depends on the length of time the sugar has been boiling.

2d *Degree* is *The Pearl*. This takes place when the sugar has been boiled a few minutes longer. Small bubbles will rise to the surface which look like pearls. These will increase in size and number the longer it is boiled. If tried as before, the thread will snap quickly when drawn out. Syrups are boiled to this degree.

3d Degree is *The Blow*. If the boiling is continued a few minutes longer, and the skimmer is dipped into the sugar and then blown upon, the sugar will form itself into small globules on the back, which gives the name to the degree.

4th Degree is *The Feather*. This degree is ascertained by dipping the skimmer into the sugar and shaking it, the sugar will form on the edge like a fringe.

5th Degree is *The Ball*. When, by dropping the sugar into cold water, it can be made into a ball by rolling it on the hand, it has reached this degree.

6th Degree is *The Crack*. This degree is reached when it has been boiled sufficiently that when tried as in the first degree, it will draw in a thread and break quickly, and be hard and dry. Taffy, lemon, twist and cream candies are boiled to this degree.

7th Degree is *The Caramel* or *Hard-baked*. As soon as the sugar begins to give out a strong, acid odor and grows more or less dark colored, it has reached this last degree. This is the degree for caramels and cocoanut candies.

When boiled hard enough, the candy is poured upon an oiled, marble slab, a smooth piece of thick tin will answer nearly as well, and then cut into small pieces, which are drawn out into sticks of the desired size. Candy lumps are made by cutting the sticks into small lumps with a sharp knife before they are cold.

FLAVORING AND COLORING.

The flavoring and coloring matter should never be *boiled*, but should be added just as it is about to be taken from the fire. Boiling destroys the fineness of the flavor, and brilliancy of the color. White candy may easily be stripped or decorated with colored designs, by taking a little of the syrup from the kettle while yet soft, and coloring as may be desired; then boil the remainder brittle, cut into lumps or sticks, and then stripe on the outside with the soft, colored candy.

All mineral substance, except pure ultra marine and

Prussian blue, are poisonous. Brilliant colors can be produced without using poisonous substances. For red, use cochineal, carmine or Brazil-wood; for blue, Prussian blue, blue lake, indigo precipitate and pure ultra marine; for yellow, saffron, marigold and turmeric. All of these, which are but a few of the many used, mix well to produce different shades, and are harmless. If one-half teaspoon of soda be used for one quart of molasses it will make that kind of candy much whiter and tenderer.

Everton Taffy.

3 ounces butter melted.
1 pound of brown sugar.
Grated rind of a lemon or teaspoon of ginger.

Boil the mixture over a clear fire until the syrup, when dropped into cold water, breaks between the teeth, without adhering to them. Fifteen minutes is usually long enough for boiling. Pour into buttered pans. If lemon peel is used, put it in when the sugar is half done; if ginger is used, stir it in when the sugar is dissolved.

Almond Taffy.

5 ounces butter, melted.
1 pound brown sugar.
2 ounces of almonds.

The almonds must be blanched, split and thoroughly dried in a slow oven. Peanuts, hickory nuts or cocoanut may be substituted for almonds. Lemon or rose water used for flavoring. Boil the mixture to caramel, then pour quickly into buttered pans. A single minute suffices to burn and spoil the candy at this stage.

Best White Molasses Candy.

1 pound granulated sugar.
1 pint Stewart's syrup.
Boil till quite thick when dropped into cold water.
Then add 1 pint best Porto Rico molasses.
3 or 4 tablespoonfuls vinegar.

Boil to the snap, remove from the fire and stir in quickly one-half a small tablespoonful soda, and flavor with essence of lemon. Pour on the slab and work white. This makes a better candy than that which is usually sold by confectioners. Good candy can be made in this way by using all Porto Rico molasses; it can also be made with no sugar.

CREAM CANDY.

½ pound loaf sugar.
1 gill water.
Set it over a slow fire for half an hour, then add
½ teaspoonful gum arabic (dissolved).
½ tablespoon of vinegar.
Boil till it is brittle, then take off and flavor to suit your taste, Rub the hands with sweet butter and pull the candy till it is white, after which cut in any shape desired.

COMMON LEMON CANDY.

1 pound of brown sugar (clarified).
Extract of lemon or lemon juice; if wanted especially sour use a little tartaric acid.
Peppermint, rose or hoarhound may be used instead of lemon. Boil till it is brittle, pour on buttered pans or on a slab, and cut it in sticks.

CARAMELS.

Boil clarified sugar till it is very brittle and has a slight odor of burning. Pour it on the slab. As soon as cool enough to receive an impression with the finger, stamping it in small squares, about an inch in size, with a caramel mould. Turn over the mass, wipe the bottom to remove any oil that may adhere to it, put it in a dry place to harden. If you have no caramel mould it can be scored with a knife, after which they are glazed with another coating of sugar. Caramels should be kept tightly closed.

Lemon Caramels.

Prepare the syrup as for caramels; when nearly done add the lemon which has been prepared by grating the yellow peel with a lump of sugar and to the grated peel a few drops of the juice with water enough to dissolve the sugar completely, stir this in a few minutes before taking from the fire. Orange and Lime caramels are prepared in the same way from these fruits.

Coffee Caramel.

2 ounces coffee.
1 pound sugar.

Make an infusion of the coffee using as little water as possible, strain it through a cloth and stir gradually into the boiled syrup a few minutes before taking it from the fire.

Chocolate Caramel.

½ pound chocolate.
2 cups sugar.
¼ cup milk.
Small lump of butter.

Scrape the chocolate in the milk, add it to the boiled sugar and stir in the butter, same as in coffee caramel.

Cream Coffee Caramels.

2 pounds sugar.
1 cup cream.
2 ounces butter.
2 ounces coffee.

Boil the sugar in a large sauce-pan to give room for expansion. As soon as it begins to bubble, stir in the cream very slowly; add next the butter, then the coffee infused with a little butter. Stir constantly over a good fire. When the syrup is brittle and has a slight odor of caramel, pour it on a slab, let it cool and imprint with a caramel mould.

Cream Chocolate Caramel.

2 pounds sugar.
4 ounces chocolate.
2 ounces butter.
1 cup cream.
Made the same as cream coffee caramel.

Ginger Candy Tablets.

1 pound loaf sugar.
Juice of half a lemon, or a few drops of acetic acid.
1 dessert spoonful essence of Jamaica ginger.

Take just enough water to dissolve the sugar, and boil it to the ball degree; then add the acid and essence. Rub the sugar with the back of the bowl of a silver spoon against the sides of the kettle, until it is whitened or grained, and somewhat resembles an opal in color. After the sugar has been so worked pour it immediately into very small moulds measuring half an inch or an inch square, a tin pan which is divided into small squares can be used; when the candy has dried, it can then be snapped apart into the tablets. Smear the moulds slightly with oil of almonds. The tablets should be dried hard under a screen for half an hour.

Vanilla Candy Tablets.

1 pound loaf sugar.
A few drops essence of vanilla.
A few drops acetic acid.
No color. Made same as ginger candy tablets.

Cinnamon Candy Tablets.

1 pound loaf sugar.
A few drops essence cinnamon.

Boil the sugar to the crack. This may be colored rose-pink. The color is added while the sugar is boiling.

Nut Candy.

2 cups sugar.
1 table spoon vinegar.
1 cup nuts.
Piece of butter size of a walnut.
Tartaric acid size of a small bean.

Boil twenty minutes, stirring all the time. Stir in the nuts when ready to pour out.

DRINKS.

TEA.

Tea consists of the prepared leaves of the tea plant, a hardy shrub which grows from three to six feet high, chiefly in China.

The plant is raised from the seed, and matures in from two to three years, yielding usually three crops of leaves each season. The leaves are picked by hand in May and June. The plant yields leaves from four to six seasons.

Many varieties of tea of all grades of quality are known in the market. These depend *first* upon the soil, climate, culture, etc., of the locality where it is grown. *Second*, upon the time of picking; the young leaves that are first gathered being tender and delicate, while the second and third are more bitter, tough and woody. *Third*, the mode of treatment or preparation, which consists in drying and roasting and rolling in the hand, by which the leaves acquire their twisted appearance, and finally, sifting and winnowing.

All the different varieties of tea are classed as either *green* or *black*. What constituted the real difference was long a matter of doubt. It was first supposed that they came from different species of plants, but the latest accounts agree that they come from the same species, but differ on account of being differently treated.

Green tea is cultivated in manured soil. The leaves are steamed, withered and roasted, almost immediately after gathering. They are dried quickly after the rolling process, the whole operation being brief and simple.

Black tea is grown chiefly on the slopes of hills and ledges of mountains. The leaves are allowed to be spread out in the air for some time after they are gathered, and are then tossed about until they become soft and flaccid, they are then roasted for a few minutes and rolled, after which they are exposed to the air a few hours, in a soft, moist state, and lastly, are slowly dried over a charcoal fire.

Green tea gives up much less of its juice in the drying process, which explains its more energetic action upon the nervous system.

The most important teas of commerce are arranged according to their grade, and price per pound paid for them in Canton:

GREEN TEAS.			BLACK TEAS.		
Twangay,	18 to 27	cts.	Bohea,	12 to 18	cts.
Hyson Skin,	18 " 30	"	Congou,	22 " 25	"
Young Hyson,	27 " 40	"	Campoi,	22 " 30	"
Hyson,	40 " 56	"	Souchong,	20 " 35	"
Imperial,	45 " 58	"	Caper,	20 " 40	"
Gunpowder,	45 " 60	"	Pekoe,	35 " 75	"

The Chinese method of making tea is to throw some tea into a cup and pour boiling water over it, then cover the cup with a shallow saucer, and let it rest for some time. After standing sufficiently they pour the clear liquid into a saucer and drink it hot. Various methods are pursued in different countries, but it is desirable to obtain from the leaves the largest amount of matter which water will extract and retain in the liquid, therefore the best plan is to pour boiling water upon the tea in a close vessel and let it gently heat for a few minutes.

Teas of all sorts are liable to the grossest adulterations. Green teas are extensively stained or painted by the Chinese to heighten their green color. Other leaves are often mixed with the tea leaves. A crude and worthless preparation of sweepings, dust, sand, leaves and other impurities of the tea warehouse, are cemented together with gum or rice water, which the Chinese honestly call *lie tea*, is employed to mix with other tea.

In England, exhausted leaves are bought up and their astringent property restored by the addition of catachu (a tanning extract), and colored with black lead, logwood, etc., and sold as genuine tea. These adulterations are carried on so extensively, that it is said we *never* get pure green tea.

To detect indigo or Prussian blue in tea, let a portion of it be shaken with cold water and thrown upon a bit of muslin, the fine coloring matter will pass through the muslin and settle to the bottom of the water. When the water is poured off, the blue matter may be treated with a solution of chloride of lime. If it is bleached, the coloring matter is indigo. If potash makes it brown, and afterwards a few drops of sulphuric acid make it blue again, it is Prussian blue.

Dr. Edward Smith says: "The conclusions at which we arrived after our researches in 1858, were that tea should not be taken without food, unless after a full meal; or with insufficient food, or by the young or very feeble, and that its essential action is to waste the system, or consume food by promoting vital action which it does not support, and they have not been disproved by any subsequent scientific researches." He also says: "The perceptible effects of full doses of tea, which are generally, if not universally, admitted are:

1st. A sense of wakefulness.

2d. Clearness of mind, and activity of thought and imagination.

3d. Increased disposition to muscular exertion.

4th. Reaction, with sense of exhaustion in the morning following the preceding efforts, and in proportion to them."

Tea is a strong narcotic, and like all other narcotics produces a morbid state of brain and nervous system. It is especially hurtful to persons of a nervous temperament, and to growing children of this constitution it should be strictly denied. Dr. Settson declares that it is the main cause of scrofula. Those to whom it is best suited are the plethoric and sanguine. It is used with benefit as a common drink at the commencement of fevers, and inflammatory complaints. Persons of gouty and rheumatic natures find weak tea one of the least objectionable of all drinks. Some cases of severe nervous headache may be relieved by a cup of strong green tea.

COFFEE.

The coffee plant was originally a native of Arabia and Abyssinia, but has been naturalized over a large part of the tropics. It is supposed to have been introduced into the new world by the French in 1717, who first planted it in the island of Martinique. On examining the present state of coffee production throughout the world, we find it has undergone great revolutions within the past thirty years.

Thus Brazil, which at the beginning of the century was hardly known in the coffee market, now furnishes nearly as much as all the rest of the world beside.

Java ranks next to Brazil among coffee producing countries. According to Agassiz, "more than half the coffee produced by the world is of Brazilian growth. And yet the coffee of Brazil has little reputation simply because a great deal of the best produce of Brazilian plantations is sold under the name of Mocha or Java, as coffee of Martinique or Bourbon. A great part of the coffee which is bought under those names, or under that of Java coffee, is Brazilian, while the so called Mocha coffee is often nothing but the small round beans of the Brazilian plant, found at the summit of the branches, and very carefully selected." The plant requires a deep, good soil, with plenty of moisture, and a temperature not lower than 65°, and is usually grown on a hillside very much after the manner of the tea plant.

The plant is very prolific for it remains in flower during eight months of the year, and produces a succession of crops of fruit, so that there are usually three harvests anually, but at the same time the fruit is in all stages of development, and the picking of it requires great care.

When left to a free growth of nature, the tree attains a hight of fifteen to twenty feet, but when cultivated, it is pruned so as to remain about six feet, by which process it throws out a large quantity of branches at its lower part, and produces more fruit. Its leaves are opposite, evergreen, and not unlike those of the bay tree. Its blossoms are white, resembling the flower of the jasmine. The fruit is called a bean, or berry, but the former is the more correct expression. The beans are in pairs, which are placed face to face in a hard, leathery skin, surrounded by a fleshy covering, somewhat resembling the cherry. After the thick pulp has been removed, the seeds are left in a cistern till fermentation sets in, the mucilage is then washed off, and the coffee is in a fit state to be taken to the drying ground.

Much of the superior quality of the coffee from Mocha is attributable to the slower method of drying, which is done by allowing the berries to remain in the sun; but in the larger plantations of Brazil, it is necessary to resort to quicker means of freeing the beans from their coverings, which is performed by machinery.

The object of roasting is not only to make it more easy to crush or grind but also to create or develop an aromatic volatile oil, and care must be taken in the roasting that the good effects of the latter may not be destroyed by burning the substance of the bean. The natural color of the bean is a dull, pale green, but in roasting, it acquires three colors according to the degree, viz: yellowish-brown, chestnut-brown and black. The proper degree of roasting is that of chestnut-brown, and when the color approaches black, it gives a burnt, dry flavor to the infusion.

The modes of preparing the beverage are almost infinite, but all should combine two principles, namely, to extract the greatest amount of aroma and body, and to render the fluid quite clear and separate from the grounds.

Ground coffee is very extensively adulterated. Various substances are employed for this purpose, as roasted peas, beans and corn, and dried and roasted roots, such as turnips, carrots, potatoes, etc. But the most common adulterant is chiccory, a plant of the dandelion tribe, which has a large, white, parsnip-like root abounding in a bitter juice.

Cheats in coffee may be quite easily detected by pouring cold water upon the coffee, if pure, the liquid acquires color very slowly, and does not become very deep after remaining in the water for a considerable time. If chiccory root is used, it quickly becomes a deep brown, and in a short time becomes very dark; with boiling water the change is more quickly seen. The mixture of burnt and ground peas and beans is not so quickly seen, and the most certain method is by examining the coffee through a microscope.

Coffee acts upon the brain as a stimulant, inciting it to increased activity, and producing sleeplessness; hence it is of great value as an antidote to narcotic poisons. Coffee, unlike tea, does not increase the vaporising action of the skin, but decreases it, and therefore dries the skin. It increases the action of the heart, and the fullness of the pulse, and excites the mucous membranes. It is more fitted than tea for the poor and feeble. It is also more fitted for breakfast, inasmuch as the skin is active, and the heart's action feeble; whilst in good health and with sufficient food, it is not needful after dinner; but if drank should be taken soon after the meal. There probably is not the same degree of reaction after taking strong coffee as follows strong tea, and none of these effects may be marked, if the infusion be very weak.

Cocoa and Chocolate.

These are closely allied to tea and coffee, as respiratory excitants, and are valuable as food, as they possess a large amount of fat, which is its chief nutritive element, as well as other food materials.

Chocolate is produced from the seeds of the cocoa palm. The seeds are inclosed in a fruit somewhat resembling the cucumber in size. They are about the size of an almond, and when extracted are reduced to a powder, after which they are mixed with sugar and rolled into a very thick paste, which takes the name chocolate.

Cocoa nibs are the nuts roughly broken, and may be boiled in that state, but it is necessary to boil them for several hours to extract the strength from them.

COFFEE. (*To Make.*)

Delmonico uses one and one-half pounds of coffee to a gallon of water, pouring the hot water on the coffee which is placed on a strainer. The coffee is never boiled. Another method, better adapted for family use, is to allow one heaping tablespoonful of ground coffee for every person, and if wished quite strong, two extra spoonfuls for the pot. Mix with the ground coffee a part or whole of an egg, according to the amount made. Pour over half as much water as you need. Let the coffee froth up, then stir down the grounds and let it boil three minutes; then set it where it will keep hot—not boil—for fifteen or twenty minutes longer. Those who use the "National Coffee Pot" need to keep it over the fire a longer time, and will have most delicately flavored coffee. A mixture of three-fourths Java and one-fourth Mocha is a most excellent mixture. Keep the coffee closely covered when making.

TEA. (*To Make.*)

Allow one teaspoonful of tea to each cup. Have the water in the teakettle *boiling* when poured on the tea. Cover the teapot closely, and let it set where it will keep hot ten or fifteen minutes, then add more boiling water. Keep the teapot sweet and clean.

CHOCOLATE. (*To Make.*)

6 tablespoonfuls grated chocolate to each pint of water, with the same quantity of milk as water. Sweeten to taste. Rub the chocolate smooth in cold water. Pour on the water boiling hot. Boil twenty minutes and then add the milk and boil ten minutes longer. The sugar can be added to the chocolate on the fire or in the cups.

Cocoa Nibs or Shells.

Wet the shells in a little cold water. Use one cupful of shells for one quart of water, which must be boiling. Cook one hour or more and then add a quart of milk. Let it heat to nearly boiling, and then take from the fire.

Hop Beer.

One handful of hops, boil one hour, strain, and add one pint of molasses, and enough water to make two gallons. When milk-warm, add one cup or cake of yeast; let it stand over night; skim, and pour it off from the yeast carefully; add one tablespoonful of wintergreen, or any other flavoring, and bottle for use.

Spruce and Boneset Beer.

Boil a small handful each of hops and boneset for an hour or two, in a pailful of water; strain it, and dilute it with cold water until it is of the right strength. Add a small tablespoonful of essence of spruce, sweeten, ferment and bottle it, like the spring beer.

The essences of hops, checkerberry, ginger and spruce, put into warm water in suitable proportions, then sweetened, fermented and bottled, make good beer.

Jamaica Ginger Beer.

1½ ounces of Jamaica ginger extract.
1 ounce cream tartar.
1 pound of sugar.
4 quarts of boiling water.
2 lemons sliced thin.

Stir until the sugar is melted. Let it cool to a blood heat, then add two gills of good yeast, and let it work for twenty-four hours, then bottle. It improves by keeping several weeks, unless the weather is hot.

Spring Beer.

Take a handful of checkerberry (wintergreen), a few sassafras roots cut up, half a handful of pine-buds, while they are small and gummy, and a small handful of hops. Put all these into a pail of water over night, and in the morning boil them two or three hours; fill up the kettle when it boils away. Strain it into a jar or firkin that will hold a half pailful more of water. Stir in a pint and a half of molasses, then add the half pailful of water. If not sweet enough add more molasses. It loses the sweetness a little in the process of fermentation, and should be made rather too sweet at first. Add two or three gills of good yeast, set it in a warm place, and let it remain undisturbed till it is fermented. When the top is covered with a thick dark foam, take it off; pour off the beer into another vessel, so gently as not to disturb the sediment; then bottle it, and set it in a cool place. It will be ready for use in two days. The sediment should be put into a bottle by itself, loosely corked, and kept to ferment the next brewing.

Lemonade.

3 lemons to a quart of water.
6 tablespoonfuls of sugar.

Pare the yellow peel from the lemons, and unless you intend to use the drink immediately, leave it out. It gives a bitter taste to the sugar if left long in it. Slice and squeeze the lemons upon the sugar, add a very little water, and let them stand fifteen minutes. Then fill up with water; ice well.

Orangeade

Is made in the same manner, substituting oranges for lemons.

Egg Nogg.

6 eggs, whites and yolks beaten separately, and very stiff.

1 quart rich milk.
½ cup of sugar.
½ pint of best brandy.
Flavor with nutmeg.

Stir the yolks into the milk with the sugar, which should first be beaten with the yolks. Next comes the brandy. Lastly whip in the whites of three eggs.

BLACKBERRY WINE.

Measure your berries and bruise them; to every gallon add one quart of boiling water. Let the mixture stand twenty-four hours, stirring occasionally; then strain into a cask. To each gallon add two pounds of sugar, stir until well dissolved. Cork tightly and let it stand in your cellar one year before you open it for use.

BLACK CURRANT WINE.

Pick the currants, measure them, and to every four quarts, put one quart water; then break the currants, add the water, stir them up, let them stand three days; then squeeze out the juice, and to each quart add one pound of sugar, put in a vessel and let it work. Skim it frequently, and when it is clear, cork it up, and in the course of five months draw off and bottle.

RAISIN WINE.

1½ pounds of white sugar.
2½ pounds raisins, seeded and chopped.
2 lemons, all the juice and half the grated peel.
2½ gallons boiling water.

Put all into a stone jar, and stir every day for a week. Strain, then, and bottle it.

CHERRY WINE.

1 gallon of bruised cherries.
1 gallon of rain water.
5 pounds of sugar.

Let the cherries and water stand twenty-four hours, strain and add the sugar. Let it stand three weeks, strain again and bottle.

Currant Wine.

Pick, stem, mash and strain the currants, which should be very ripe.
To 1 quart of juice add
¾ pound white sugar.
½ pint of water.
Stir all together long and well; put into a clean cask, leaving out the bung, and covering the hole with a bit of lace or mosquito net. Let it ferment about four weeks, rack off when it is quite still, and bottle.

Rhine Wine.

Take one gallon of the Rhine variety of black grapes; or if you cannot get them, use the real Delaware grapes; and add one gallon of water, after bruising the grapes. Let it stand for eight days and then draw it off; now add to each gallon of wine three pounds of sugar, stirring it in. Let it stand ten or twelve hours, when it can be bottled or barreled for use. If allowed to stand for a sufficient length of time, it will in every respect prove equal to the imported wine.

Elderberry Wine.

8 quarts of berries.
4 quarts of boiling water poured over the berries.
Let it stand twelve hours, stirring now and then. Strain well, pressing out all the juice. Add
3 pounds of sugar to 4 quarts of juice.
1 ounce of powdered cinnamon.
½ ounce of powdered cloves.
Boil five minutes, and set away to ferment in a stone jar, with a cloth thrown lightly over it. When it has done fermenting, rack it off carefully, not to disturb the lees. Bottle and cork it well.

Raspberry Shrub. No. 1.

Cover the raspberries with best vinegar, and lay over night. In the morning mash the berries, and squeeze through a coarse bag. To every pint of the juice, add one pound of sugar. Boil twenty minutes; when cool, bottle. This will make quite a thick syrup, which must be diluted with water when drank.

Raspberry Shrub. No. 2

Fill a jar with red raspberries; pour in as much vinegar as it will hold. Let it stand ten days, then strain it through a sieve. Don't press the berries, but let the juice run through. To every pint add one pound of loaf sugar. Boil it like other syrup; skim, and bottle when cold.

Blackberry Shrub

Is made in the same manner as raspberry, allowing one pound and a quarter of sugar to a pint of the juice.

Blackberry Syrup.

1 pint of juice.
1 pound of white sugar.
½ ounce of powdered cinnamon.
¼ ounce of mace.
2 teaspoonfuls cloves.
1 glass of best French brandy to every pint of the mixture.

Procure perfectly ripe high blackberries, as they have more of the medicinal quality than the low berries. Put them in a porcelain-lined kettle over a moderate fire. Let them remain until they break in pieces; then mash and strain through a flannel bag. Boil all together (except the brandy) for fifteen minutes, stirring occasionally; then strain the syrup again, and add the brandy. Put into bottles, cork and seal them tight, and keep in a cool place. This syrup, mixed with cold water, is an excellent remedy for bowel complaint.

*Strawberry Sherbet.

1 quart of strawberries.
3 pints of water.
Juice of 1 lemon.
1 tablespoonful orange-flower water.
¾ pound white sugar.

Select fresh and ripe strawberries. Crush to a smooth paste; add the rest of the ingredients (except the sugar), and let it stand three hours. Strain over the sugar, squeezing the berries through a cloth hard; stir until the sugar is dissolved, strain again and set on ice for two hours or more before you use it.

HYGIENIC EFFECT OF DRINKS.

[For Hygienic Effects of Tea and Coffee, see pps. 280 and 283.]

ALCOHOLIC.

All alcoholic drinks are the result of the decomposition of sugar. Nature will only assimilate such substances as come to her in an organized state. Alcohol has the same elements as sugar—carbon, hydrogen and oxygen—but the latter being organized for digestion, is agreeable to the taste, and is readily appropriated as heating food, while alcohol, being disorganized, creates rebellion and is expelled as an intruder. Alcoholic stimulants may be beneficial, however, in rare cases, to give strength till natural food can be taken and digested, but if continued longer, react, and produce only harm.

BEER AND LIGHT WINES

are less injurious, as many of the elements have not become sufficiently disorganized so but that much nutriment in the form of sugary and starchy matter is supplied to the system. But this might better be taken in any other form without the deleterious element always entering with them—that of alcohol.

COCOA

is supplied with all the requisite elements of food, and to those who like its flavor it is a very agreeable and useful beverage, having all the advantages of tea and coffee without their deleterious qualities. Its nutritive elements are, however, too concentrated to agree with very delicate stomachs.

It contains a large share of oily matter with four per cent. of phosphates and also some albumen.

THE SICK ROOM.

Milk Porridge.

1 tablespoonful Indian meal, and
1 tablespoonful white flour wet to a paste with cold water.
2 cups boiling water.
2 cups milk.
A *good* pinch of salt.
Boil the paste in the hot water twenty minutes; add the milk and cook ten minutes more, stirring often.

Corn Meal Gruel.

2 quarts of boiling water.
1 cup of Indian meal, and
1 tablespoonful flour, wet up with cold water.
Salt to taste, and, if you like, sugar and nutmeg.
Wet the flour and meal to a smooth paste, and stir into the water while it is boiling. Boil slowly half an hour, stirring up well from the bottom. If a cathartic is desired omit the wheat flour altogether.
Oat meal gruel is made in the same way.

Rice Flour Gruel.

Make this exactly like Indian meal gruel, using less of the rice flour than of the Indian meal for the same quantity.

Flour Gruel.

Tie a teacup of flour in a strong cloth, and boil it six hours; when it is done it will be a hard cake of flour; dry it, and grate a large teaspoonful, mix it in paste with cold water, and stir it in boiled milk; let the gruel boil gently ten minutes, and add salt. This is excellent for patients suffering with bowel complaints.

Barley Gruel.

Boil pearl barley until tender, reduce it to a pulp, pass it through a sieve, add water until of the right consistency, boil fifteen minutes and season to suit the taste.

Rice Jelly.

½ cup whole rice, well washed and soaked two hours in a little warm water; then added with the water to that in the kettle.
3 pints cold water.
1 small pinch of salt put into the water.
Sweeten to taste with loaf sugar.

Simmer the rice half an hour; then boil until it is a smooth paste, and the water is reduced one half. Strain through double tarletan, sweeten and give to the child. This is an admirable preparation for an infant suffering with weakness of the bowels. If there is no fever, you may put one-third part milk, boiled with the rice.

Arrowroot.

1 cup boiling water.
1 cup fresh milk.
2 teaspoonfuls best Bermuda arrowroot, wet with cold water.
1 *small* pinch of salt.
2 even teaspoonfuls white sugar dissolved in the milk.

Stir the arrowroot paste into the salted boiling water; stir and boil five minutes, or until it is clear; add the sweetened milk, and boil ten minutes slowly, still stirring.

Farina.

1 cup boiling water.
1 cup fresh milk.
1 large tablespoonful Hecker's Farina, wet with cold

2 teaspoonfuls white sugar.
A little salt.

Stir the farina into the boiling water (slightly salted) in the farina kettle (i. e. one boiler set within another, the latter filled with hot water). Boil fifteen minutes, stirring constantly until well thickened. Then add the milk, stirring it in gradually, and boil fifteen minutes longer. You may make enough in the morning to last all day; warming it up with a little hot milk as you want it. Keep in a cold place. This is very nice for children.

BEEF TEA.

Chop a pound of lean beef as fine as sausage meat; pour on it a pint of cold water, let it soak for half an hour, then put it over a slow fire; when it has boiled five minutes, pour it off and season with salt.

MUTTON BROTH.

1 pound lean mutton or lamb, cut small.
1 quart cold water.
1 tablespoonful rice, or barley, soaked in a very little warm water.
4 tablespoonfuls milk.
Salt and pepper, with a little chopped parsley.

Boil the meat, unsalted, in the water, keeping it closely covered until it falls to pieces. Strain it out, add the soaked barley or rice, simmer half an hour, stirring often; stir in the seasoning and the milk, and simmer five minutes after it heats up well, taking care it does not burn. Serve hot.

CHICKEN BROTH

Is excellent made in the same manner as mutton, cracking the bones well before you put in the fowl.

CHICKEN JELLY.

Half a raw chicken pounded with a mallet, bones and meat together.

Plenty of cold water to cover it well—*about* a quart.

Heat slowly in a covered vessel, and let it simmer until the meat is in white rags, and the liquid reduced one-half. Strain and press, first through a colander, then through a coarse cloth. Salt to taste, and pepper, if you think best; return to the fire, and simmer five minutes longer. Skim when cool. Give to the patient cold, just from the ice. You can make into sandwiches by putting the jelly between thin slices of bread spread lightly with butter.

Toast Water.

Slices of toast, nicely browned, without a symptom of burning.

Enough boiling water to cover them.

Cover closely, and let them steep until cold. Strain the water, sweeten to taste, and put a piece of ice in each glassful. If the physician thinks it safe, add a little lemon juice.

Jelly Water.

1 large teaspoonful currant or cranberry jelly.
1 goblet ice water.

Beat up well, for a fever patient. Wild cherry or blackberry jelly is excellent, prepared in like manner, for those suffering with summer complaint.

Apple Water.

1 large juicy pippin, the most finely flavored you can get.

3 cups cold water, 1 quart, if the apple is very large.

Pare and quarter the apple, but do not core it. Put it on the fire in a tin or porcelain saucepan with the water, and boil, closely covered, until the apple stews to pieces. Strain the liquor *at once,* pressing the apple hard in the cloth. Strain this again through a finer bag, and set away to cool. Sweeten with white sugar, and ice for drinking. It is a refreshing and palatable drink.

Milk Punch.

1 tumbler milk, well sweetened.
2 tablespoonfuls best brandy, well stirred in.

Patients in a very low condition have been kept alive for days at a time by this drink, until nature could rally her forces. Give cold with ice.

ADDITIONAL RECIPES.

ADDITIONAL RECIPES.

MISCELLANEOUS.

Cure for Burns and Scalds.

The first thing to be done is to remove the clothes, if the body is scalded. Then apply a thick layer of flour, and when it falls off lay on more. The object is to shield the wound from the air. Cotton wool is another good application. Lay a thick fold of it on, and then wet with good sweet oil; let the cotton remain until a new skin is formed. A soft bandage should be put outside the cotton. If the cotton is removed for the sake of putting on fresh, there will be a scar; if suffered to remain as directed, there will be no scar.

To Clean Kid Gloves.

1 drachm carbonate of ammonia.
1 drachm chloroform.
1 drachm sulphuric ether.
1 pint deodorized benzine.

Wash the glove in a little of the mixture, as you would a piece of cotton; then slip it on your hand while wet, and wipe with a clean, soft cloth, until thoroughly dry. Let them hang in the air awhile to remove the unpleasant odor of the benzine. They will be soft and pliable and look nearly as well as new.

Prepared Glycerine for the Hands.

Equal parts of glycerine, camphor and ammonia.

To Prepare Earth for House Plants.

Put together equal parts of the three following things, soil from the sides of a barnyard, well-rotted manure, and leaf mould from the woods, or earth from the inside of an old tree or stump. Add a small quantity of sand. For cactuses put as much sand as of the other materials and a little fine charcoal.

To Wash Silk.

1 tablespoonful honey.
1 tablespoonful soft soap.
2 cups of cold water.
1 wineglass of alcohol.

Mix and shake up well; lay a breadth of the silk at a time on a table, and sponge both sides with this, rubbing it well in; shake it well up and down in a tub of cold water; flap it as dry as you can, but do not wring it. Hang it by the edges, not the middle, until fit to iron. While it is very damp, iron on the wrong side. Dark silks may be treated in this way.

To Clean Black Silk.

Into one quart of water put a black kid glove and boil down to a pint; sponge the silk with this, and iron on the wrong side while damp.

To Clean Alpaca.

Sponge the alpaca with spirits of ammonia and water, and iron on the wrong side while damp.

To Renew Wrinkled Crape.

Stretch over a basin of boiling water, holding it smooth, but not tight, over the top, and shifting as the steam fairly penetrates it. Fold, while damp, in the original creases, and lay under a heavy book or board to dry. It will look nearly as well as new.

To Restore the Pile of Velvet.

Wet on the wrong side; let some one hold a hot iron bottom upward, and pass the wet side of the velvet slowly over the flat surface. When the steam rises thickly through to the right side, it will raise the pile with it.

To Curl Tumbled Feathers.

Hold over the top of a hot stove, but not near enough to burn; withdraw, shake them out, and hold them over it again until curled.

To Clean Straw Matting.

Wash with a cloth dipped in clean salt and water; then wipe dry at once. This prevents it from turning yellow.

To Remove Paint from Windows.

Rub the paint spots with spirits of ammonia, or with a copper cent.

To Remove Fruit Stains.

Hold the stained article, before it has been wet, tightly over a bucket or tub, and pour boiling water upon the spots until they disappear. Do not allow the fabric to touch the water below.

To Remove Iron Rust and Ink Stains.

Oxalic acid is infallible in removing iron rust and ink stains. Use in the proportion of one ounce to a quart of soft water. The article must be spread with this mixture, over the steam of hot water, wetting occasionally. It will remove indelible ink and other stains. It is very poisonous, and must be kept in a bottle corked. Wash the article afterward, or the liquor will injure it. This will apply only to white goods, as the acid will change the color of colored goods.

To Remove Iron Mould.

If the mould is fresh and not very dark, tie up a teaspoonful of cream tartar in the moulded place, and put it into cold water without soap, and boil it half an hour.

To Destroy Rats and Mice.

Take equal quantities of rye meal and unslacked lime, mix them without adding any water. Put small quantities in places infested by rats; they will devour it, be thirsty, and the water they drink slackens the lime and destroys them.

To Remove Grease.

For grease spots of any kind, benzine or gasoline are much used, applied with a small sponge or linen rag. They do not injure any colors, but they have to be used with a good deal of perseverance, or they will spread the spot without removing it. Tailors use equal parts of alcohol and ammonia to clean coats and pants, and nothing is better. For very nice articles, chloroform is better than anything else; it will remove all kinds of grease, paint or varnish. Magnesia or powdered French chalk rubbed on the wrong side, will often remove grease spots.

To Remove Tar.

Rub well with clean lard, afterwards wash with soap and warm water. Apply this to either hands or clothing.

Camphor Ice.

1 ounce of lard, or sweet oil.
1 ounce of spermaceti.
1 ounce of camphor.
1 ounce of almond oil.
½ cake of white wax.
Melt and turn into moulds.

To Remove Discoloration from Bruises.

Apply a cloth wrung out in very hot water, and renew frequently until the pain ceases. Or apply raw beefsteak.

For Sudden Hoarseness.

Roast a lemon in the oven, turning now and then, that all sides may be equally cooked. It should not crack or burst, but be soft all through. Just before going to bed take the lemon (which should be very hot), cut a piece from the top, and fill it with as much white sugar as it will hold. Eat all the sugar, filling the lemon with more, as you find it becoming acid. This simple remedy induces gentle perspiration, besides acting favorably upon the clogged membranes of the throat.

Perspiration.

The unpleasant odor produced by perspiration may be removed by putting a spoonful of spirits of ammonia in a basin of water and bathing in this. This is especially good for bathing the feet.

White Soap for Toilet Use.

6 pounds of washing soda.
6 pounds of lard or fat.
3 pounds unslacked lime.
1 teacupful of salt.
5 gallons of soft water.

Put the soda and lime in a tub and pour over them the water boiling hot. Stir to dissolve. Let it stand until clear and all dissolved; then pour off the clear liquid. Add the fat and salt, and boil four hours, then pour into pans to cool. Should it be inclined to curdle or separate, if the lime be too strong, pour in water and boil over again.

To Clean Flat-Irons.

Tie up a piece of yellow beeswax in a rag, and when the iron is almost, but not quite hot enough to use, rub it quickly with the wax, and then with a coarse cloth.

Stove Polish.

Stove lustre, when mixed with turpentine and applied in the usual manner, is blacker, more glossy, and more durable than when mixed with any other liquid. The turpentine prevents rust, and when put on an old, rusty stove will make it look as well as new.

Cleaning Pots, Kettles and Tins.

Boil a double handful of hay or grass in a new iron pot, before attempting to cook with it; scrub with soap and sand, then set on full of clear water and let it boil half an hour. After this it can be used with safety. As soon as a pot or frying-pan is emptied of that which has been cooked in it, fill with hot or cold water, and set back upon the fire to scald thoroughly. New tins should stand near the fire, with boiling water in them, in which has been dissolved a spoonful of soda, for an hour; then be scoured with soft soap, afterwards rinsed with hot water. Use sifted wood ashes or whiting for cleaning them. Copper utensils should be cleaned with brick-dust and flannel.

Starch.

To Make the Starch. Dissolve three tablespoonfuls of the best starch in cold water; stir it very fast into a quart of boiling water; boil a few minutes. Five minutes before it is done stir in a piece of spermaceti the size of a walnut, and stir till it is well mixed.

Starching. As soon as you can bear your hands in the starch dip the linen in, and be careful to rub the starch into every part, or you will have blisters in the bosom. Fold the shirts so as to bring the two bosoms together, and fold the collars in a dry towel. Let them lie over night.

A bosom board is an indispensable article, and is made by taking a board eight inches by eighteen, and covering one side with three thicknesses of flannel fastened to the edge with small tacks; then cover the flannel with three thicknesses of cotton cloth, sewed on tight and perfectly smooth.

Iron the shirt and bosom on the board; when the bosom is dry, brush it over with water till slightly damp, and then with a polishing iron (which can be got at any hardware store) rub the surface of the linen hard until you have a fine polish. If the irons are rough, rub them over with salt or smear the face slightly with beeswax, which must be cleaned off before using. The pan used for starch should not be used for any thing else.

COLD STARCH.

Dissolve three tablespoonfuls of starch in a pint of cold water. Dip the linen in and thoroughly wet every part; then *rinse* the articles starched, in clear water to take *off* the starch which will adhere to the linen. Do not be afraid to rinse the linen well, for it will be stiff enough when ironed. They may be ironed in ten or fifteen minutes, but should not be allowed to remain in the cloths longer, as they will not iron well. Lay a thin cloth upon them when you pass the iron over the first time. The irons should be quite hot. This mode of starching is preferred by many persons to the use of boiled starch. The starch which is not taken up by the linen, will settle in the water and can be used again.

TO CLEAN HAIR BRUSHES.

Put a few drops spirits of ammonia in soft water and dip the bristles in, taking care not to wet the handles. Soda can be used instead of ammonia. Combs can be cleaned in this mixture.

PATENT SOAP.

5 pounds hard soap.
1 quart of ley.
¼ ounce of pearlash.
Place on the fire and stir well until the soap is dissolved; add
½ pint spirits of turpentine.
1 gill hartshorn.
Stir well; it is then fit for use. The finest muslin may be put to soak in this suds, and if left for a time will be

come very white. A small portion of this soap put in a little hot water, and a flannel cloth, will save labor and a brush in cleaning paint.

Soap Made with Potash.

Allow sixteen pounds each of grease and potash for a barrel of soap. The grease should be such as has been well taken care of, viz: tried before it became wormy and mouldy. The color of the potash should be about that of pumice stone. That which is red makes dark soap unfit for washing clothes. Cut the grease into pieces of two or three ounces, put it into a tight barrel with the potash, then pour in two pailfuls of rain water. The soap will make sooner if the water is hot, but will be as good made of cold. Add a pailful of soft water every day until the barrel is half full, and stir well each day. When the barrel is half full add no more water for a week, but stir it daily. After that add a pailful a day until the barrel is full. It is better to keep soap three or four months before using it, it spends more economically, and is less sharp to the hands. When half of it has been used, put two pails of soft water to the rest, and stir up well from the bottom; the lower half is always the strongest. It is good economy to make soap, and it is so little work to make it with potash, and the result is so sure, that no one need be deterred from it by the fear of trouble or ill success.

Tooth Powder. No. 1.

2 ounces of Peruvian bark.
2 ounces of myrrh.
1 ounce of chalk.
1 ounce Armenian bole.
1 ounce orris root.

Tooth Powder. No. 2.

Equal parts of orris root, pulverized pumice stone and prepared chalk. Use once a week.

Wash for the Teeth.

One ounce of myrrh, powdered and dissolved in one pint of spirits of wine. A little of this dropped on the tooth brush is excellent for the teeth and gums.

To Keep Suet.

Pull off the skin or membrane from fresh suet, sprinkle salt upon it, tie it up in a cloth or bag, and hang it in a cool dry place. It will keep sweet the year round.

To Clear Sugar.

Dissolve in hot water a little gum arabic and isinglass; pour it into sugar when boiling and all sediment will rise to the top of the pan to be skimmed off.

To Cleanse Lard or Butter.

Rancid lard or butter may be purified and made sweet for cooking purposes by trying it over with a little water added and a few sliced raw potatoes.

Crackers.

Crackers, after being kept for some time, lose their tenderness and delicacy. To renew these qualities, put the crackers into a broad shallow pan, and let them stand in a moderately hot oven for half an hour. Upon taking them out, they will be fresh and crisp.

To Clean Furniture.

An old cabinet maker says the best preparation for cleaning picture frames and restoring furniture, especially that somewhat marred or scratched, is a mixture of three parts linseed oil and one part spirits of turpentine. It not only covers the disfigured surface, but restores wood to its natural color, and leaves a lustre upon its surface. Put on with a woolen cloth, and when dry rub with woolen.

Papering Whitewashed Walls.

To make paper stick to whitewashed walls, make a sizing of common glue and water, of the consistency of linseed oil, and apply with whitewash or other brush to the walls, taking care to go over every part, and especially the top and bottom. Apply the paper as soon as you please, in the ordinary way, and if the paste is properly made it will remain firm for years.

Rules for Keeping Goldfish.

1. Have the diameter of the globe at least five times the fish's length.
2. Change the water no oftener than three times a week, and have it moderately warm.
3. In changing, lift the fish in a cup or linen net; never in the hand.
4. Feed with fine bread crumbs, and the yolks of eggs boiled hard and powdered.
5. Furnish the globe with water-plants, to give refreshing shadow, to purify the water and afford food.

The following weeds are procurable in fresh water ponds: Water Starwort, Water Milfoil, Ditch Moss, Eel Grass, Pennywort, Hornweed, Duckweed. The Duckweed is especially liked for its seeds.

To Purify a Sink or Drain.

Dissolve a pound or two of chloride of lime in plenty of water, and pour down; or use carbolate of lime.

The Best Deodorizer.

Use bromo-chloralum in the proportion of one tablespoonful to eight of soft water; dip cloths in this solution and hang in the rooms; it will purify sick-rooms of any foul smells. The surface of anything may be purified by washing well and then rubbing over with a weakened solution of bromo-chloralum. It is an excellent wash for sores and wounds that have an offensive odor.

To Soften Old Putty or Paint.

Soft soap mixed with a solution of potash or caustic soda; or pearlash and slacked lime mixed with sufficient water to form a paste. Either of these may be applied with a brush or rag, and when left for some time will render its removal easy.

Cement for Fastening Wood and Stone.

Melt together four parts of pitch and one part of wax; then add four parts of powdered brick-dust or chalk. It must be warmed before use, and thinly applied to the surfaces to be joined.

Sealing Wax.

6½ pounds of rosin.
½ pound of beeswax.
1½ pounds of Venetian red.
Melt all together.

To Remove Bottle Stoppers.

A few drops of ammonia will loosen glass stoppers in jars or bottles.

To Make Hens Lay.

Give one teaspoonful powdered cayenne pepper every other day, to every dozen fowls.

Antidotes for Poison.

For *any* poison swallow instantly a glass of cold water with a heaping teaspoonful of common salt and one of ground mustard stirred in. This is a speedy emetic. When it has acted, swallow the whites of two raw eggs. If you have taken corrosive sublimate, take half a dozen raw eggs besides the emetic. If laudanum, a cup of *very* strong coffee. If arsenic, first the emetic, then half a cup of sweet oil or melted lard.

ARRANGING THE TABLE.

SHAPE AND SIZE OF TABLE.

Regarding the setting of the table, and the serving of the food we start with the supposition that the ordinary oval "extension" table is used. Some authors recommend a circular table about five feet in diameter, and think this plenty large for six or even eight persons. This would do well if all the dishes were to be carved and served by the servant in what is known as the Russian style. But most Americans, with Addison, do not like all their food both bestowed and distributed like rations to paupers. And then, too, we like plenty of room—elbow-room—at table. Be sure that you have the table large enough so that not only the guests need not jostle or crowd each other, but that you may have sufficient room to arrange the dishes with taste, and also to place such ornaments upon the table as are needed to give it a bright and cheery look. Nothing looks more vulgar and unpleasant than a crowded or overloaded table devoid of ornaments, so do not not fail to provide plenty of room for dishes and ornaments.

TABLE LINEN.

Too much cannot be said about the pleasant effect produced by having the linen of the most spotless whiteness.

There should be a thick baize placed under the table-cloth. It prevents noise, and the heaviest table-linen will look comparatively thin and sleazy when placed upon a bare table. Few people afford such table-cloths as need no starch, but when starch is used there should be so little that it cannot be detected by the eye. Napkins should not be starched. It makes them stiff and disagreeable.

TABLE ORNAMENTS.

Nothing is so pretty and so indicative of a fine taste as flowers. If you have no *epergne* (an ornamental stand for a large dish in the center of the table) use a *compatier*, or raised dish, with a plate upon the top for cut flowers ; or place flower-pots with blossoming plants on the table. A net-work of wire painted green, or of wood or crochet work, may be used to conceal the roughness of the flowerpot, or it may be set into a *jardiniere* vase. The flowers form a handsome center-piece around which to place two or four fancy dessert dishes. The dessert will consist of fruit, fresh or candied, fancy cakes, candies, nuts, raisins, etc.

SERVING FRUITS.

MIXED FRUITS.

Always choose a raised dish for fruits. Arrange part of the clusters of grapes to fall gracefully over the edge of the dish. Mix any kind of pretty green leaves or vines which may also fall and wind around the stem of the dish. Arrange firmly, so that when the dish is moved there will be no danger of an avalanche.

WATER-MELON.

A water-melon should be thoroughly chilled. It should be kept on the ice until about to be served. It may be simply cut in two with a slice cut from the convex ends to enable the ends to stand firmly on the platter. Then the pulp is scooped out in egg-shaped pieces, with a tablespoon, and served.

PEACHES.

Choose large, fresh, ripe and juicy peaches, pare and cut them into two or three pieces. They should be large, luscious looking peaches, not little chipped affairs. Sprinkle over granulated sugar, put them into the freezer and half freeze them; this will require about an hour, as they are more difficult to freeze than cream. Do not take them from the freezer till the moment of serving, then sprinkle over a little more sugar. Serve in a glass dish. Canned peaches can be treated in the same way.

COMBINATION OF DISHES.

SOUPS.

Soup is generally served alone; however, pickles and crackers are a pleasant accompaniment for oyster soup, and many serve grated cheese with macaroni or vermicelli soups. Hot boiled rice is served with gumbo soup. This the hostess serves *in* the soup, a ladleful of soup and a spoonful of the rice. Cold slaw is sometimes served at the same time with the soup, and eaten with the soup or just after the soup-plates are removed.

FISH.

The only vegetable to be served with fish is potato. They may be served boiled whole, or some stuff the fish with seasoned mashed potatoes.

BEEF AND VEAL.

Almost any vegetable may be served with beef. At dinner parties, mushroom sauce is generally served with beef. Horse-radish is a favorite accompaniment for beef. Tomatoes, parsnips and oyster-plant are especially suitable for veal.

CORNED BEEF.

This should be served with carrots, parsnips, turnips, cabbage or pickles around it.

TURKEYS.

Cranberry sauce or some acid jelly should be served with turkey. Any vegetable may be served with it.

CHICKENS.

A boiled chicken is generally served on a bed of boiled rice. A row of baked potatoes is a pretty garnish for a roast chicken. Serve salads with chicken.

LAMB AND MUTTON

are nice with green peas, spinach, cauliflower or asparagus.

PORK.

The best combinations for pork are fried apples, apple sauce, sweet potatoes, tomatoes or Irish potatoes. Pork sausages should always be served with fried apples or apple sauce.

ROAST GOOSE

calls for apple sauce and turnips.

GAME

should be served with some kind of acid jelly, as currant or plum. Spinach, tomatoes and salads are especially suitable for game.

PREPARING THE TABLE.

Put a knife and fork by the side of, and a napkin on, each plate. Place water glasses by the plates ready to be filled just before the dinner is announced. At a dinner party, place a little bouquet by the plate of each lady in a glass or silver bouquet-holder. At each gentleman's plate put a little bunch of three or four flowers, called a *boutonniere* in the folds of the napkin. As soon as the gentlemen are seated at table they may attach them to the left lappel of the coat.

Have the plates intended for dessert already prepared, with a finger-bowl on each plate. The finger-glasses should be half filled with water with a slice of lemon in each, or a geranium leaf and one flower.

The warm dishes—not *hot* dishes—keep in a closet or on the top shelf of the range till the moment of serving.

Place the soup tureen (with soup that has been brought to the boiling point just before serving) before the seat of the hostess.

Dinner being now ready it should be announced by the butler or waiting-maid. Never ring a bell for a meal.

If the company be so large that the hostess cannot place her guests without confusion, have a little card on each plate bearing the name of the person who is to occupy the place.

Bills of fare when they are used are often written in French, but good sense would lead one to prefer our own language, as it is almost impossible to find a company all of the members of which could read the French.

SERVING THE DINNER.

The soup, salad and dessert should be placed invariably before the hostess, and all other dishes before the host.

As each plate is ready, the host puts it upon the small salver held by the butler who then with his own hand places this and the other plates on the table before each guest. If a second dish is served in the course, the butler, putting a spoon in it, presents it on the left side of each person, allowing him to help himself. As soon as any one has finished with his plate, the butler should remove it without waiting for the others to finish. When the plates are all removed, the butler should bring on the next course. It is not necessary to use the crumb-scraper till just before the dessert is served.

TABLE ETIQUETTE.

"Chatted food is half digested."
—*Old Proverb.*

The first essential is to catch the hare, and the second to cook it well, but the third is undoubtedly to eat it properly. Human beings were never intended to be the mere guzzlers of food that they too often are. A due attention to the grace and decency of feeding is often the surest means of provoking the taste of the nice. A well presented meal will entice the languid appetite, when the same food ill served will repel all desire. Cheerfulness of mind is as essential to a good digestion, as a good digestion is essential to cheerfulness of mind. Sterne said, "A man's body and his mind are like a jerkin and a jerkin's lining; rumple the one, you rumple the other."

The first duty of an entertainer is to see that his friends are well served. "The host who has compelled a guest to ask him for anything, is almost a dishonored man." He should anticipate the wants of all. An excessive entreaty to eat is, however, not in good taste, and a refined guest never expects it.

The guest should commence eating as soon as helped, and not wait, as some people with a strain of excessive politeness do, until all are served, and thus produce an awkward pause of staring expectancy.

We need not go so far back into the elements of good breeding as some writers on etiquette have, and remind our well-bred readers that it is not considered polite to pick one's teeth with a fork at the table, and that the water in the finger-glasses is not to be drank, but to be used to wash the fingers. The various observances of table ceremony are not so frivolous as they may appear. For example, soup should not be taken the second time, as it is too much fluid for any stomach at the beginning of a dinner. The knife should be used for cutting food and *not* for conveying it to the mouth. The waiter should not be allowed to serve from the right hand, for nothing can be more awkward than to attempt to take anything from the waiter on the wrong side, which is the right hand.

At a large dinner party it is better to confine your powers of entertainment to your immediate neighbors, and avoid brawling out to those opposite, or at a considerable distance from you. When the waiters are limited in number, the gentlemen present should attend carefully to the wants of the ladies in their vicinity. Avoid all gross heaping up of your plates. As a general rule, refuse to be served with more than one kind of meat and vegetable at a time. There is one good rule, which, if followed, will make you an acceptable guest everywhere: Be not obtrusive; do everything smoothly and quietly; talk in a low tone of voice, and handle you knife, fork and plate without clatter, and eat without any audible gulping and smacking of the lips.

By common consent many of the usual table formalities are dispensed with at breakfast; at this informal repast, each person is left free within certain limits, to consult exclusively his own convenience. It is not expected that there should be a gathering in the drawing-room or elsewhere, of the whole party, and a simultaneous movement to the breakfast table as at dinner. The presence of the host and hostess is not exacted, although where there is a family of children requiring the discipline of order and punctuality, no parent should fail to set the example of regular observance of the hour of breakfast, as of every other meal.

The breakfast table should be, in accordance with the unceremoniousness of the repast, very simply dressed. The damask tablecloth and napkins, the white china, the shining urn, the glittering glassware symmetrically arranged, will of themselves contribute to entice a morning appetite. The center of the table should always be adorned with flowers, if they can be obtained, or fruit when in season. The mistress of the house takes her place at the head or side of the table and before her she has the tray with the various vessels for the usual domestic beverages, tea and coffee. The hot water should be freely used, not so much to temper the tea and coffee, as to rinse out the cups. The slop-bowl is a necessary vessel, which, however, is too often wanting. Fastidious people do not care to see the "jetsams" and "flotsams" of their first cup floating in their second.

It is not customary for fastidious people to accept of more than two cups of tea or coffee; but we do not know why good breeding, though moderation and temperance in all things is one of its cardinal principles, should confine itself to precisely that number. It has always been recognized as a symbol—the origin of which we do not pretend to know—of having had enough when the drinker leaves his spoon in his cup, and of his wanting more when it is left in his saucer.

It is always considered good breeding to get through the breakfast with as little formality of service as possible. The well-bred on such occasions whatever force they may have of servants, dispense as far as possible with their presence, and content themselves with a neatly dressed and unobtrusive maid, who knows when to make a timely exit.

The simplest costume is always regarded as the most becoming for breakfast. The matron should make her appearance in white cap and early morning indoor dress; and the master of the house may present himself in his ordinary dress, or even in shooting jacket.

The wedding or formal official breakfast is a stereotyped affair. It is little else than the fashionable ball supper, lighted up by day instead of gaslight.

The proper costume at wedding and formal breakfasts, as at all festivals before dinner, is a morning dress. The gentlemen should wear frock coats and light vests and trousers, and the ladies with their usual morning visiting drapery. The gentleman ordinarily enters the drawing-room with his hat in his hand, and the lady will always, unless very intimate, present herself with her bonnet on her head. The guests take their places with all the ceremony of a formal banquet. The bride and bride-groom always have the precedence in the procession to the refreshment room, and others take their position according to their age and rank. The gentleman in escorting his lady, should always give her his right arm.

Of late years the luncheon, or *déjeûner à la fourchette* —the breakfast with a fork—has been dignified by its formal recognition by society as a cermonious repast. There is, however, much less formality in the serving of a lunch than a dinner. It is seldom in this country, though generally in France, composed of several courses. The whole repast, whatever it may be, is set before the guests at the same time. When only one or two are to partake of the meal, a tray is served; but when more, the whole table is spread, but everything to be eaten ordinarily appears upon it. The formal breakfast or lunch is more especially the feast of literary men, fashionable women, and other idlers. At their "receptions" the dames generally serve up chocolate and cake.

The origin of dinner eating is coeval with the creation of man, but dinner giving is the late product of advanced civilization. A popular author says: "It may be received as an axiom that the social progress of a community is in direct proportion to the number of its dinner parties." It is unquestionable that more enduring alliances have been struck by diplomatists across the mahogany than were ever agreed upon in ministerial cabinets.

In regard to eating, parsimony is by no means the best economy of time. It is particularly necessary to lengthen the American dinner, and we know of no better means of doing this than by dividing it into courses, and interspersing between them cheerful interludes of social talk. The old proverb, that "chatted food is half digested" is worth remembering. A full hour, at least, should be spared from the busiest day for the main repast. Let each one make the most of his dinner, whatever it may be; let it be prolonged and freed from grossness by a graceful ceremony; and above all, let it be partaken of in company, for nothing is so depressing to mind and body as solitary feeding.

The number of persons at a dinner party, according to an old saying, should never be "more than the muses (nine), or less than the graces (three)." Brillat-Savarin says, "Let not the number of the company exceed twelve;" for he, like all of his country-men, stops suddenly short of the thirteen—an ominous number in the superstitious fancy of the French. It is too much the practice, particularly in this country, to invite people of the same profession or occupation to dine together. Brillat-Savarin, than whom there is no better authority, says, "that the guests invited to a dinner should be so selected that their *occupations shall be varied*, and their tastes analogous, and with such points of contact, that there shall be no necessity for the odious formality of a presentation."

The invitations, if the party is a formal one, should be sent about a week or ten days before the dinner. The usual formula is simply this, either written in a note or printed on a card:

Mr. and Mrs. —— request the pleasure of Mr. ——'s company, —— —— (date and No.), at —— o'clock.

The favor of an answer is requested; (or) R. S. V. P.

A formal acceptation should read thus:

Mr. —— accepts with pleasure Mrs. ——'s invitation to dinner, at —— o'clock, on ——.

All written invitations should be answered immediately in writing, but especially invitations to dinner, and should be complied with at all hazards. If, by any mischance—as the death of a relative, or some other serious cause—the guest, after having once accepted an invitation, is unable to comply with it, he must be careful to send notice of the fact, with his regrets, at the earliest possible moment.

At all dinner parties, the ladies and gentlemen are expected to present themselves in full evening costume. The host and hostess, particularly when the occasion is not a very formal one, will take care to keep their own dresses in due subordination, lest they may possibly outshine too evidently some of their guests, and unnecessarily put them to the blush.

Punctuality is essential to the perfection of dining, as it is to the proper performance of every social duty. Fashion now sanctions what common sense has always inculcated, and men of society are expected, alike with men of business to be exact in their engagements.

On arriving at the house, the gentleman if accompanied by a lady, gives her his arm on entering the drawing-room, and the first person addressed should be the hostess. Very fashionable people have a footman at the door to announce the names of the guests as they present themselves. If this is not done, the host or hostess may introduce their visitors to each other, taking care to make as little fuss as possible about it. When introductions are dispensed with, as they may be with propriety, the guests should have no hesitation in conversing freely with each other as mutual acquaintances.

When the dinner is announced, a procession is at once formed. The host gives his right arm to the female guest who, from age, rank or strangeness, has the precedence, and leads her to a place at the dinner table at his right, he being at the head or at one side; after whom comes the most distinguished male guest with the hostess. In England, the hostess often remains with the most important male person until the last, and performs the duty of pairing the guests. The hostess will seat herself at the other extremity, or at the opposite side of the table, with her escort on her right. The rest follow in couples, ranked generally according to age, and as they enter the dining-room are placed so that the host may be flanked on either side by a lady, and the hostess by a gentleman. The rest of the guests are arranged in successive couples, so that each gentleman will be between two ladies, and each lady between two gentlemen, provided the guests will allow of such an arrangement. It is usual to separate the husband from the wife, and temporarily sever other domestic relations.

If you value your health you will take a substantial meal at an early hour of the day, say at noon, or thereabouts. The appetite is almost universally strong at this time, and the corporeal energies being in their fullest strength, the function of digestion is more readily and effectively performed. The mistake which is made by many who take a late dinner is, that they make it serve the purpose of both dinner and supper. It is dangerous to abandon the early dinner without an equivalent in the form of a solid luncheon. All epicures agree, moreover, that to appreciate a fine dinner, it must not be eaten with the voracity of the man famished by a whole day's hunger. In England, people seldom sit down to a dinner before seven, or half past seven or eight o'clock. In France six is the usual hour, and the fashionable people of the United States seem generally inclined to follow the French in this, as in other things. If our advice, and a substantial lunch at noon be taken, we would recommend the ceremonious repast of the day never to be eaten earlier than half past five.

The ordinary mode of serving a dinner is the French one. The various dishes are placed upon the table just as they leave the hands of the cook, and being carved by host and hostess are distributed by the servants to the guests. For formal occasions, however, the Russian mode, or the *dîner a la Russe*, has become fashionable. The dishes, when this style is adopted, are not served until cut up, when they are handed in succession to each guest by the waiters. The table is adorned in the center with flowers and fruit, various gelatines and ornamental confectionery. The plates of soup are generally put on the table before the guests are called in, and a bill of fare, as well as the name of each person, to indicate the seat he is to occupy, printed or written upon a card, is placed on the napkin. Under each soup-plate is one of the ordinary kind of plates. When the dessert is to be eaten, a silver knife, fork and spoon are served upon a small plate with the finger bowl and d'oylay. The guest on receiving these, spreads his d'oylay on his left, deposits the finger-bowl upon it, and noiselessly sets his knife on the right, and his fork and spoon on the left.

Soup should be placed on the table first. Some old fashioned people place fish and soup together, but "it is a custom more honored in the breach than in the observance." All well ordered dinners begin with soup, which the hostess should serve and send round. If wine is served, it should follow the soup.

For ordinary dinner, the following *ménu* is sufficient: One kind of soup, one kind of fish, two *entrées*, a roast, a boil, game, cheese, ices, dessert and coffee.

For more ceremonious dinners, two soups (one white, the other clear), two kinds of fish, and four *entrées* are necessary. Bread should not be cut less than an inch thick, rolls are preferred.

Entrées are those dishes which are served in the first course after the fish.

Entremênts are those served in the second course after the roast.

It is a foreign custom, and an excellent one, to serve the coffee in the dining-room before the ladies retire, as it puts an end to the prolonged wine drinking, now so universally condemned by all well-bred people.

The hostess gives the signal by rising from the table, and the gentlemen and ladies return to the drawing-room in the order in which they left.

It is seldom that a person takes a seat, but all remain standing or walk about the drawing-room conversing or admiring the pictures, articles of *vertu*, and whatever else may invite notice. The visit to the drawing-room being merely designed to graduate the farewell, and thus render the departure less abrupt, is naturally informal. The stay after dinner, unless additional company has been invited, and there is a supplementary evening party, is seldom prolonged beyond half an hour, when leave is quietly taken.

BILLS OF FARE.

BREAKFAST. NO. 1.

Mutton Chops,   Minced Codfish with **Eggs,**
     Stewed Potatoes,
Rice Cakes,   Gems,
     Cold Bread,
Tea,   Coffee.

BREAKFAST. NO. 2.

Codfish Balls,   Cold Venison,
     Muffins,
Corn Bread,   Rolls,
Tea,   Coffee.

BREAKFAST. NO. 3.

Broiled Beefsteak,   Cold Tongue,
     Baked Potatoes,
Cracker Toast,   Corn Meal Muffins,
Tea,   Coffee.

BREAKFAST. NO. 4.

Broiled Fresh Fish,   **Beefsteak,**
     Fried Potatoes,
Cream Toast,   Graham Biscuit,
     Rolls,
Tea,   Coffee.

BILLS OF FARE.

DINNER. No. 1.

Ox-Tail Soup,
Salmon,
Roast Beef,   Roast Pork,
Mashed Potatoes,   Boiled Rice,   Apple Sauce,
Stewed Tomatoes,   Onions,   Squash,
Horse Radish,   Chow Chow,
Apple Pie,   Cream Pie,
Apples,   Raisins,   Nuts,
Tea,   Coffee.

DINNER. No. 2.

Oyster Soup.
Baked Halibut,
Turkey,   Roast Mutton,
Boiled Potatoes,   Cabbage,   Parsnips,   Hominy,
Cranberry Sauce,   Currant Jelly,
Tapioca Pudding,   Mince Pie,
Assorted Cake,
Lemon Ice Cream,   Nuts,   Oranges,   Apples,   Raisins,
Tea,   Coffee.

DINNER. No. 3.

Asparagus Soup,
Fresh Mackerel,
Roast Lamb,   Boiled Tongue,
Mashed Potatoes,   Green Peas,   Squash,
Cucumbers,   Onions,   Horse Radish,   Pickled Beets,
Cocoanut Pie,   Jelly Cake,
Ice Cream,   Wine Jelly,
Tea,   Coffee.

Dinner. No. 4.

Pea Soup,
Rock Fish,
Spare-rib of Pork,   Roast Veal Stuffed,
Boiled Potatoes,   Escalloped Tomatoes,   Onions,
Pickled Beets,   Apple Sauce,   Chow Chow,   Celery,
Horseradish,   Anchovy Sauce,   Tomato Catsup,
Boston Lemon Pudding,   Squash Pie,
Blanc Mange,   Charlotte Russe,
Oranges,   Apples,   Nuts,   Raisins,
Tea,   Coffee.

Supper. No. 1.

Cold Pickled Salmon,   Cold Boiled Tongue,
Bread and Butter,
Crackers and Cheese,   Selected Cake,
Tea, Coffee.

Supper. No. 2.

Cold Roast Meat,   Raw Oysters,
Bread and Butter,   Canned Fruit,
Selected Cake,   Tea, Coffee.

Supper. No. 3.

Cold Ham,   Lobster,
Biscuit and Butter,
Preserved Pine Apple,   Sponge Cake,   Cup Cake,
Tea,   Coffee.

Supper. No. 4.

Cold Fowl,   Sardines,
French Rolls and Butter,   Crackers and Cheese,
Preserved Fruit,   Selected Cake,
Tea,   Coffee.

INDEX.

SOUP.
MEAT AND VEGETABLE.

	PAGE
Asparagus	17
Beef	13
Bean, Dry	17
Calf's Head, Plain	15
Corn, Green	16
Croutons	18
Flavors for	11
French Vegetable	14
Mutton	14
Mock Turtle	15
Noodles for	18
Ox-Tail	15
Pea	17
Powder for	12
Turkey	13
Tomato	17
Veal with Macaroni	13
Vegetable	16

FISH SOUP.

Catfish	20
Clam	19
Lobster	20
Oyster (*No.* 1)	19
Oyster (*No.* 2)	19

FISH.

	PAGE
Catfish, fried	26
Codfish, (*fresh*) boiled	21
Codfish (*salt*) boiled	22
Codfish Sounds and Tongues	22
Codfish Balls	23
Codfish (*salt*) and Eggs	22
Codfish and Potato Stew	23
Eels, stewed	29
Eels, fried	29
Fish, broiled	23
Fish Chowder (*No.* 1)	24
Fish Chowder (*No.* 2)	24
Halibut, boiled	28
Halibut, baked	28
Halibut Steak	28
Mackerel (*salt*)	23
Mackerel (*fresh*) broiled	24
Rock Fish	22
Salmon, broiled	25
Salmon, boiled	25
Salmon, baked	25
Shad, (*fresh*) broiled	27
Shad, (*salt*) broiled	28
Shad, (*fresh*) boiled	26
Shad, (*salt*) boiled	27
Shad, fried	27
Shad, baked	27
Smelts	29
Trout, Salmon, boiled	26
Trout, Salmon, baked	25

	PAGE.
Trout, Brook, fried	26

SHELL FISH.

	PAGE.
Clams, To Open	30
Clams, boiled	30
Clam Chowder (*No.* 1)	30
Clam Chowder (*No.* 2)	30
Lobster, To Select	31
Lobster, To Serve	31
Oysters, fried	32
Oyster Fritters	31
Oyster Omelet	34
Oyster Pie	33
Oysters, Pickled	33
Oyster Patties	32
Oysters, Raw	33
Oysters, Scalloped	32

MEAT.

BEEF AND VEAL.

	PAGE.
Beef, Directions for Boiling	37
Beef, Directions for Roasting	38
Beef, (*corned*) boiled	39
Beef, To Corn	43
Beef Croquettes	42
Beef, (*dried*)	40
Beef, French Method	40
Beef, hashed	41
Beef's Liver	41
Beef Omelet	42
Beef Pickle	42
Beef Tongue	39
Beef Steak (*No.* 1)	38
Beef Steak (*No.* 2)	39
Beef Steak, Tough	39

	PAGE.
Crust for Meat Pie	42
Meat Pie	41
Sweetbread, fried	46
Sweetbread, broiled	46
Veal, broiled	44
Veal Chops	43
Veal Cutlets	43
Veal Fillet	44
Veal Loaf	45
Veal Loin	45
Veal Omelet	46
Veal Pot Pie	45
Veal Pie	44
Veal Steak	43

MUTTON.

	PAGE.
Mutton, boiled	48
Mutton or Lamb Chops Broiled	47
Mutton Cutlets	48
Mutton Leg, boned	48
Mutton, roast	47
Mutton, stew	46

PORK.

	PAGE.
Ham, broiled	53
Ham and Eggs	53
Ham or Shoulder, boiled	52
Hams, (*molasses cured*)	52
Head Cheese or Souse	54
Lard	49
Pig, roast	49
Pork Steak	51
Pig's Feet	54
Pork and Beans, baked	55
Shoulder of Pork	50
Sausages, To Make	51
Sausages, To Fry	51

	PAGE.
Sausage, Bologna	52
Salt Pork, fried	53
Spare-rib or Chine	50
Tripe	54

POULTRY.

	PAGE.
Chicken, broiled	58
" fried	58
" fricasseed	58
" Pie	59
" Pickled	58
" Prairie, Quails. etc	59
" Prairie broiled	59
" Prairie, Fricasseed	60
Duck, roasted	60
Goose, roasted	60
Pigeon Pie	61
Pigeons, roasted	60
Turkey or Chicken boiled	57
Turkey or Chicken dressing	57
Turkey or Chicken pressed	57
Turkey or Chicken roasted	56

GAME.

	PAGE.
Fawn, roasted	63
Game, To Keep	62
Partridges, boiled	63
" roasted	63
Rabbits and Squirrels	62
Venison	62

GRAVIES AND SAUCES
FOR FISH AND MEAT.

	PAGE.
Butter, drawn or melted	64
Gravies	64
Sauces, Anchovy	66
" Caper	66
" Celery	65
" Egg	65
" Mint	66
" Oyster	65
" Mayonaise	66

EGGS.

	PAGE.
Boiled	67
Dropped	70
Elements of	67
Fried	69
Omelet Fried	68
" Plain	68
Packing	70
Poached	68
Poached á la Créme	69
Scrambled	67

MILK, BUTTER AND CHEESE.

	PAGE.
Butter	72
" Making	74
Cheese	75
" Making	76
" Cottage	77
Milk	71

MEAT MAXIMS .. 78

HYGIENIC EFFECT OF ANIMAL FOOD.

	PAGE.
Cheese	82
Eggs	82
Fat Meats	81
Fish	81
Lean Meats (*fresh*)	80

	PAGE.
Salt Meats	81
Shell Fish	82

VEGETABLES.

	PAGE.
Asparagus (*No.* 1)	93
" (*No.* 2)	93
" (*No.* 3)	93
Beans, shelled	97
" string or snap	96
Beets, boiled	96
Broccoli and Eggs	91
Cabbage, boiled	90
" boiled in milk	90
" ladies'	90
Cauliflower	91
Carrots, boiled	95
Celery	98
Corn, green, boiled	94
" " stewed	94
" Patties	95
" Hulled	94
Cucumbers, fried	92
" raw	92
Elements of	83
Egg Plant fried	98
Greens	99
Maccaroni with Cheese	100
" baked	99
Mushrooms, stewed	99
" broiled	99
" To Select	98
Onions, boiled	94
" fried	94
Oyster Plant (*See Salsify.*)	
Peas, green	93
Parsnips, boiled	96
" fried	96

	PAGE.
Parsnips, stewed	96
Potato balls	88
Potatoes, boiled	88
Potato Cakes	89
Potatoes, fried	89
" old, To Cook	89
" heated in milk	89
" mashed	88
" sweet	90
Radishes	98
Squash, summer	97
" winter	97
" baked	97
Salsify or Oyster Plant	95
Succotash	95
Spinage	95
Sauer Kraut	90
Turnips, mashed	92
Tomatoes, stewed	91
" scalloped	91
" raw	92

VEGETABLE ACIDS.

Acetic acid	103
Citric acid	102
Malic acid	102
Oxalic acid	103
Pectic acid	103
Tartaric acid	102

FLAVOR'D VINEGARS.

Celery	104
Horseradish	104
Oyster	104
Peach	104

PICKLES.

Bean	108

INDEX.

	PAGE.
Butternut and Walnut	107
Cucumber or Gherkin	105
Cucumber, salt	106
Cabbage, red	107
Cauliflower	106
Chow-Chow	109
" Cucumber	109
" English	110
Mangoes	108
Nasturtiums	108
Peppers	106
Tomato, green	108

SWEET PICKLES.

Cucumbers	111
Cantelope	111
Damsons	111
Peaches	112
Plums, spiced	112
Tomatoes	111
Watermelon Rind	113

CATSUPS.

Currant	115
Ever Ready	117
Gooseberry	116
Horseradish	116
Tomato	115
Walnut	115
Worcestershire, Imitation	216

SALADS.

Celery	119
Chicken, Suggestions	122
Chicken	122
Chicken Salad Dressing	122
Cold Slaw	119
Dressing for	121
Horseradish	119
Lettuce	119
Lobster (*No.* 1)	126
Lobster (*No.* 2)	121
Made Mustard	118
Sydney Smith's	118
Tomato	120

YEAST.

Hop Yeast (*No.* 1)	126
Hop Yeast (*No.* 2)	127
Milk or Salt Rising	126
Potato Yeast (*No.* 1)	125
Potato Yeast (*No.* 2)	126
Yeast Cakes	127
Yeast without Hops	128

BREAD.

Bread, buttermilk	131
" hop yeast	131
" for large baking	132
" milk	132
" milk yeast or salt rising	126
" Patterson	132
" sponge	133
" Graham (*No.* 1)	133
" Graham (*No.* 2)	134
Biscuit, baking powder	135
" butter-milk or sour milk	136
" cream	134
" cream tartar	134
" raised (*No.* 1)	235
" raised (*No.* 2)	135
" soda	135

INDEX.

	PAGE.
Buns	136
" Easter	136
" plain	137
Crackers	137
Crumpets	138
Gems, Graham	143
Muffins (*No.* 1)	141
" (*No.* 1)	141
" buttermilk	141
" sour milk	141
" corn meal	143
" Graham	142
" Graham raised	142
" rice	142
Puffs	137
Rolls (*No.* 1)	138
" (*No.* 2)	139
" French (*No.* 1)	139
" French (*No.* 2)	139
" Graham	143
Rusk	140
Rusk sweet	140
Strawberry shortcake	134
Sally Lunn (*No.* 1)	140
Toast, French	143
" milk	144
Wafers	138

CORN BREAD.

Brown bread	145
Boston brown bread	145
Brown bread, raised	146
Graham and Indian	145
Johnny cake (*No.* 1)	144
" (*No.* 2)	144
" (*No.* 3)	144
Steamed brown bread	145

GRIDDLE CAKES AND WAFFLES.

	PAGE.
Cakes, buckwheat(*No.*1)	154
" " (*No.*2)	154
" bread	150
" green corn	151
" rice	152
Griddle cakes (*No.* 1)	152
" (*No.* 2)	153
Waffles, rice	153
" risen	153
" quick	153

FRITTERS.

Fritters	156
"	155
" egg plant	155
" snow	155

VEGETABLE MAXIMS | 157

HYGIENIC EFFECTS OF VEGETABLES.

Beans and Peas	159
Buckwheat	159
Carrots	158
Fruits	159
Indian Corn	158
Oats	158
Parsnips	158
Rye	159
Squashes	158
Turnips	158

SUGAR | 160

CAKE.

Almond	172

INDEX.

	PAGE.
Citron	158
Chocolate	168
Cream	170
Coffee	172
Cocoanut	176
Currant	177
Cornstarch	179
Delicate	168
Feather	167
Fruit	173
Fruit, everyday	173
Fruit, farmer's	174
Fruit and nut	174
Gold	167
Hickory nut (*No.* 1)	171
Hickory nut (*No.* 2)	171
Ice Cream	170
Jelly	177
Lemon	165
Marble (*No.* 1)	177
Marble (*No.* 2)	178
Myrtle's	176
Orange (*No.* 1)	164
Orange (*No.* 2)	165
One, two, three, four	171
Pound	172
Plain	175
Pork	179
Ribbon	166
Raspberry roll	180
Sea foam	165
Silver	167
Spice	176
Sponge (*No.* 1)	175
Sponge (*No.* 2)	175
Snow drift	179
Tri-color	167
Tea	180
Watermelon	169
Wedding	173
White	177

ICING.

Icing (*No.* 1)	180
Icing (*No.* 2)	181

COOKIES AND SMALL CAKES.

Cookies	182
" ammonia	182
" rich	181
Cocoanut drops	182
Kisses	183
Macaroons	183
Ring jumbles	183

GINGERBREAD AND SNAPS.

Breakfast cookies	186
Ginger snaps (*No.* 1)	185
Ginger snaps (*No.* 2)	185
Gingerbread, hard	184
" sugar	184
" soft	184
" sponge	185

CRULLERS AND DOUGHNUTS

Crullers	187
Doughnuts (*No.* 1)	186
" (*No.* 2)	186
" raised	187

SWEETMEAT MAXIMS

Measures	189

PIES.

Apple custard	199
Apple (*No.* 1)	198
Apple (*No.* 2)	198

	PAGE.		PAGE.
Blackberry	199	Arrowroot	220
Cherry	199	Black	210
Cocoanut	200	Bird's Nest	212
Chocolate custard	200	Bread	213
Custard	200	Berry	215
Cornstarch	201	Boston Lemon	217
Cranberry	201	Boston Orange	217
Cream	201	Batter	223
Currant	199	Cracker	211
Gooseberry green	199	Cocoanut	215
Lemon (*No.* 1)	202	Cornstarch, boiled	220
" (*No.* 2)	202	Cornstarch, baked	220
" (*No.* 3)	202	Cottage	221
" (*No.* 4)	203	Custard, baked	224
Mince	197	Cracked Wheat	225
Mock Mince	198	Delicate	222
Orange	203	English Plum (*No.* 1)	208
Pie Crust (*No.* 1)	196	English Plum (*No.* 2)	209
Pie Crust (*No.* 2)	196	Farina	214
Puff Paste, French	197	Fruit Valise	215
Peach	203	Food	219
Plum	199	German Puffs	221
Potato, sweet	200	Graham	226
Pumpkin	204	Hen's Nest	212
Raspberry	199	Hominy	226
Rhubarb	199	Hasty	226
Strawberry	204	Indian	223
Squash (*See Pumpkin*)	204	Indian and Suet	223
TARTLETS.		Lemon	216
Lemon Tart Filling	204	Minute	225
Orange	204	Orange	216
Raspberry Cream	205	Oatmeal	225
PUDDINGS.		Porcupine	209
		Plum (*No.* 1)	210
Apple Dumpling, baked	222	Plum (*No.* 2)	211
Apple Dumpling, boiled	222	Plum, Thanksgiving	224
Apple and Tapioca	213	Pineapple	219

	PAGE.		PAGE.
Queen of Puddings	210	Jelly, Orange	241
Rice	217	Lemon Snow	237
Rice with Eggs	218	Meringues	236
Rice and Tapioca	218	Orange Souffle	237
Rice, boiled	218	Raspberry Trifle	236
Sago	213	Stained Froth	238
Snow	221	Whipped Syllabubs	236
Steam	222		
Tapioca	214		
Velvet	219		

ICE CREAM.

		Chocolate	247
		Ice Cream (*No.* 1)	236

PUDDING SAUCES.

		Ice Cream (*No.* 2)	247
Cream, sweetened	228	Lemon (*See Orange*)	
Foaming	230	Orange	248
Hard	227	Pineapple	248
Jelly	228	Raspberry	248
Lemon	227	Strawberry	248
Plain	227	Self-Freezing, Directions for	246
Sauce for English Plum	229		
Sauce for Velvet	228		

ICES.

Sauce for all kinds	229	Currant and Raspberry	250
Wine	229	Lemon	249

FANCY DISHES FOR DESSERT.

		Orange	249
		Strawberry	249
Blanc Mange, cornstarch	228		
Blanc Mange, moss	239		

SAUCES, PRESERVES AND FRUIT JELLIES.

Blanc Mange, velvet	238		
Custard, boiled	235	Apples	253
Charlotte Russe	235	" Sweet (*See Quinces*)	
Cream, Lemon	239	Apple Butter	258
Cream, Spanish	240	Apples steamed	253
Cream, Tapioca	239	Citron	252
Floating Island	235	Cherries	253
General Directions	235	Cherries, dried	254
Jelly, Wine	240	Cherry Sauce	255
Jelly, Calf's Foot	241	Cider Apple Sauce	254
Jelly, Lemon	242	Crab Apples	254

INDEX.

	PAGE.		PAGE.
Cranberry Sauce	254	Strawberry	260
Currant	255	Wild Plum	262
Damsons	256		
Egg Plums	256	**CANNED FRUIT.**	
Figs	257	Berries	265
Gages, green	256	Pears	266
Jam, Blackberry	259	Peaches	265
Jam, Grape	260	Plums	266
Jam, Gooseberry	260	Pineapple	265
Jam, Raspberry	259	Tomato	266
Jam, Strawberry	259		
Marmalade, Crab apple	262	**CONFECTIONERY.**	
" Grape	264	Boiling Sugar	271
" Peach	263	Clarification of Sugar	271
" Pear	263	Coloring and Flavoring	272
" Sweet apple	262	Candy, Cream	274
" Quince	263	Candy, Lemon	274
" Wild Plum	263	Candy, Molasses, white	273
Orange Peel	257	Candy, Nut	272
Peaches	252	Caramels	274
Peach Butter	257	Caramels, Coffee	275
Pears	252	Caramels, Chocolate	275
Pears, baked	253	Caramels, Cream Chocolate	276
Pineapple	253		
Quince and sweet apple	258	Caramels, Cream Coffee	275
Strawberries	255	Caramels, Lemon	275
Tomato, Ripe	255	Tablets, Cinnamon	276
Watermelon Rind	258	Tablets, Ginger	276
		Tablets, Ginger	276
FRUIT JELLIES.		Tablets, Vanilla	276
Apple	262	Taffy, Almond	273
Blackberry	260	Taffy, Everton	273
Currant	260		
Curarnt	261	**DRINKS.**	
Crab Apple	261	Beer, Hop	285
Green Grape	262	Beer, Spring	286
Quince	261	Beer, Spruce and Boneset	285
Raspberry and Currant	262		

INDEX.

	PAGE.
Beer, Jamaica Ginger	285
Chocolate, to make	284
Coffee	281
Coffee, to make	284
Cocoa and Chocolate	283
Cocoa Nibs or Shells	285
Egg Nogg	286
Lemonade	286
Orangeade	286
Shrub, Blackberry	289
Shrub, Raspberry (*No.*1)	289
Shrub, Raspberry (*No.*2)	289
Sherbet, Strawberry	290
Syrup, Blackberry	289
Tea	278
Tea, to make	284
Wine, Blackberry	287
Wine, Cherry	287
Wine, Elderberry	288
Wine, Raisin	287
Wine, Rhine	288

HYGIENE OF DRINKS.

Alcoholic	291
Beer	291
Cocoa	221
Light Wines	291

SICK ROOM.

Arrowroot	293
Beef Tea	294
Broth, Chicken	294
Broth, Mutton	294
Farina	293
Gruel, Barley	293
Gruel, Flour	292
Gruel, Corn Meal	292

	PAGE.
Gruel, Oat Meal (*See Corn Meal*)	292
Gruel, Rice Flour	292
Jelly, Chicken	294
Jelly, Rice	293
Milk Punch	296
Milk Porridge	292
Water, Apple	295
Water, Jelly	295
Water, Toast	295

MISCELLANEOUS.

Antidotes for poisons	310
Burns and Scalds, cure for	300
Crackers	308
Cement for Wood or Stone	310
Cleanse Lard or Butter	308
Clean Furniture	308
" Kid Gloves	300
" Alpaca	301
" Black Silk	301
" Straw Matting	302
" Flat Irons	304
" Pots, Kettles and Tins	305
" Hair Brushes	306
" or wash Silk	301
Crape, wrinkled, to Renew	302
Camphor Ice	303
Deodorizer, best	309
Earth for House Plants	300
Feathers, to curl	302
Fruit Stains, to remove	302
Grease, to remove	303
Glycerine, prepared	300

INDEX.

	PAGE.
Goldfish, to keep	309
Ironrust and Ink stains, to remove	302
Ironmould, to remove	302
Make Hens Lay	310
Paint from Glass, to remove	302
Perspiration	304
Putty or Paint, to soften	310
Papering Whitewashed Walls	309
Remove Bottle Stoppers	310
Remove Discolorations from Bruises	303
Rats and Mice, to destroy	303
Sugar to clear	308
Sink or Drain, to purify	309
Sealing Wax	310
Sudden Hoarseness	303
Stove Polish	304
Suet, to keep	308
Starch, cold	306
Starch, boiled	305
Soap, Patent	306
Soap made with Potash	307
Soap, White Toilet	330
Tar, to remove	307
Tooth Powder (*No.* 1)	304
Tooth Powder (*No.* 2)	307
Tooth Wash	308
Velvet, to restore	301

ARRANGING THE TABLE.

	PAGE.
Shape and Size of Table	311
Table Linen	311
Table Ornaments	312

SERVING FRUITS.

Mixed Fruits	312
Peaches	312
Watermelon	312

COMBINATION OF DISHES.

Beef and Veal	313
Chickens	314
Corned Beef	313
Fish	313
Game	314
Lamb and Mutton	314
Pork	314
Roast Goose	314
Soups	313
Turkeys	313
Serving the Dinner	315

TABLE ETIQUETTE 316

BILLS OF FARE ..342

www.ingramcontent.com/pod-product-compliance
Lightning Source LLC
Chambersburg PA
CBHW031858220426
43663CB00006B/682